DONALD E. K

BIBLE TEXTS
ILLUMINATED

 A-R Editions, Inc.

Library of Congress Cataloging-in-Publication Data

Knuth, Donald Ervin, 1938–
    3:16 Bible texts illuminated / by Donald E. Knuth.
    iii, 268 p.   24 cm.
    Includes indexes.
    ISBN 0-89579-252-4
    1. Bible—Criticism, interpretation, etc.   2. Calligraphy.
I. Bible. English. Selections. 1990.   II. Title.   III. Title:
Three, sixteen.
BS511.2.K58 1990
220.6—dc20
                                        90-44038

A-R Editions, Inc.
801 Deming Way
Madison, Wisconsin 53717-1903
(608) 836-9000

Third printing, 2012

to Victor M. L. Selle
and Norman G. Pfotenhauer

FOREWORD

THE BIBLE is an incomparable book. Millions of people have devoted a major portion of their lives to Bible study. Hundreds of thousands of books have been written about the subject, and we now have ready access to dozens of translations and dozens of commentaries. The Bible is an inexhaustible resource that has been challenging people's minds and hearts for centuries.

As a child I learned many Bible stories and memorized many Bible passages. I heard Bible readings every Sunday morning. But I never appreciated the richness and depth of the Bible until I was an adult, a graduate student at the California Institute of Technology. My wife talked me into going to Sunday morning Bible classes in addition to church, and at that time our class was being taught by Dr. Walter A. Schroeder of Caltech's chemistry department. Walt led discussions that concentrated on one book of the Bible at a time; when I joined, we were studying the Acts of the Apostles. His class was wonderful because he let the discussions proceed at their own pace. Instead of using published course materials, he prepared himself by reading a number of commentaries, and we spent the class time discussing details of the text. Some Sundays we would cover only one or two verses; at other times we were able to finish half of a chapter.

The course ran on for months, but it was constantly interesting. I hadn't realized that Bible study could provide such long-term stimulation for a person who was already fairly well educated about most things. But soon after joining Schroeder's class I knew that I would never tire of it.

About fifteen years later, I decided that I should try to lead a Bible class myself, instead of merely being a participant and taking advantage of other people's preparation. I had thought of a different way to organize such a class, based on some scientific principles I had learned in the meantime, and I found a dozen or so people who were willing to serve as guinea pigs in my experiment. In fact, our pastor and his wife even decided to sit in on my lectures; this kept me on my toes.

During the next four months I found that the selected material unfolded itself almost magically. The class succeeded beyond my wildest dreams. Attendance was high; the discussions were animated and thought-provoking. The experience was so inspiring, for me in particular, that I knew it should be shared with many others. The things I had learned were too exciting to keep to myself. Therefore I decided to write a book about the approach to Bible study that had clicked in such an amazing way. This is that book.

Before I explain the approach I used, I should mention that my normal job as a college professor is to teach computer science; I also write books about computers and mathematics. I'm only an amateur at theology, so I've probably made lots of mistakes while preparing this material—although I do know how to use a library pretty well. I can't say that my scientific background makes me a better Bible student, but I don't think it's a handicap either. Indeed, I believe that God wants the Bible to be read by scientists as well as by people who don't have such strange ways of thinking.

Scientists nowadays rarely write about things outside their narrow fields of expertise, and it's especially unfashionable for a scientist to say much about religion. Yet I sense that many people are eager to learn what a contemporary scientist like me really thinks about theological matters; the relative scarcity of such information is another reason I decided to prepare this book. Many of the greatest mathematicians of the past—including Pascal, Newton, Euler, and Cauchy—wrote about theology, so I am not ashamed to follow in their footsteps.

There are two ways to read the Bible. Method 1: We can read it straight through, for context. By reading at normal speed, we can follow the flow of ideas and get intuitive impressions, just as the first readers and hearers of those words might have done. Or, Method 2: We can single out isolated verses, for meditation and/or scholarly study. By focusing on small details, it's possible to understand the deeper significance of a passage.

Both of these ways are important. Method 2 is most satisfactory for group study, since Method 1 works best when a person can read at leisure and without interruption.

I planned my Bible class around Method 2, although I wanted to be careful to keep my eyes on the forest as well as the trees. I knew that my duty as discussion leader would be to put each selected verse into its proper context— to explain how the parts fit into the whole. A computer scientist is supposed to be good at keeping both a local and a global perspective on whatever is being studied, because computer programming requires the ability to switch rapidly between the consideration of fine details and the perception of overall structure. Therefore I had some confidence that I'd be able to avoid the pitfalls of Method 2 without losing its advantages.

But what verses should we choose for study? If we always turn to the Bible from the same direction, there's a danger of getting into a rut. It seems best to have a variety of approaches, for in this way we will clearly appreciate the fact that the more we learn, the more we find is yet to be learned.

Before I began to teach my course, I had participated in many stimulating Bible classes that had studied the scriptures at close range. These classes could be grouped into three categories:

a) Systematic study of one book. I've already mentioned Dr. Schroeder's class about the Acts of the Apostles, which proved to be so enlightening for me. There also were many others in subsequent years, based on the gospel of John, the epistle of James, the book of Revelation, the Psalms, various letters of Paul, and so on.

b) Themes in the Bible. Effective courses can be based on particular types of Bible passages, like the parables of Jesus; on particular aspects of Christian life, like the principles of good stewardship; on specific doctrinal issues, such as the work of the Holy Spirit, the role of women in the church, the creation of the universe, the concept of immortality; or on other themes such as playfulness and humor.

c) Lectionaries. Over a period of many centuries the Christian churches have compiled lists of special Bible passages that are recommended for reading on various occasions during the church year. At present the major liturgical church bodies—Catholic, Anglican, Lutheran, Presbyterian, etc.—make use of a three-year cycle of gospel lessons, epistle lessons, psalms, and readings from the Old Testament. These selections often determine the themes of Sunday sermons and hymns, hence many people like to prepare for worship by making a study of the appointed readings before attending church.

My idea for a Bible class was based on a fourth way to select Bible verses for study, making use of a mathematical principle that provides an effective way to gain knowledge about complicated things: A large body of information can be comprehended reasonably well by studying more or less random portions of the data. The technical term for this approach is *stratified sampling*. It's something like the Gallup poll, in which a lot can be learned from studying comparatively little. Stratified sampling is a surprisingly good way to magnify our perceptual abilities.

Of course I am not about to claim that a randomization technique is going to replace any of the other methods. But I do believe that it adds a new dimension to our understanding of the Bible and of the related literature; it gives fresh insights that we might miss with the traditional approaches. I'm excited about presenting the method in this book because the experiences I've had with it have proved its worth. I am convinced that this fourth method, in combination with the other three, will be a good basis for Bible study throughout my life.

What is this glorious mathematical method? It's easy to understand. The Bible contains approximately 30,000 verses. Let's suppose that each verse has been written on a slip of paper, and that all the slips have been put into an enormous bowl. A random sample can be obtained by stirring the contents of the bowl thoroughly and then selecting, say, 60 of the slips. After studying those 60 Bible verses very carefully, we might not expect to know a whole lot about the other 29,940; but in fact, mathematicians have found that a surprising amount of information about a large subject can often be derived with a high degree of confidence, even when only a small sample has been investigated.

Putting this another way, let's consider the city of Menlo Park, California. (Menlo Park is the site of Bethany Lutheran Church, where I first gave the Bible class that led to this book.) The population of Menlo Park is roughly 30,000. If you were to interview 60 of those people, selected at random—asking them about their goals, their living conditions, and so on—you would have a pretty good idea of what sorts of people live in Menlo Park. You could serve on the city council and feel that you represented the entire city reasonably well. Of course, the choice of 60 interviewees should be unbiased; you shouldn't give special prominence to the people who go to church, or the people who contributed to your election campaign. It seems reasonable to say that a council member who bases decisions on a knowledge of 60 randomly selected citizens of Menlo Park will do a much better job than one who simply meets 60 people through normal channels, even though 99.8 percent of the population has not been contacted.

To get a good statistical sample, we should choose people who aren't too much the same. We should try to obtain a realistic mixture of men and women, of children and adults, of rich and poor, of different races and religions, etc. That's what the Gallup poll does. In Menlo Park, we might select one person from each of 60 neighborhoods. Choosing from different "strata" makes the sample "stratified"; mathematicians have proved that stratified sampling tends to give more reliable results than completely random samples do.

But let's return from politics to Bible study. The statistical theory suggests that we will be better off choosing *one* random verse from *each book* of the Bible, instead of choosing 60 random verses from the total of 30,000. Taking one verse from each book leads us to consider essentially all of the Bible's authors, although it also tends to discriminate against longer books. In this way we get representation analogous to what happens in the U.S. Senate, where Nevada counts as much as California although it has fewer people.

If we decide to choose one verse out of each book in the Bible, the verse itself should be chosen in an unbiased way. We want to understand the Bible as a whole, so we don't want to assume that the preparers of lectionaries and other selected lists have found all of the really valuable passages; nor do we want to take a chance that some well-meaning people have unwittingly introduced their own prejudices. Let us therefore agree to select verses by some rule that does not depend on reading the book in advance.

One way to obtain an unbiased selection is to roll dice (or to "cast lots" as the Bible says). A more modern approach would be to use microcomputers or pocket calculators that generate random numbers. This idea is appealing, but it's not ideal, because participants in a Bible class ought to be able to study the texts in advance. Truly random choices could be made a week ahead of time, but a simpler rule is preferable when we consider that people sometimes must miss a class or two.

From the title of this book, you can readily guess the rule I decided to use: My proposal was to study *Chapter 3, verse 16* of every book in the Bible. Of course, I have to admit that this suggestion loaded the dice a bit, since John 3:16 is perhaps the most famous verse of all. You might say that my choice of verse 3:16 revealed a certain lack of faith, since I enriched the sample by making it better than a truly random selection. Perhaps I was secretly afraid that the whole Bible class would turn out to be a dud, so I needed to make sure that I could at least get the Gospel message across. On the other hand, my choice of 3:16 affected only one data point; the 3:16 rule didn't cause any significant bias at all, except with respect to the study of John's gospel. And the fame of John 3:16 is actually a plus, because it makes the selection rule easy to remember.

The idea of looking at randomly chosen Bible verses isn't new; it has a distinguished history. For example, John Wesley wrote in 1746 that

> at some rare times, when I have been in great distress of soul, or in utter uncertainty how to act in an important case which required a speedy determination, after using all other means that occurred, I have cast lots, or opened the Bible. And by this means I have been relieved from that distress, or directed in that uncertainty.

(I found this quotation in Volume 5 of his collected works, on page 316. The page number is a pleasant coincidence.)

On the other hand, I don't recall ever hearing a suggestion that random page turning might lead to a systematic procedure—one that helps a reader understand the Bible by making a thorough investigation of verses that have been selected haphazardly. In the scheme I am proposing, the selected verses must be studied very intensively. They must be understood in context and compared carefully to related passages found elsewhere. It is this methodology that I think is new and valuable.

Chapter-and-verse designations weren't part of the Bible until long after the words were written, and no theological significance was attached to the numbers when they were assigned. Therefore verse 3:16 has no special reason to be unusual in any way, and we can expect it to be a "typical" Bible passage (except, of course, in the gospel of John). That is exactly what we want, for stratified sampling. There is a slight bias because Chapter 3 tends to be near the beginning of a story; for example, in the gospels of Matthew, Mark, and Luke, we will be studying events that come very early in Jesus's ministry. But 3:16 isn't so close to the beginning that the effects are significant. A narrative is generally well under way by the time we get to Chapter 3.

When I first announced that I would be leading a new type of Bible class, I asked everyone to prepare for the first session by reading Genesis 3:16, Exodus 3:16, Leviticus 3:16, Numbers 3:16, and Deuteronomy 3:16. I hadn't read those verses yet myself, but I had faith that they would prove to be informative.

A few days later, when I began to prepare for the first class, I found that some books of the Bible don't *have* 16 verses in Chapter 3. In such a case it's natural simply to ignore the division between Chapters 3 and 4, continuing to count as if the verses in Chapter 4 were actually a continuation of the previous chapter.

For example, Psalm 3 has only eight verses; the modified rule calls for the study of Psalm 4, verse 8. This modification needs to be used ten times, for the books of Ezra, Esther, Psalms, Song of Solomon, Hosea, Amos, Jonah, Micah, Zechariah, and 1 Thessalonians.

Some books of the Bible are so short, they don't even get as far as Chapter 3, or they end with a short third chapter. This phenomenon sent me back to the drawing board again. I decided to omit all such books, because they turn out to be similar to other books that are long enough to be included. Thus, in the Old Testament we will miss Obadiah and Haggai because of their brevity; in the New Testament we will lose Titus, Philemon, 2 John, 3 John, and Jude. That leaves 37 books of the Old Testament to consider, and 22 of the New; all told, there are 59 instances of the 3:16 rule.

Now let's recapitulate and summarize the basic idea of this book: We are going to study 59 verses of the Bible, starting with Genesis 3:16 and ending with Revelation 3:16. In each sufficiently long book of the Bible we will look at the sixteenth verse after the beginning of the third chapter. We will study those verses in great detail, and we'll also consider how they relate to neighboring verses and to the book as a whole.

The main body of this volume consists of 59 four-page sections, one for each book of the Bible that is long enough to have a 3:16. One page in each section discusses the Biblical book as a whole; another page contains the 3:16 verse, interpreted visually by a calligrapher. These calligraphic pages can stand alone as works of art. The remaining two pages are devoted to an analysis of the verse and its context.

From a careful scrutiny of each 3:16 text, and from the fact that the verses have been chosen by an arbitrary rule, we'll be able to grasp the scope of the entire Bible in a new way. Not all of the passages we study will be full of profound, spiritual insights; but the proportion of good ones to ordinary ones will say a lot about the Bible's total resources.

After growing fond of the 3:16s, I wanted to put them into my own words, so I decided to prepare my own versions of the 59 Bible verses featured here. Fortunately for me, the task of rendering only 1/500 of the Bible into English was quite easy by comparison with translating the whole text. Since I had to deal with only a limited number of words, I was able to spend more time on each verse than any Bible translator could reasonably afford. Although I am by no means a scholar of Greek or Hebrew, I tried to render each phrase into contemporary English as best I could, by looking carefully at more than a dozen of the best available translations and by analyzing other appearances of the same words. Sometimes I made slight changes so that the 3:16 verse could stand by itself; for example, if the original text used a pronoun like 'he', I sometimes changed it to the name of the person involved. No translation can be perfect, but I have attempted to preserve the original meaning as faithfully as possible. I hope that the style I've chosen is neither too formal nor too breezy.

As I said, three out of every four pages in this book are filled with commentary. But I'm sure that you'll get the most enjoyment from the other pages (which contain nothing but Bible verses), because those pages are the work of many of today's finest calligraphers. A wonderful thing happened to me shortly after I first taught the 3:16 Bible class: My research at Stanford began to be concerned with the problems of publishing beautiful books, and I had the great privilege of getting to know Hermann Zapf. One day I told Hermann about my dream of writing a book based on the 3:16s of the Bible; and I was overjoyed to find that he shared my excitement. He immediately agreed to design the cover and to provide an illustration for John 3:16. Furthermore, he volunteered to introduce me to 58 other calligraphers from around the world, so that this book could be a special feast for the eyes as well as for the spirit.

It's important to remember that the goal of this study is not to find a shortcut by which we can learn all of the Bible's facts, or by which we can encounter all of its doctrines or master any particular topic. These 59 verses certainly do not distill the whole Bible into a super-mini reader's digest. Yet if we keep in mind that the Bible is roughly 500 times as great as the passages we will be analyzing, we can develop a good picture of the whole.

Will the method of stratified sampling work for you? I hope you'll try it and see. Keep your Bible open as you study the material, since you'll find that the 3:16s lead to many other interesting verses.

The following pages contain numerous references to specific Bible passages, because I think it's best to interpret the Bible by letting the Bible interpret itself. I recommend that you keep your favorite Bible open as you read these comments, so that you can easily look up this additional material. I have tried to limit the cross-references to verses that are especially relevant; therefore I don't think you'll be wasting your time if you page through your Bible in order to find each of the cited passages.

When a reference is given to chapter and verse, without the name of a Biblical book, it refers to the book that is currently under discussion. Likewise, a reference to a verse without a chapter number is an implied reference to Chapter 3. For example, in the section on Genesis, a reference to '1:22' stands for 'Genesis 1:22'; a reference to 'verse 14' stands for 'Genesis 3:14'. A series of references like 'Jeremiah 38:4, 50:43' stands for both 'Jeremiah 38:4' and 'Jeremiah 50:43'.

I have adopted a computer scientist's gimmick of using 'single quotes' to designate words or phrases that are being considered primarily as letters or symbols of written text, while "double quotes" designate ordinary quotations. English phrases in single quotes often represent my attempt to express the literal equivalent of a Hebrew or Greek word.

The Boston Public Library and the libraries of Harvard University and Stanford University were of enormous help to me as I was preparing this book for publication. I've also had the opportunity to make brief visits to the Bodleian Library in Oxford, and to the libraries of Yale Divinity School, Westminster Theological Seminary, Pittsburgh Theological Seminary, the Graduate Theological Union in Berkeley, and St. Patrick's Seminary in Menlo Park. What a joy it is to study the accumulated wisdom of many centuries, in a great research library! In addition, I've had special help from many people. For example, Prof. Frank Moore Cross graciously provided me with some previously unpublished information about the Dead Sea Scrolls. Dozens of volunteer readers with a wide variety of backgrounds made important comments on early drafts of my manuscript; I'm deeply grateful for the remarks they made.

+ + +

There's an Afterword, following the section on Revelation 3:16, that discusses my own conclusions about this experiment. But please, read the main part of this book first. I have tried to present the viewpoints of many great students of the Bible, so that people of all persuasions will find good questions to ask themselves as they contemplate the 3:16s. [Caution: Each chapter is pretty much independent of the others, so you will probably find it best to read the material in small doses.]

THE BOOK OF GENESIS starts at the beginning of time and ends with the story of the pioneering ancestors of the Jewish people. It sets the scene for the rest of the Bible by discussing how things began. It is simultaneously a great work of literature—filled with memorable stories and piquant details—and a great theological statement. It affirms that there is a God who created the world and continues to shape its history, a God who has inspired the faith of its people from the beginning.

Careful study of the text has led most Bible scholars to believe that Genesis is not the work of a single author. According to this consensus, Genesis is a compilation of three independent documents, something like what we would obtain by combining the books of Matthew, Mark, and Luke into a single Gospel. However, such an analogy isn't perfect, because the styles of Matthew, Mark, and Luke are rather similar; the three sources of Genesis are sufficiently distinct from each other that it is possible in most places to reconstruct each one from the composite text that we have.

The so-called J-document included in Genesis has a warm, earthy, incisive style and calls God 'Yahweh' ('Jehovah'). The E-document describes a slightly more remote God called 'Elohim'. The P-document is more formal and concerned with priestly matters such as orderly lists and specific dates. Each of these documents was based on ancient traditions that had been carefully preserved. Reverent editors have carefully woven the separate accounts together so that the original documents remain essentially intact.

Chapters 1–11 deal with primeval history, from the time of creation to the aftermath of the great flood. The remaining chapters introduce God's special relationship with a single community. They relate the stories of Abraham and Sarah (Chapters 12–24), Isaac and Rebekah (25–26), Jacob and Rachel (27–36), Joseph and his brothers (37–50).

For thousands of years the book of Genesis was the most rational account available about the world's origins. Therefore people began to regard it as a scientific document as well as a work of theology; they forgot that a book of such antiquity had to be consistent with the outlook of its own time. Some people even today expect this book to have the precision that we require of a modern historian or scientist. The surprising thing is that Genesis is as accurate as it is: Archaeology keeps shedding new light on long-forgotten facts recorded in this book, indicating that centuries of orally transmitted history did not actually blur the details by very much.

Turning to the woman,
GOD SAID:
"Great will be your troubles
during pregnancy, and your
LABORS during childbirth;
yet you will be filled with desire
for your husband, and he will
DOMINATE you."

THE TRIALS AND TRIBULATIONS OF WOMEN are highlighted in this provocative passage. The scene is the Garden of Eden, where the first man and woman have just disobeyed God by eating forbidden fruit. In the preceding verses, 14 and 15, God has pronounced judgment on the serpent who tempted them to eat. In the following verses, 17–19, God will speak of hardships that the man will face. Verse 16 is addressed to the woman.

Before we try to look for the deeper significance of this verse, let us try to understand the original Hebrew words. A more literal English translation might read 'Greatly multiplied will be your troubles', because the same Hebrew term occurs in the phrase 'be fruitful and multiply' found in 1:22 and 1:28. Instead of 'troubles' we might also say 'anguish'; it is the same word that is applied to the man in verse 17, 'in anguish you shall eat'. The root word for 'labors' can be found also in Proverbs 14:23, where we are told that hard labor is profitable. Finally, the verb 'dominate' appears also in 1:16, which says that the sun dominates the day and the moon dominates the night; this Hebrew word refers to influence and power, but it does not imply subjugation. A quite different term is used in 1:26 to describe the relation between human beings and animals.

GENESIS 3:16
Turning to the woman, God said:
"Great will be your troubles during
pregnancy,
and your labors during childbirth;
yet you will be filled with desire
for your husband,
and he will dominate you."

People have interpreted this verse in many different ways. Some think that the story in Chapter 3 is essentially a verbatim record of an actual encounter. But the details—the talking serpent, the description of God walking in the garden, and the use of Hebrew poetry—suggest rather that it is a parable or an allegory meant to teach us an important lesson.

One school of thought simplifies verses 14–19 to something like this: "If Adam and Eve hadn't sinned, snakes would have feet, women would deliver babies painlessly, and men wouldn't have to sweat." But I believe that the message of these words is quite different; let us look at them closely, in connection with other parts of the Bible.

Giving birth to a child is an agonizing experience. For example, 35:16–18 tells how Rachel died in severe pain as Benjamin was born. The anguish of childbirth is mentioned in Isaiah 13:8, Jeremiah 4:31, Micah 4:10, Revelation

12:2. We also know that men have often dominated their wives. Thus, God's statement in verse 16 certainly agrees with what actually happened.

But we must be careful not to read too much into these words. Some people, both men and women, have twisted verse 16 into a supposed decree for the subjugation of women, just as others have mistakenly found support for anti-Semitism in other Bible passages; this is a tragedy. God wants husband and wife to be a team, "one flesh" (2:24; Mark 10:8).

Verse 16 links 'domination' to the mystery of sexuality in an interesting way. The woman will yearn for her husband—in spite of the traumas of childbirth—and he will dominate her. An almost identical construction occurs in the Hebrew text of 4:7, where we read that 'sin yearns for you, and you can dominate it'. In both cases the object of yearning becomes dominant. Thus we might paraphrase the closing words of verse 16 by saying, "He will fill your thoughts and your actions"; the domination being referred to here is taking place within the woman, not being imposed by the man. In the same way men are dominated by women (Song of Solomon 7:10; 1 Esdras 4:22).

Men and women have differing physical characteristics that once made it appropriate for men to function as bread-winners and women as child-rearers; but these differences are no longer very important. The meaning of verses 16–19 for members of modern society is that, whatever our situation in life, we will not have an easy time of it. We will experience serious troubles.

God spoke these words after Adam and Eve had sinned. They had disobeyed his instructions because of their thirst for knowledge. It is clear from other Bible passages that human beings are rebellious by nature (see, for example, 6:5), and that everybody is guilty of sin (1 Kings 8:46; Proverbs 20:9; Ecclesiastes 7:20; 1 John 1:8).

Do verses 16–19 simply describe God's punishment for sin? No; the book of Job says that there is more to the story than reward and punishment. We don't know why God didn't create a world that is free of suffering, but Genesis 3 suggests that a pain-free world would be incompatible with the kind of knowledge that humans prize. Without troubles and hard labor, progress might be impossible. Would things be better if everyone were in a state of constant euphoria and painlessness?

Let us note in closing that God is reprimanding Eve but not repudiating her. There will be trials, but she remains a woman. Jesus points out in John 16:21 that the joy of birth overcomes the travail that precedes it.

THE BOOK OF EXODUS describes a series of events that are crucial to the Old Testament as a whole. The exodus is to Judaism as the incarnation is to Christianity. The corresponding Hebrew word, *yâtsâ'* (which appears frequently in this book, for example in verses 3:11 and 19:1), stands for both physical departure and spiritual liberation, and both senses are significant here. Many generations of parents have repeated this epic tale to their children: "We were slaves in Egypt, and God freed us with a mighty hand.... Then he commanded us to keep his laws and to revere him, for our lasting good" (Deuteronomy 6:21–24).

The first half of this book is about departure. We learn first about Moses, the great leader (Chapters 1–6). Then the Egyptians are afflicted by a series of plagues, culminating in the first Passover (Chapters 7–12). The Israelites escape from Egypt to the freedom and adventure of the wilderness (Chapters 13–19). At the end of this section they stand poised before God's presence on Mount Sinai; in several senses this is the high point of the story.

The remaining chapters tell how God establishes a covenant with his people. He introduces the Ten Commandments and other laws (Chapters 20–24); then he gives detailed plans for a center of worship, the Tabernacle (Chapters 25–31). The people rebel, but they soon renew the covenant (Chapters 32–34). Finally the Tabernacle is completed (Chapters 35–40); Moses dedicates it exactly one year after the exodus had begun (40:17).

The events described here probably took place in the 13th century B.C., during the so-called 19th dynasty of Egypt. Most scholars believe that the present form of Exodus, like Genesis and Numbers, is an amalgam of ancient documents consisting primarily of three sources called J, E, and P. The three strands are interwoven more intricately here than in the other books, presumably because they have so many features in common when they relate such important events. Thus Exodus can truly be called a mosaic about Moses.

God's guiding and sustaining hand is the dominant theme in this book. The children of Israel left Egypt almost against their will; the exodus was more a deliverance than a departure. God chose to have an active relationship with them: He summoned them to a new land, as he had summoned Abraham (Genesis 12:1); he expected them to trust him as Abraham did (Genesis 15:6; Exodus 14:31); he insisted on high standards of individual piety and moral conduct (20:3–17). Indeed, as he says in Isaiah 43:21, "They are the people I shaped for myself, and they will broadcast my praise."

GO AND CALL

the leaders of Israel together.
Tell them that

Jehovah

the God of their ancestors -
the God of Abraham, Isaac, and Jacob -
has appeared to you and said,
"I have paid close attention
to you here in Egypt
and I have seen
how you are being treated."

Exodus 3 : 16

Evert van Dijk

MOSES is receiving his divine commission as the words of this text are being spoken. He has spent the past several years in the desert with a group of Midianites, who are nomadic people somewhat like the Bedouin of today; according to Judges 6:5, "they and their camels are innumerable." Moses has just come to Horeb, the mountain of God (verse 1), also known as Mount Sinai (see 19:11; Deuteronomy 1:6). The exact location of Horeb is disputed; ancient traditions associate it with a peak that is now called Jebel Musa, 'Mount of Moses', near the southern tip of the Sinai peninsula, but researchers have proposed at least ten alternative sites for the events described here.

God has suddenly appeared in a bush that burns without being consumed (verse 2). He calls to Moses (verse 4), and the decisive encounter begins.

EXODUS 3:16

Go and call the leaders of Israel together. Tell them that Jehovah, the God of their ancestors — the God of Abraham, Isaac, and Jacob — has appeared to you and said,

"I have paid close attention to you here in Egypt, and I have seen how you are being treated."

Verse 16 contains several points of interest. In the first place, it is the first time that the Bible mentions the 'leaders of Israel'. We know from later references (e.g., 24:1 and Numbers 11:16) that this group included at least 70 people. They are sometimes called 'elders' because the Hebrew word means, literally, 'old people'; they were evidently venerable members of the community. Such social structure was known to be present in Egypt long before this, as early as the sixth dynasty.

'Israel', incidentally, was a special name given to Joseph's father Jacob (Genesis 32:28 and 35:10); it means 'May God persevere'. Exodus 1:1 refers to 'children of Israel who came with Jacob', which sounds somewhat curious because Israel and Jacob were the same person; however, if you think about it, this way of speaking is quite natural because 'children of Israel' was a common phrase by the time Exodus was written.

God has a message for the leaders of Israel: He wants to engineer an exodus (verse 17). But he needs to establish his credibility first (verse 13). He identifies himself as Jehovah (or 'Yahweh' in Hebrew), a name that he has just interpreted for Moses in verse 14. The exact significance of verse 14 is not completely clear, and it has been the subject of much scholarly speculation. 'Yahweh' is evidently related to the verb 'to be', and the King James Version of the Bible renders it as 'I AM THAT I AM'. The best translation is probably either 'I AM; that is who I am' (New English Bible) or 'I am the one who is' (New Jerusalem Bible). Revelation 1:8 speaks of the Lord God "who is, who was, and who is to come." God is the Being who exists and needs no further introduction, since he is the context for everything else.

God also identifies himself in verses 6, 15, and 16 as the God of Abraham, Isaac, and Jacob. This has become a familiar phrase in the liturgy of many churches; for example, one of the Eucharistic prayers in the Book of Common Prayer refers to "Lord God of our fathers; God of Abraham, Isaac, and Jacob." Jesus refers to this passage in Mark 12:26, where he says it carries the implication that Abraham, Isaac, and Jacob are still living.

God announces in verse 16 that he has paid close attention to the Israelites in Egypt. He has seen their misery; he has heard them cry out (verse 7). The Hebrew words *pâqôd pâqadti*, translated here as 'paid close attention', are somewhat difficult to render in English, hence there is considerable variation in the existing translations of this part of verse 16. The verb *pâqad* is repeated twice for emphasis. The King James Version says "I have surely visited you"; similarly, in Psalm 65:9 we read, "Thou visitest the earth, and waterest it." Apparently a visit from God is a wonderful thing; but Exodus 32:34 presents another side of the coin: "When I visit I will visit their sin upon them." The King James translators did not always render *pâqad* as 'to visit'; they also chose the verb 'to punish' in several places (for example, Isaiah 13:11; Zephaniah 1:8); and they used other words like 'appoint', 'avenge', 'bestow', 'count', 'muster' in other parts of the Bible.

It is hard to translate *pâqad* because it is difficult to find human terms that describe divine actions. The ordinary meaning of *pâqad* is 'to take notice' or 'to pay attention'; when God does that, we have a case of heavenly intervention, so it is an especially important happening. Indeed, God's attention to the world is not only a primary theme of this verse; it is a primary theme of the whole book of Exodus and the whole Bible.

The precise wording of verse 16 is significant, because Joseph had predicted in Genesis 50:24–25 that God would "pay close attention" to the Israelites and bring them back to their homeland. Joseph's phrase was well remembered (see 13:19); therefore the leaders of Israel had reason to know, when Moses repeated God's words of verse 16, that the real thing was about to happen. Indeed, Moses did call the leaders together (4:29); they believed his message and worshipped God when they had heard it (4:31).

THE BOOK OF LEVITICUS is filled with rules and regulations, not actions. Therefore it has been called "the dullest book in the Bible," and readers often skip it. The primitive rites described here have long been superseded, so they seem to have no practical value for modern life. However, a person who reads between the lines will discover interesting details about ancient life throughout this book. The laws of Leviticus illuminate many other parts of the Bible; for example, 12:6–8 explains the offering presented by Joseph and Mary in Luke 2:24 and gives us an idea of that couple's social status.

Leviticus also teaches an important lesson that is valid for all time: "God's people should be holy, since God is holy" (11:45, 19:2, 20:26). God is present with his people (26:12); he makes them holy, set apart, by teaching them the right way to live (22:31–32). This emphasis on consecration and purity is confirmed and strengthened in the New Testament (Matthew 5:48; 1 Peter 1:16).

The basic forms of sacrifice, both bloody and bloodless, are prescribed in Chapters 1–7. Then the story of Exodus advances slightly, as Aaron and his sons are ordained to be the first priests (Chapters 8–10); this is the only narrative section in the book. The next part contains laws about clean and unclean food and people (Chapters 11–15). The annual Day of Atonement ('Yom Kippur') is inaugurated in Chapter 16; then comes a collection of miscellaneous ordinances called the Law of Holiness (Chapters 17–26). The "golden rule" is found here (19:18, 34). Chapter 27 is an appendix that discusses cash values.

Aaron was from the tribe of Levi (Exodus 4:14), and the Levites were responsible for religious ceremonies (Numbers 3:6); therefore it is not surprising that this ceremony-conscious book has been called Leviticus. But if you examine the first seven books of the Bible closely, you will find that Leviticus contains the fewest explicit references to Levi and his sons. They are mentioned only incidentally, in 25:32–33. The reason for this curious fact is that priests were generally selected from the descendants of Aaron, while the other Levites performed subsidiary duties.

Almost every chapter begins with God speaking to Moses and telling him to relay instructions to the people or to the priests. This literary device makes it possible to embed lists of laws into a story; but many of the detailed regulations found here were inappropriate for the Israelites at the time of Moses. Indeed, the rest of the Bible gives little indication that the rules of Leviticus were obeyed very faithfully until a much later time. Therefore the present form of Leviticus is probably an expansion of a much older and shorter legal code.

וְהִקְטִירָם
הַכֹּהֵן
הַמִּזְבֵּחָה

THE PRIEST
SHALL BURN
THESE PIECES
ON THE ALTAR.

לֶחֶם אִשֶּׁה
לְרֵיחַ נִיחֹחַ

AS A FOOD
OFFERING
OF PLEASING
AROMA
MADE BY FIRE.

כָּל חֵלֶב לַיהֹוָה

ALL OF THE FAT
BELONGS TO

GOD.

Leviticus 3 : 16   Ismar David

19

THE SACRIFICE OF ANIMALS was the central symbol of worship, the chief way to show piety, in almost every nation of antiquity. Burnt offerings must somehow be intimately connected with the very essence of religion. The symbolism and the slaughter repel us today, but the underlying motivation—to communicate earnestly and to make peace with God—remains.

Chapter 3 is about a particular type of sacrifice that is often called a "peace offering" in English, because the Hebrew word *sh*e*lâmim* and its Ugaritic equivalent *šlmm* found in clay tablets at Ras Shamra appear to be a plural form related to the word *shâlôm*, 'peace'. Other translators call it a "communion offering" or a "shared offering," because the priest and people would eat the meat that was left after the prescribed parts had been burnt (7:15, 32); it was a meal shared with God.

The priest shall burn these pieces on the altar, as a food offering of pleasing aroma, made by fire. All of the fat belongs to God.

Abel brought an early peace offering in Genesis 4:4, and many more peace offerings are recorded in the Bible (for example, in Exodus 24:5; Joshua 8:31; Judges 20:26; 1 Samuel 11:15). The greatest of these was by Solomon, who reportedly offered up 22,000 oxen and 120,000 sheep when the Temple was dedicated (1 Kings 8:63).

Verses 1–5 deal with peace offerings of cattle; verses 6–11 give almost identical rules for peace offerings of sheep; and verses 12–16 repeat the rules again, this time for goats. In all three cases, specific animal parts that are covered with fat are to be burnt on the altar. The only real difference is that sheep may have fatty tails, and these too should go into the fire (verse 9).

A priest (Hebrew *kôhên*) was to officiate at this ritual. Verse 16 mentions only one priest, while verse 5 (for the corresponding case of cattle) calls for priests. Some scholars interpret this as evidence of hasty editing that may have occurred when an old book of sacrificial laws was being incorporated into Leviticus. But cattle may have been sacrificed with more fanfare than goats.

The word 'burn' in verse 16 actually means 'cause to smoke'. Another Hebrew word is used for burning wood in 6:12; the bush in Exodus 3:2 was burning in this other way. A third kind of burning, more fiery, occurs in 4:12.

One of the chief characteristics of sacrificial offerings was their agreeable aroma, which was thought to bring special pleasure to God as well as to the human participants of the sacred meal. For example, Noah made an offering after the flood waters subsided, and Genesis 8:21 says that God was moved by the

20

pleasing smell. In the corresponding passage from epic tablets of ancient Babylonia (*Gilgamesh* 11:160–161), we find a similar statement: "The gods smelled the sweet savor; they crowded like flies around the sacrificer." Homer tells us that Greek gods, too, enjoyed "the sweet vapor of the fat" (*Odyssey* 12:369).

The concluding words of verse 16 sound strange to modern ears, since we think of fat as something to get rid of. But to the people of ancient times, fat was associated with richness. The "fat of the land" in Genesis 45:18 was the choicest part. The Hebrew word that means 'fat' in verse 16 means 'best' in Numbers 18:12 and 2 Samuel 1:22. (A different word is used for 'corpulence' in Judges 3:17.)

Verse 17 reinforces verse 16 by saying that fat should not be eaten. This prohibition is repeated in 7:23–24. Modern readers might assume that a taboo against eating fat was God's way of controlling the cholesterol level in his people; but the Israelites certainly didn't think of it that way. They regarded burning of fat as a sacrifice of the most delectable parts. The corrupt sons of Eli were killed in battle soon after disobeying this rule (1 Samuel 2:16, 29; 4:11).

One might think that God is automatically pleased whenever somebody goes through the motions of a sacrificial ritual. But other passages in the Bible make it clear that the important thing is really the sacrificer's attitude. An offering means nothing unless God accepts it; God cannot be bribed. For example, God says in 26:31 that he will refuse to inhale smells that are intended to please him, if the Israelites do not also obey his commandments. Humility is better than sacrifice (Psalm 51:16–17). Empty formality in religion should be replaced by true justice (Amos 5:21–24).

Let us conclude our discussion of Leviticus 3:16 by considering it from the standpoint of New Testament theology. The strict laws of Leviticus help us realize the greater freedom Christians have. We need have no scruples about eating fat, pork, and other foods that were proscribed in the Old Testament (see, for example, Romans 14:14). Yet Jesus never did eat those things.

Hebrews 10:4 tells us that the blood of animals cannot take away guilt; but when Jesus offered his own body as a sacrifice, we all were made holy (Hebrews 10:10). Our study of peace offerings makes it easier to understand Ephesians 5:2, where we read that Christ lovingly gave himself for us as an offering and sacrifice to God, "of pleasing aroma." We are therefore encouraged to present our own bodies as a living sacrifice, holy and acceptable to God (Romans 12:1; Hebrews 13:16).

THE BOOK OF NUMBERS tells how God uses the rugged discipline of the desert to prepare his chosen people for entry into the land he has promised them. Thus it provides an important historical link between the epic tales of the exodus from Egypt and the conquest of Canaan.

The traditional title of this book is somewhat misleading, because only 9 of its 36 chapters have a preponderance of numerical data. Another name like 'Grumbles' might be more appropriate, because Israel's rebellious complaints are a recurring part of the story. Incidentally, 'Numbers' is the first book in English Bibles to have a purely English title. Most of the traditional names come from an ancient Greek translation in which the first books were called *Génesis, Éxodos, Leuitikón, Arithmoí, Deuteronómion, Iēsoús, Kritaí, Roúth.* St. Jerome's ancient Latin version set the standard of nomenclature by translating the Greek titles as follows: *Genesis, Exodus, Leviticus, Numeri, Deuteronomium, Josue, Judicum, Ruth.*

As the book begins, Moses has achieved the initial objective of leading the people to Mount Sinai, the site of his original encounter with God. Chapters 1–12 describe the journey from Sinai to Kadesh (approximately one month); Chapters 13–20 cover the encampment at Kadesh (38 years); and Chapters 21–36 describe the journey from Kadesh to Transjordan (five months). The text has evidently been compiled from a variety of ancient traditions and lists.

The Israelites were forced at this time to eke out a sparse existence in typical Bedouin fashion, but with an important difference. God was present at the center of the camp (2:2) in the form of a fiery cloud (9:16). He continually kept the community together and guided it by giving instructions to Moses.

We frequently read that God became angry with people who did not follow his laws (see, for example, 11:1, 12:9, 14:11, 16:46, 25:3); these episodes are generally followed by punishments of some sort. Then Moses and/or the priests intercede (see 11:2, 12:13, 14:19, 16:48, 25:11). Thus, God's firm justice is accompanied by his firm promises to adhere to the covenant he has made.

The Bible shows us later that rewards and punishments are not really related to obedience and disobedience in such a simple way. But strong medicine is necessary to cure the disease of faithlessness, so God decides that the Israelites should wander in the wilderness for forty years (14:33, 32:11). These forty years were well remembered later (e.g., Psalm 95:10; Amos 2:10; Acts 7:36; Hebrews 3:9). St. Paul sums up the book of Numbers aptly in 1 Corinthians 10:11 when he says that these things "were recorded for our instruction."

MOSES
enumerated
the sons of Levi,
as he had been
commanded by
GOD.

Numbers 3 : 16

Erkki Ruuhinen

23

A CENSUS OF THE LEVITES is one of several tallies that are recorded in the book of Numbers. The first of these, in Chapter 1, enumerates men of age 20 or over who are fit for army duty (1:3). In this case all of the Israelites are involved *except* for the tribe of Levi (1:49), whose members are exempt from military service because of religious duties (1:51). Now in Chapter 3 the Levite males are being counted; this census is to include everyone who is at least one month old (verse 15). The number will turn out to be 22 thousand (verse 39).

The word 'enumerated' in verse 16 stands for the Hebrew verb *pâqad*, which was translated as 'paid attention to' in Exodus 3:16. When *pâqad* occurs in the opening chapters of Numbers, it means more exactly 'to muster or enroll for service'. The censuses in Chapters 1 and 26 were both taken when military maneuvers in Canaan were being planned. The meaning of *pâqad* is quite different from *châshab*, 'to compute' (see Leviticus 25:52).

NUMBERS 3:16

Moses enumerated the sons of Levi, as he had been commanded by God.

Moses is obedient in verse 16 to God's command; the phrase 'commanded by God' can be translated more literally 'commanded by the mouth of Jehovah', a common Hebrew figure of speech. God issues commandments frequently in the Old Testament, beginning in Genesis 2:16. He repeatedly gives instructions by speaking to Moses (for example, in 1:1, 48; 2:1; 3:5).

If we want to penetrate further into the meaning of verse 16, we need to understand more about the census that it describes. And this leads to difficult questions about large numbers that can only be understood in connection with the results of other censuses. So let's take a look at the individual statistics for non-Levite tribes, as reported in Chapters 1 and 26:

Reuben	Simeon	Gad	Judah	Issa-char	Zeb-ulun	Eph-raim	Manas-seh	Ben-jamin	Dan	Asher	Naph-tali
46500	59300	45650	74600	54400	57400	40500	32200	35400	62700	41500	53400
43730	22200	40500	76500	64300	60500	32500	52700	45600	64400	53400	45400

The grand totals are respectively 603,550 (1:46) and 601,730 (26:51); thus there are about 600 thousand men of military age (11:21; Exodus 12:37).

Almost every Bible scholar agrees that these numbers are impossibly large. They imply a population of more than two million, when women and children are included. All of these people came from Goshen in Egypt, which has an area of about 70 square miles; two million people would make the population density more than three times that of Singapore or Hong Kong. By comparison, Manhattan Island has 22 square miles and about 1.5 million people in high-rise apartments. Furthermore, the Israelites have large flocks and herds (11:22; Exodus 12:38). There isn't enough level land in the Sinai area to accommodate so many people and animals. Thus it is clear that an alternative population estimate of 40 thousand (Judges 5:8) is much more reasonable.

Closer inspection shows that the individual counts all have a remarkable property: The number of "hundreds" is always between 2 and 7; it is never 0, 1, 8, or 9. The odds against this happening consistently, in 24 separate census items, are more than 200,000 to 1. (Imagine throwing 24 dice; it is quite unlikely that no 1's or 6's will show up. The stated census data is even less likely.) Thus a phrase like '46 thousands and 5 hundreds', which is a literal translation of the total given for Reuben in 1:21, probably does not mean '46,500'. We don't know what 'thousands' and 'hundreds' were, but it is extremely unlikely that one 'thousand' was the same as ten 'hundreds'; otherwise those 24 numbers would have been different.

Indeed, the Hebrew words for 'thousand', 'hundred', 'fifty', and 'ten' were used also to mean organizational units (Exodus 18:25; Deuteronomy 1:15). Clay tablets with ancient census data have been found at Mari and Alalakh, north of Canaan, and these records state the number of military units followed by the number of fighting men; individual units often had fewer than ten men. Therefore verse 1:21 may well mean '46 units, a total of 500 men'. This leads to a grand total of 5550 fighters, a number that is consistent with the descriptions of subsequent battles and still large enough to be impressive.

On the other hand, the totals in 1:46 and 26:51, and the related calculations in Chapter 2 and in Exodus 38:25–26, are based on the assumption that 10 hundred = 1 thousand, because they "carry" from one place to another. This indicates that the person who edited Numbers into its final form was working at a time when the old meaning of 'thousand' had been forgotten; so it provides good evidence for the great antiquity of the original census data.

Since some numbers in Chapter 1 are original but others were evidently added later by an editor, we can expect to have further questions about the numbers in other chapters; many problems remain. For example, the significance of 32 thousand virgins in 31:35 is far from clear. Sometimes a number will be multiplied by ten when a story is being retold (compare 2 Samuel 10:18 with 1 Chronicles 19:18). We should be aware that the authors of the Bible considered symbolic values to be more important than mathematical precision.

THE BOOK OF DEUTERONOMY completes the Pentateuch, the 'five scrolls' at the beginning of the Bible. These five books are also called the Torah, from the Hebrew word for 'law'. They came to be known as the Law of Moses (Ezra 3:2 and 7:6), because Moses is the great leader and law-giver whose personality dominates most of the material. God speaks to Moses and Moses communicates with the people. Therefore Martin Luther's translation of the Bible calls the first books 1 Moses, 2 Moses, and so on; this book is 5 Moses in his scheme.

Deuteronomy means 'the second law', and this book can be regarded as a second edition of the law, a reaffirmation and summary of essential principles in the previous books. It is primarily an exposition of Israel's faith, with practical applications for daily life; it faces basic questions about the meaning of God's acts. Thus it is a deeply theological book, a fitting conclusion to the books that precede it and a fitting introduction to the books that follow.

Most of Deuteronomy consists of three farewell addresses by Moses to the people he has led to eastern Palestine. The first address (Chapters 1–4) summarizes the events in the book of Numbers; the second (Chapters 5–28) is the main statement of the covenant or treaty between God and Israel; the third (Chapters 29–30) emphasizes the benefits and dangers of compliance and non-compliance. The remaining chapters (31–34) continue the story where Numbers left off; they contain poems composed by Moses and describe his death.

The style of Deuteronomy is distinctly different from that of the preceding books. Its warm, flowing, persuasive eloquence has been compared to sermons preached by fine orators. The content of Deuteronomy also has distinctive features; for example, there are no kind words here about Moses's brother Aaron, who is so prominent in Exodus, Leviticus, and Numbers. Therefore this material seems to stem from an independent source. Scholars disagree widely about when it was written, some believing that it comes almost entirely from the hand of Moses himself (see 31:24) and others believing that it originated 200 or 400 or 600 years later.

The highlight of Deuteronomy is the *Shema*, the monotheistic creed of Judaism: "Listen, Israel! Our God is One" (6:4). God owns the universe (10:14); he loves and sustains his people (4:37, 7:8), who ought to love and serve him (6:5, 10:12). Everybody is urged to "choose life" (30:19). Jesus called 6:5 the "greatest commandment" (Matthew 22:38); he also quoted Deuteronomy 8:3, 6:16, and 6:13 when he was tempted in the wilderness (Matthew 4:4, 7, 10).

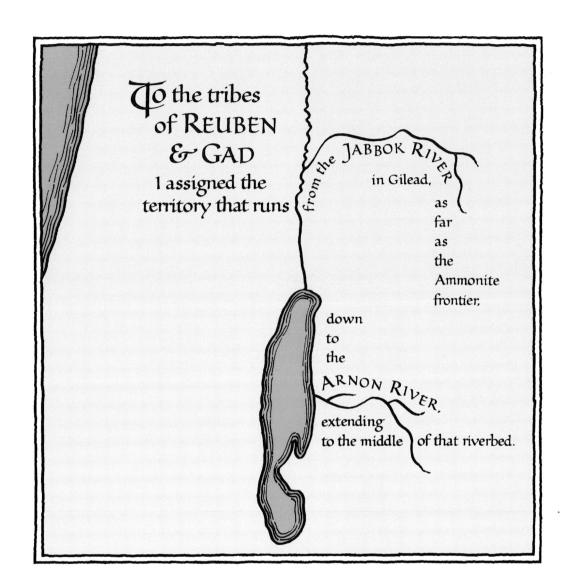

To the tribes of REUBEN & GAD I assigned the territory that runs from the JABBOK RIVER in Gilead, as far as the Ammonite frontier, down to the ARNON RIVER, extending to the middle of that riverbed.

Deuteronomy 3:16

John Prestianni

TERRITORIAL RIGHTS were important in ancient times, just as property deeds are important today. Indeed, this is one of the principal subsidiary themes of Deuteronomy, where 'possessing land' is mentioned more than sixty times. A study of verse 16 provides a useful geography lesson that will help us visualize the scene of much Old Testament activity.

The land of Palestine is bisected by the Jordan River, which flows due south into the Dead Sea. Canaan lies to the west of the Jordan, and Gilead lies to the east. The Jabbok River, which more or less cuts Gilead in two, is one of the principal tributaries of the Jordan. Its ancient name *Yabbôq* is thought to mean 'pouring forth', and its modern name Nahr ez-Zerqa means 'blue river'. Jacob wrestled with God near the Jabbok (Genesis 32:22–28); there is an interesting play on words relating Jacob, Jabbok, and the Hebrew for 'wrestle', which is *'âbaq*.

DEUTERONOMY 3:16

To the tribes of Reuben and Gad, I assigned the territory that runs from the Jabbok River in Gilead, as far as the Ammonite frontier, down to the Arnon River, extending to the middle of that riverbed.

The Arnon River is about 50 miles south of the Jabbok. It empties into the Dead Sea from the east. It becomes nearly dry in the heat of summer; however, seasonal flows have left an impressive gorge, up to 1700 feet deep and 2 miles wide. This gorge makes it a natural boundary. The city of Aroer (verse 12) was on the north rim of the Arnon, in the tableland about 15 miles east of the Dead Sea.

Verse 16 describes a northern border (the Jabbok) and a southern border (the Arnon); the Jordan and the Dead Sea are understood to be the border on the west (verse 17). But what about the east? A glance at a map provides some clarification: The Jabbok flows roughly north for a while before it turns and heads west toward the Jordan. Thus it serves as the northeast corner of a well-defined region. The east bank of the upper Jabbok was Ammonite territory. There is no need to specify a southeastern boundary, because that land is desolate (see 4:43; 1 Chronicles 5:9).

Ammonite heritage survives today in the name Amman, capital city of the Hashemite Kingdom of Jordan. This city lies near the headwaters of the Jabbok. In ancient times it was known as Rabbah Bene Ammon, 'Great (city) of the Sons of Ammon' (verse 11).

The territory south of the Dead Sea belonged to the Edomites, who were descendants of Abraham's grandson Esau (Genesis 25:30). The territory east of the Dead Sea and south of the Arnon belonged to the Moabites, who were—like the Ammonites—descendants of Abraham's nephew Lot (Genesis 19:37–38). This land had been allocated to them by God, so the Israelites were not supposed to touch it (2:5, 9, 19).

The tract described in verse 16 once belonged to the Moabites, but it had been taken by an Amorite king (Numbers 21:26). The Israelites captured it in a bloody battle, at which time all the former inhabitants were annihilated (2:34–36). The Israelites had also conquered another Amorite kingdom, north of the Jabbok (verses 1–8); but they still had five more Amorite centers to face, west of the Jordan (Joshua 10:5). God supported these victories because the Amorites' religious practices were so abominable (20:18). Many years earlier, Sodom and Gomorrah had been destroyed for the same reason (Genesis 18:20). In principle, God is the owner of all land (Leviticus 25:23).

The tribes of Reuben and Gad had asked to remain east of the Jordan instead of sharing in the promised land of Canaan. Moses agreed, provided that they would fight in Canaan with the other tribes (Numbers 32:1, 32). This they did (Joshua 4:12, 22:2). Reuben was the first-born son of Israel's first wife (Genesis 29:32); he is always mentioned first when the tribes are listed. Gad was the first-born of Israel's fourth wife (Genesis 30:11).

The Bible doesn't give a clear idea of how the Reuben-Gad parcel was divided between the two tribes. "Gad chose the best land" (33:21). According to Numbers 32:34–38, the Reubenites occupied a relatively small cluster of cities centered around Heshbon, in the middle of the region, while the Gadites spread out over the remaining territory. But Joshua 13:15–28 reports a quite different distribution, with Reuben in the south. The Moabite Stone, a famous relic from 840 B.C. now in the Louvre, agrees with the Numbers account.

The Reubenites apparently suffered serious casualties when this land was taken, because they are strong in the censuses of Numbers but weak in 33:6. Since the land has no definite eastern boundary, it is relatively exposed; Gad is warned about future raiders in Genesis 49:19. Ammonites try unsuccessfully to annex the property in Judges 11:13. Ultimately the Reubenites and Gadites both disappear from historical records; their territory is taken by Hazael of Damascus, an Aramean king who is a contemporary of Elisha (2 Kings 10:32–33). Many years later, Isaiah 15–16 and Jeremiah 48 will refer to this region as Moabite country. The present name of the Arnon, Wadi el-Mujib, preserves the name of Moab.

THE BOOK OF JOSHUA describes the triumphant conclusion to the story of the exodus: The children of Israel reach the promised land and settle in their divinely ordained place of rest. A spirit of joyful optimism and fulfillment prevails; the scorecard at the end of Chapter 12 reads "God 31, Canaanites 0."

Joshua, the successor to Moses, leads the activities on God's behalf. His name is the Hebrew equivalent of the Greek name Jesus. It is an appropriate name for a liberator because it means 'Jehovah saves'.

Chapters 1–5 describe the Israelites' entry into Canaan. The cities are conquered in Chapters 6–12, and the land is parceled out in Chapters 13–21. Then the covenant between God and Israel is reaffirmed (Chapters 22–24), in accordance with Joshua's farewell exhortation: "Decide today whom you will serve...; as for my family and myself, we will serve Jehovah" (24:15).

This book was evidently compiled from folklore and early documents, because it makes frequent reference to things that remain "to this day" (for example, in 4:9, 5:9, 6:25, 7:26). Verse 10:13 mentions one of the sources, a book of poetry that also includes a lamentation by King David (2 Samuel 1:18). Joshua himself wrote some things down (24:26). The author's chief purpose is to illustrate theological principles rather than to write history, so he presents an idealized and simplified account of complex events. On the other hand, he duly notes that the conquest of Canaan was incomplete (13:1–6, 15:63, 16:10, 23:4).

Pacifists are not fond of this book. Although God had said, "You shall not kill" (Exodus 20:13), God now directs the Israelites as they massacre every living thing in Jericho (6:21). According to Psalm 106:34, God wanted them to destroy even more than they did. How can we reconcile this with other instructions to seek peace (Psalm 34:14), to turn the other cheek (Matthew 5:39), and to put away our swords (Matthew 26:52)?

Sometimes things must get worse before they can get better. God's ultimate goal of universal peace (Isaiah 2:4) cannot be achieved instantaneously, with the world as it is; there must also be justice, and immorality cannot be condoned. (See Genesis 15:16.) The pagan fertility cults that were rampant at the time of Joshua were so diametrically opposed to God's will that it was best to obliterate them and to teach the world a better way. The tension between good and evil had to be faced. Therefore I guess Joshua took a step in the right direction; but I'm glad I was not in his shoes.

The water came to a standstill
JOSHUA 3:16   and accumulated
far upstream at Adam,
the town near Zarethan.
This completely cut off
the flow down to the Sea
of the Arabah (the Salt Sea),
so the people
were able to cross opposite Jericho.

Joshua 3:16   Jean Larcher

31

THE HISTORIC ENTRY of the Israelites into Canaan was associated with a miraculous parting of the waters, just as in the exodus from Egypt (see 4:23). In this case the water accumulated upstream—literally, 'formed one heap'—in the River Jordan; previously it had been driven back by a strong wind in the Red Sea (Exodus 14:21). A somewhat rare Hebrew word, *nêd* ('heap'), links these two events, since it appears both here and in Exodus 15:8. In later years, Elijah and Elisha are said to have crossed the Jordan in a similar way (2 Kings 2:8); there is also a legend in the Apocrypha about Israel's ten lost tribes crossing the river Euphrates on dry land (2 Esdras 13:44).

God generally uses human agents and/or natural forces to carry out his plans. A plausible mechanism for the damming of the Jordan was discovered by archaeologists who experienced a series of earthquakes in July 1929. The shaking caused a large section of cliff to fall across the river bed, completely shutting off the flow of water for 21 1/2 hours. This happened just opposite Tell ed-Damiyeh, the ruins of the ancient town of Adam, about 16 miles north of Jericho. An interesting photo of the scene appears in John Garstang's book *Joshua, Judges* (1931), facing page 138. A similar landslide, which took place on December 8, 1267, was recorded by Nowairi, an Arab chronicler of the Crusades. The event of verse 16 might have been caused by such a slide, or by supernatural intervention, or both; according to verses 5 and 13, it had been predicted before it actually occurred. The waters returned again in 4:18 after everyone was safely across.

JOSHUA 3:16

The water came to a standstill and accumulated far upstream at Adam, the town near Zarethan. This completely cut off the flow down to the Sea of the Arabah (the Salt Sea), so the people were able to cross opposite Jericho.

This dramatic event was a big morale booster for the Israelites, who commemorated it with two monuments: one in the middle of the river (4:9) and one on the western shore (4:20). It also frightened the Canaanites, whose hearts 'melted' when they heard the news (5:1). Ancient clay tablets record Canaanite rituals that celebrate the victory of Baal over the sea-dragon Leviathan (see Psalm 74:14); to these people, conquering the sea or the river was a supreme example of divine power over the cosmic forces under the earth.

The Jordan River flows through the northernmost part of the Great Rift Valley, a massive depression in the earth's surface that extends thousands of miles southward, reaching as far as Mozambique. Geologists believe that this land has been subsiding for a long time, because continental plates are spreading out underneath, far below the surface. The lowest point on earth occurs where the Jordan empties into the Dead Sea, about six miles south of where Joshua and the Israelites crossed over.

The Jordan, whose name means 'downcomer', doesn't look broad and straight like the Mississippi; it meanders in a sinuous path about 200 miles long, while covering a distance of only 65 miles as the crow flies. Most of the year it is only about 75 yards wide and 3 feet deep, but when the snow melts on the slopes of Mount Hermon in Lebanon the river overflows its banks and fills a flood plain more than a mile wide. At such times the Jordan is very difficult to cross, and verse 15 tells us that it was indeed in a flood stage.

The Dead Sea is usually called the Salt Sea in the Bible, because the lack of an outlet has made its water extremely salty. It is also called the Sea of the Arabah, after the desert that surrounds it. Recent discoveries of ancient scrolls hidden in nearby caves have made the Dead Sea especially famous.

Two of these scrolls contain the earliest known Hebrew manuscripts of the book of Joshua (c. 100 B.C.); but unfortunately the leather has been eaten away by worms, and only a few scraps are still readable. One of the legible fragments includes the end of verse 15 and the first four words of verse 16. It is interesting because it agrees with the standard Hebrew text known from later times, except for the addition of the word 'wheat' after verse 15. This extra word appears in the Septuagint, an ancient Greek translation of the Old Testament (c. 200 B.C.), and scholars had speculated that the Greek translators might perhaps have inserted extra words for clarity. Now it appears that the original verse 15 did refer to wheat. This makes sense, because the wheat harvest occurs at the same time of year as high water in the river, shortly before the Israelites celebrate the Passover (5:10).

Verse 16 mentions two towns. The site of Adam has been identified, just south of where the Jabbok meets the Jordan, but archaeologists still disagree about the location of Zarethan. Some place it 12 miles north of Adam, on Tell es-Sa'idiyeh; but a more ancient ruin, Tell Umm Ḥamad, seems more likely. The latter site is near both Adam and Succoth (see 1 Kings 7:46).

One lesson we can learn from Joshua 3:16 is to let God lead our way across dangerous barriers. William Williams expressed it well in his 18th-century hymn: "When I tread the verge of Jordan, Bid my anxious fears subside; ... Death of Death and Hell's destruction, Land me safe on Canaan's side!"

THE BOOK OF JUDGES describes the turbulent times when the Israelites began to establish themselves in Canaan. Joshua had died without naming a successor, and each tribe had settled on its own territory; now each tribe began to do its own thing (21:25). This was a period of revolutionary social upheaval, lasting about 150 years, characterized by growing urbanization and by great tension between monotheism and the established fertility-cult religions. It was also a significant time of transition in military tactics, as the Bronze Age gave way to the Iron Age. The Philistines on the west coast had iron chariots (1:19) and a monopoly on iron weapons (1 Samuel 13:19).

Local rulers called judges were now in charge. We might well call them "sheikhs," since their responsibilities were rather different from the judges of today. According to archaeological records from that time, a judge was supposed to muster troops and provide protection from wandering nomads as well as to administer justice. Ancient justice also implied vindication and revenge.

Chapters 1–2 introduce the material, then Chapters 3–16 present stories about individual judges: Othniel, Ehud, Shamgar (3); Deborah, Barak (4–5); Gideon (6–8); Abimelech (9); Jephthah and five minor judges (10–12); Samson (13–16). The final chapters describe further incidents of that era: the migration of Dan (17–18) and the scandal of Benjamin (19–20).

This may well be the most fascinating book in the Bible from a historical standpoint, because it consists largely of ancient folk tales that have been preserved almost intact. Individual tribes loved to retell the heroic exploits of their former leaders, and these colorful sagas have lively details and touches of humor. We learn, for example, that Ephraimites could not pronounce the *sh* in *shibbôleth* (12:6). We learn of people's faults as well as their faith.

The independent stories are connected by editorial remarks that place most of the events in a cyclic pattern: (1) The Israelites forget their God and practice idolatry. (2) God allows their neighbors to subjugate them. (3) They cry for help. (4) God inspires someone to save and/or judge them. (5) There is peace for forty years. (6) Return to step 1. The individual instances of this pattern usually involve only one or two tribes, hence the actual incidents probably overlapped in time; they may not even be presented in chronological order, because careful records were probably not kept.

As the Israelites continued to backslide into pagan practices, God continued to straighten them out. Hebrews 11:33 praises the faith of the judges and prophets who held the nation together during this difficult period.

Ehud
Made·himself
a·short
double·edged
sword and
strapped·it·to
his·right·thich
underneath
his·clothes

Judges 3:16

Judges 3 : 16   Robert Borja

35

EHUD'S STORY, in verses 12–30, is a particularly fine example of folk literature from ancient Canaan. German scholars call it *Kunstprosa*, 'artistic prose', because the Hebrew text is highly rhythmic, although it is not quite poetry.

Ehud is a hero of left-handed people (verse 15), for reasons that will soon be clear. Left-handedness was evidently prized by the tribe of Benjamin, to which Ehud belonged—even though Benjamin literally means 'son of the right hand'. For example, 20:16 mentions 700 left-handed Benjaminite soldiers, each of whom could sling a stone at a strand of hair without missing. Ambidextrous Benjaminites are also mentioned in 1 Chronicles 12:2. British commentators on these verses note that the Kerr clan in Scotland reputedly once trained its fighting men to be lefties; a left-handed Scotsman is sometimes called Kerr-handed, probably because the word *caerr* means 'left' in old Gaelic.

JUDGES 3:16

Ehud made himself a short, double-edged sword, and strapped it to his right thigh, underneath his clothes.

The name Ehud itself means 'united'. It is still a fairly common Jewish name, sometimes associated in America with the nickname Woody. (Another name Yehudi, which corresponds to 'Judah', might seem related to Ehud, but it is not.) Ehud's adversary is named Eglon, which means 'young bull' or 'fatted calf'.

As the story begins, Moabites have captured the city of palms (verse 13). This is the oasis of Jericho, according to Deuteronomy 34:3 and 2 Chronicles 28:15; it had been allocated to the tribe of Benjamin (Joshua 18:21). Jericho itself was in ruins (see Joshua 6:26 and 1 Kings 16:34), but people were presumably still making use of the plentiful spring water in that area. Since the Israelites had established themselves west of the Jordan with comparatively little difficulty, the Moabite king Eglon was no doubt tempted to follow their example; indeed, verse 12 says that God himself gave Eglon the strength to capture this land.

Now we get to our chosen verse 16: Ehud conceals a dagger or short sword on the inside of his right leg. This position was convenient for him, being left-handed; and it also was a good hiding place, because Eglon's security guards were less likely to notice a tell-tale bulge in that area or to feel there for a concealed weapon. The sword must have been sharp, since the same Hebrew word *chereb* is used for an instrument of circumcision in Joshua 5:2.

Ehud is bringing a gift to Eglon (verse 15). The Hebrew word used here is slightly ambiguous. Sometimes it denotes the tribute or protection money demanded by an occupying power (2 Samuel 8:2), but it could also be a means of ingratiation (2 Kings 8:9). In either case, Eglon is undoubtedly in a mellow mood after receiving what Ehud has brought, and this gives Ehud the chance for a private interview (verse 19).

Ehud says, "I have a message for you from God," and King Eglon arises (verse 20). Then Ehud quickly draws the hidden dagger with his left hand and thrusts it into Eglon's belly (verse 21); it lodges in the fat (verse 22), and the king dies (verse 25). The Hebrew word for 'edge' in verse 16 is actually a form of the word for 'mouth'; thus a sword can indeed deliver a message.

Ehud chose a sword of just the right length for this job. It could not be too short, since Eglon was very fat (verse 17); on the other hand, it could not be too long or it would be unwieldy. The Hebrew text of verse 16 says that his sword was a *gômed* in length, and this word has puzzled translators because it does not appear elsewhere in the Bible. Ancient documents from a few centuries later say that *gômed* means a short cubit or 'fist cubit', a cubit that is measured from the elbow to the knuckles of a clenched fist rather than to the end of extended fingertips. According to this reckoning, Ehud's sword was about 13 inches long, unless the meaning of *gômed* has changed with time. A similar sword, 16 inches long, has been excavated at Megiddo. Incidentally, the ancient Targum translation of Judges—an oral paraphrase into Aramaic, dating from several centuries before Christ—uses a word like *gômed* in verse 15 to stand for left-handedness, literally 'compressedness in the right hand'. Such ingenious wordplay in the original languages is often lost in translation.

Well, it's interesting to study the gory details of this ancient story, but we should also ponder the moral question it raises. Was Ehud an agent of God's justice, or was he an assassin? Can first-degree murder be justifiable homicide when the victim is a foreign aggressor who has taken over our property?

The Bible seems to say that Ehud did right, for a man of his time. But today we would certainly disbelieve anyone who claims that God wants him to kill. We like to think that civilization has advanced to a higher level, in which a compassionate attitude toward our enemies can lead to their reform, and where disagreements can be settled by negotiation and compromise.

The judges of old received praise and honor for their acts of chutzpah, deception, and slaughter. The standards of that age are still familiar today in television shows and movies that glorify successful violence. But Jesus tells us to love our enemies (Luke 6:27).

THE BOOK OF RUTH is a short story that provides a refreshing respite from the violence and anarchy described in the immediately preceding chapters of the Bible. It is a peaceful tale of life in the countryside. It makes no mention of wars or miracles; it reminds us that most of the world's people spend their lives doing things that don't get into the history books; it shows us that God is present in everyday events. Jewish people read this book every year at their feast of Shavuot, fifty days after Passover (analogous to the Christian festival of Pentecost).

The story is better read in its entirety than summarized. The chief character is Ruth, a young Moabite widow who emigrates to Bethlehem with her mother-in-law Naomi, where she marries Boaz, a well-to-do relative of Naomi's late husband. Ruth ultimately becomes known as King David's great-grandmother (4:17), thus an ancestor of Jesus Christ (Matthew 1:5).

Goethe praised the beauty of this book, and it is generally regarded as a magnificently crafted work of literature. Perhaps the original story was refined by wise women of the villages as they retold it from generation to generation; finally it was written down by a gifted wordsmith. One of the noteworthy literary devices found here is the frequent use of inversion: 'go/return' in 1:8 versus 'return/go' in 1:12; 'elders/people' in 4:9 versus 'people/elders' in 4:11. This is a book to appreciate on many levels, because the author is also a great teacher; we find excellent examples here of family loyalty, loving responsibility, prudence, generosity, and the care of widows.

Many scholars have concluded that this book was written primarily as a reaction against the prohibition of mixed marriages by Ezra and Nehemiah, after the Jewish exiles returned from Babylon to Israel (Ezra 9:1, 10:3; Nehemiah 13:25). According to this view, the author of Ruth was gently but forcefully pointing out that Israel's greatest king would never have been born, if overly strict laws of racial purity had been enforced in earlier days.

But more recent commentators see the racial issue as only one of many topics treated here. Careful studies have shown that linguistic elements once thought to indicate a relatively late date of composition are more probably authentic archaisms that are remnants of ancient dialects; hence scholars now tend to believe that Ruth was composed several centuries before Ezra's time. Ruth's story certainly provides insight into the vexing question of mixed marriages, a problem that was significant throughout Israel's history. But we miss much of the beauty of this book if we imagine that it has only one main theme.

WHEN RUTH CAME BACK,
NAOMI SAID,

»How did it go,
my daughter?«

AND SHE TOLD
HER MOTHER-IN-LAW
EVERYTHING THAT BOAZ
HAD DONE FOR HER.

Ruth 3:16   Jovica Veljović

ALL THREE PRINCIPAL CHARACTERS of the book of Ruth are mentioned in 3:16, a verse that encourages us to look at the context in the preceding verses.

Verse 15 has an interesting connection with the history of printing. The King James Version of the Bible, which is still popular today after having served for hundreds of years as the standard English translation, was first published in 1611. This first edition was a splendid achievement of the printer's art as well as a splendid work of Biblical scholarship; therefore original copies are highly prized by collectors. The first edition was issued in two forms, both dated 1611, and both containing the same style of type and the same verses on every page. But there are curious differences. In the first issue, now known as the Great He Bible, the closing words of Ruth 3:15 are 'he went into the citie', while the second issue (the Great She Bible) says 'she went into the citie'. There are thousands of other differences in spelling—for example, the He Bible says 'shee lay' instead of 'she lay' in verse 14, while

RUTH 3:16

When Ruth came back, Naomi said, "How did it go, my daughter?" And she told her mother-in-law everything that Boaz had done for her.

both say 'shee came' in verse 16—but the he/she change was the main distinguishing feature, because spelling variations were comparatively unimportant in those days.

As a matter of fact, scholars still debate whether verse 15 should say 'he' or 'she', because the ancient Hebrew manuscripts are not consistent on this point. The difference is unimportant, but the consensus of modern translators is that 'she' has won out.

Let us now look more deeply into the context of verse 16. Both Ruth and Naomi are widows; indeed, Naomi has lost her two sons as well as her husband (1:5). Widows in that time had no means of support; their family property was in danger of being lost. Therefore Hebrew law made special provisions for them. For example, they had the right to glean the grain remaining in the fields after the harvest (Deuteronomy 24:19). Ruth exercises this right (2:2), but she also asks specifically for permission, because of her status as a foreigner (2:10). This is how she becomes acquainted with Boaz.

The law also provides for a widow to be "redeemed" by her next of kin, who can buy the widow's property and marry her (4:5; see Leviticus 25:25, Deuteronomy 25:5, and Mark 12:19). In this story, Naomi tells Ruth to make herself attractive (verse 3) and to lie down where Boaz is sleeping; Ruth is also supposed to uncover his feet (verse 4). When Boaz awakes (verse 8), Ruth asks him to marry her, since she thinks he is her next of kin (verse 9). All this is taking place in the time of spring harvest, when love is in the air.

At this point Boaz does a heroic thing. He resists what I'm sure must have been a strong temptation, and he tells Ruth to wait, because he is not really her next of kin (verse 12). Moreover, he gives her a generous quantity of grain to take home to Naomi (verse 15).

The stage has now been set for verse 16. Naomi is obviously anxious to know what has happened. We notice that Naomi always addresses Ruth as "my daughter" $(2:2, 22; \ 3:1, 16, 18)$, as does Boaz himself $(2:8; \ 3:10, 11)$. This is one of the stylistic devices by which the narrator implies that Naomi and Boaz belong to an older generation. Otherwise Ruth is called Naomi's daughter-in-law $(1:22; \ 2:20, 22; \ 4:15)$. The same word is used in Hebrew for both 'daughter-in-law' and 'bride'.

Naomi's question in verse 16 is much more interesting in Hebrew than it appears to be in modern translations, because in Hebrew she is asking, literally, 'Who are you, my daughter?'. The question in this form is reminiscent of Isaac's 'Who are you, my son?' in Genesis 27:18, and it has caused considerable speculation. Why would Naomi ask that? The ancient translation into Syriac (c. 200 A.D.), which occasionally adds words of clarification, has Ruth answering "I am Ruth," but the other versions record no such reply. One of the Dead Sea Scroll fragments found in Qumran cave number 2 contains verses 13–18, and its version of verse 16 surprised everybody because it has Naomi asking 'What are you' instead of 'Who are you'.

Ruth came home when it was still dark (verse 14), and she may have looked strange carrying a heap of grain; so it is conceivable that Naomi might not have recognized who or what she was, just as Boaz had to ask in verse 9.

But the best solution to this mystery seems to have been found in the excavations at Ras Shamra (the ancient city of Ugarit), where archaeologists have unearthed documents that use a similar construction in an ancient Canaanite language related to Biblical Hebrew. For example, one Ugaritic tablet says 'Baal is dead; who is he?'; this question apparently means, "What has become of him?" Similarly, Naomi's 'Who are you?' probably means, "In what condition are you now? A widow or a wife? Are you Mrs. Boaz?"

In this verse and this story we see a lot of love and compassion turning a potentially tragic situation into a life of joy for Naomi, Ruth, and Boaz.

THE FIRST BOOK OF SAMUEL is the first half of what was originally a single, undivided work. It begins with the story of Israel's last two judges, Eli (4:18) and Samuel (7:15); it concludes with the story of Israel's first two kings, Saul (11:15) and David (16:1). Thus it tells about a significant turning point in Israel's history, when a loose federation of tribes became welded together into a single nation. This portion of the original Book of Samuel ends with an account of Saul's death and burial (31:6, 13).

The establishment of a monarchy was, of course, a highly controversial change in Israel's power structure and life style. Both sides of the debate are represented here. King Saul was not a smashing success, but David promised to be better. In retrospect, we can see that it was probably necessary for the Israelites to unify at this time, or they would have found it impossible to survive in the face of increased aggression from the Philistines, who had previously been content to live on the coast. The Israelites' forthcoming experiences as members of an affluent nation were destined to teach them important lessons about the dangers of material power and wealth; they gradually learned what sort of kingdom God really intended them to have.

This book can conveniently be regarded as a study of interactions between its leading characters. Chapters 1–7 are about Eli and Samuel; Chapters 8–15 are about Samuel and Saul; Chapters 16–31 are about Saul and David. The dominant personality is that of Samuel, a peaceful man who is especially influential as a spiritual leader; he points out that obedience to God is much more important than religious rituals (15:22). Later generations will remember Samuel as the first of the prophets, not only as the last of the judges (3:20; Acts 3:24, 13:20).

Like the other historical sections of the Old Testament, this book consists of a variety of heterogeneous accounts that were put together by later editors who have tried to include all the data at hand, even if the facts do not always dovetail perfectly. We find here a lively picture of Israel's early religious practices. The stories of Samuel throw considerable light on the pioneering activities of prophets and priests as well as kings.

The Hebrew text of Samuel has the dubious distinction of being the least well-preserved of all the Old Testament sources. For some reason, the ancient scribes who copied this material made more errors than usual, and the old manuscripts show considerable variation in small details. Some of the Dead Sea Scrolls have helped to resolve many of the textual riddles.

Eli called him saying

SAMUEL MY SON

And he answered

HERE I AM

THE CALL OF SAMUEL differs from the other Bible stories about God's first confrontations with prophets, primarily because of Samuel's age: Samuel is probably very young at the time of these events. His mother has dedicated his life to God's service (1:28), and she has left him in the care of Eli, the high priest (2:11) and judge (4:18).

Americans do not pronounce the names Samuel and Eli as Hebrew speakers do. We say *SAM-you-ell* and *EE-lie*, but *shmoo-AIL* and *'ay-LEE* would be more authentic. (Samuel has the same Hebrew name as the Shemuel of Numbers 34:20.) No great harm is done when we pronounce things in our own way, but it is wise to remember that English might mislead us. We might think, for example, that Eli's name is closely related to that of Elijah, because of traditional English spellings; but in fact there is no connection between those names in Hebrew.

1 SAMUEL 3:16
Eli called him, saying, "Samuel, my son." And he answered, "Here I am."

Samuel is called by God in verses 4, 6, and 8; and he answers "Here I am" to Eli each time, because he doesn't recognize God's voice. But the call to Samuel in verse 16 is genuinely from Eli, and the circumstances are completely different this time when Samuel answers "Here I am" once again. We can learn several valuable things from this story, so it will be a good idea to look at it closely.

Verse 1 tells us that visions of God were infrequent in those days; thus it was a special honor for Samuel to receive a divine message. Eli was an old man, nearly blind, who was resting in his normal place (verse 2); this may have been near the door of God's sanctuary (1:9). The main thing that held the tribes of Israel together in those days was the existence of this sanctuary, which was then in the city of Shiloh, about 20 miles north of Jerusalem (Joshua 18:1; Judges 18:31). It was nighttime, because the lamp had been kindled (verse 3) as it was each night (Exodus 27:21; Leviticus 24:3). Samuel was lying by the Ark of God (verse 3), also called the Ark of the Covenant (4:4); this was a special portable shrine, symbolic of God's presence, which was kept in the inner sanctuary (Exodus 25:22, 26:33).

After three false starts, Eli realizes that Samuel is being addressed by God, so he advises Samuel to say "Speak, your servant is listening" (verse 9). This works (verse 10), and a channel of communication is opened. We learn from the story so far that we should be alert for God's messages to us (Psalm 85:8). Do we recognize that voice when it comes?

44

God says in verse 11 that he will be sending a terrible punishment to Israel in the years to come, something so terrible that it will "make everybody's ears tingle." This presumably refers to the capture of the Ark by the Philistines, as described in the next several chapters. The religious life of Israel has reached a truly abominable state under the corrupt leadership of Eli's sons (2:17, 22), and Eli's attempt at reprimanding them has had no effect (2:24–25). Their rejection of God is unforgivable (verse 14).

God's first message to Samuel was certainly not calculated to produce peace of mind. Right from the start Samuel has to bear the prophet's cross, the painful duty of telling unwelcome truths to people he loves (see Jeremiah 15:10). He has just learned of God's anger—an anger so great that it will destroy his present home. Therefore he is afraid to tell Eli what has happened; he lies in bed, probably unable to sleep (verse 15).

However, when morning comes, Samuel opens the sanctuary doors, knowing that Eli will be nearby. It is Samuel's duty as a Korahite to tend these doors (1 Chronicles 6:33–37, 9:19). Throughout this story, Samuel performs his tasks faithfully.

Now comes verse 16, where we started. Eli calls out, "Samuel—my son!" He knows that his real sons have betrayed God's trust; his adopted son, Samuel, must be the one who will carry God's work forward. Saint Paul, similarly, calls Timothy his "true son in the faith" (1 Timothy 1:2).

Eli surely anticipates the worst, because he has already been warned (2:33). He is a man of great power, as head of both church and state in Israel; therefore we might expect him to be jealous and to give Samuel the cold shoulder. Why should God bypass the high priest for a child? But he continues to act in a fatherly way, and he presses Samuel to tell him everything. He invokes a solemn oath in verse 17, perhaps making a hand gesture something like slitting his throat when he says the words; this sort of oath was common in those days (see 14:44, 20:13, 25:22; Ruth 1:17).

Samuel holds nothing back (verse 18), and this leads to the climax of the story: Eli calmly accepts God's judgment, terrible as it is, without whining or complaining. "He is Jehovah; let him do what seems best." The same lesson is taught in many other places in the Bible when great men submit their own egos to God's divine ordinances. We learn this, for example, from Aaron (Leviticus 10:3); from David (2 Samuel 15:26; Psalm 39:9); from Hezekiah (2 Kings 20:19); and from Jesus (Luke 22:42).

THE SECOND BOOK OF SAMUEL might well be renamed the Book of David, because it is entirely devoted to the story of David, Israel's greatest king. Indeed, Samuel's name does not appear anywhere in this book except in the title. At this point in Biblical history we begin to encounter events that can be assigned fairly accurate dates; moreover, the first of these dates is easy to remember, because David's reign began very nearly in the year 1000 B.C.

We know from other sources that music, arts, and literature flourished under David's leadership, but this book emphasizes the stressful times that preceded and followed the peaceful years at the height of his reign. Chapters 1–8 describe David's consolidation of power, when he assumed full control over both the northern and southern territories. He succeeded in capturing Jerusalem, the almost impregnable Jebusite fortress that had previously kept northern Canaan separate from the south. Chapters 9–20 describe life in David's court, concentrating especially on the strife of later years. The closing chapters, 21–24, are appendices that contain miscellaneous additional records.

The middle portion of this book is a literary masterpiece that contains a remarkably vivid portrait of David's complex personality, evidently composed by an eyewitness. David was both warrior and poet, both politician and musician; he was a man of great faith and devotion, but he could also be wicked and ruthless. When confronted with his guilt he freely confessed his wrongs and accepted the punishment.

What a remarkable kingdom this was! Nowhere else in the world before that time would a priest be free to accuse the king of wrongdoing. Nowhere else would a court chronicler dare to present a frank picture of his royal patron; kings had always been painted as godlike paragons of virtue. The author of these chapters of the Book of Samuel has been called the "father of narrative history" as opposed to didactic history, because he was the first to provide an unvarnished account of a king's exploits in such a way that the facts are left to speak for themselves. Nobody knows the identity of this famous early source who penned such priceless descriptions of David's court, but several plausible guesses have been made. The author may have been Nathan (see 7:2; 1 Kings 4:4; 1 Chronicles 29:29; 2 Chronicles 9:29), or perhaps Abiathar (see 1 Samuel 22:20; 1 Kings 2:26), or perhaps Ahimaaz (see 18:19; 1 Kings 4:15). Whoever he was, we can be thankful for the insights he has given us into the qualities expected of a person who is to lead the people of God.

2 Samuel 3:16

Michal's husband walked behind her, sobbing as far as Bahurim; then Abner ordered him to go back. So he went back.

2 Samuel 3 : 16

Satyanarayan Mallayya Wadisherla

MARRIAGE AND POLITICS are intertwined in this sad episode from King David's early years. Michal was David's first wife; she also was the youngest daughter of Saul, Israel's first king. Saul had slyly offered her to David as bait in a trap, hoping that David would die before being able to meet the bride-price of "100 Philistine foreskins" (1 Samuel 18:20–27). After the trap failed, Saul tried to kill David again, but Michal foiled the plot (1 Samuel 19:11). Finally Saul took her away from David and gave her to another man (1 Samuel 25:44).

Several years went by. Saul died, and there were two rival pretenders to the throne (2:8 11). One was David, who had the support of Judah and the other territories south of Jerusalem; the other was Saul's son Ishbosheth, who had the support of the north. Ishbosheth was simply a puppet king, controlled by Saul's former army commander Abner; Abner was also Saul's cousin (1 Samuel 14:50). Bitter fighting raged, and David's forces began to gain the upper hand (verse 1).

2 SAMUEL 3:16

Michal's husband walked behind her, sobbing, as far as Bahurim; then Abner ordered him to go back. So he went back.

Our story begins when Abner quarrels with Ishbosheth and threatens to go over to David's side (verse 10). Ishbosheth is afraid to oppose him (verse 11). Then Abner sends envoys to negotiate with David (verse 12); David agrees to a summit meeting, but he imposes a condition: "You won't see me unless you bring Michal along" (verse 13). This is a way by which Abner can prove his good faith. Joseph had used similar language when he asked his older brothers to bring Benjamin to him in Egypt (see Genesis 43:3).

David may still be in love with Michal, but we are not told his real intentions. He certainly is not short of wives at this time (see verses 2–5). There are strong indications that he wants to remarry Michal primarily because of her ancestry. David knows that it would be foolish to defeat the northern armies and rule the northern tribes by right of conquest; this would surely lead to rebellion and ceaseless conflict. He wants rather to rule as Saul's legitimate successor. As Saul's son-in-law, he can have a legal claim on the throne. Of course, this means that he also needs official permission from Ishbosheth for Michal's hand; therefore he formally requests this (verse 14), knowing that Ishbosheth will knuckle under to Abner's wishes. Meanwhile Abner can maintain the fiction that he is still acting as Ishbosheth's agent. A careful study of these verses leaves a strong impression that David is a master strategist, superbly skilled in the diplomacy of his day.

48

The law of Moses forbade remarriage after divorce (Deuteronomy 24:1–4), but this law did not apply when the first marriage was annulled without the husband's consent. Archaeologists have found legal codes in nearby countries that apply to David's situation; these laws support his right to reclaim a wife who has been forcibly taken. David also strengthens his case in verse 14 by reminding Ishbosheth of the high bride-price he has paid.

Michal's temporary husband, Paltiel (verse 15), is caught in the middle, an innocent victim of state intrigue. He clearly loves Michal. Verse 16 poignantly depicts the touching scene in which Abner drives him off and he has to say goodbye. We can certainly sympathize with Paltiel, but we should blame Saul rather than David for his plight. Political maneuvers have unfortunately taken precedence over private affections. Incidentally, the Hebrew word used here for sobbing, *bâkôh* (pronounced *baw-KAW*) is suggestive of the sound Paltiel may have made.

The town of Bahurim, mentioned in verse 16, will turn out to be important in two of David's later escapades (16:5, 17:18). It probably was situated on the southwest slope of the modern hill Ras el-Temim, about one mile northeast of the Mount of Olives near an old road from Jerusalem to Jericho. This was essentially the southern limit of Benjaminite (Ishbosheth) territory.

According to 1 Samuel 25:44, Paltiel lived in Gallim, a town that Isaiah 10:30 locates in the vicinity of Anathoth just north of Jerusalem. If Paltiel is coming from Gallim in verse 16, he gets to follow Michal only briefly through the hills. On the other hand, he might be following her all the way from Ishbosheth's headquarters in Mahanaim, on the other side of the Jordan river—past Adam, Zarethan, and Succoth. David is in Hebron, about 20 miles south of Bahurim.

What does Michal think about this? We are not told, perhaps because women of her time are simply treated like property. We know that she did love David once (1 Samuel 18:20), but Paltiel's sorrow suggests that she might now be as unwilling to leave him as he is to leave her. Soon Michal will get into an argument with David about his rollicking behavior in a religious festival (6:16); she will remain childless (6:23).

David himself will soon be following Abner and sobbing, in verses 31 and 32—because Abner is about to be killed, assassinated by David's ruthless soldiers who seek to avenge a dead brother. Such are the events preceding Israel's golden age. Has the world changed much since then?

THE FIRST BOOK OF KINGS traces the history of the Israelite monarchy during the first hundred years or so after David's reign. This period begins gloriously with the rule of King Solomon, one of David's sons; but Solomon's imperial excesses eventually lead to a great religious decline and everything begins to fall apart. After Solomon's death, his descendants continue to rule in Jerusalem over the tribes of Judah and Benjamin, but the tribes north and east of Benjaminite territory split off into an independent kingdom whose capital is established in Samaria. Henceforth the southern kingdom calls itself Judah and the northern kingdom adopts the name Israel.

Like the Bible's other historical books, this one is a patchwork quilt of instructive material that has been pieced together from a variety of sources. In this case the connecting threads are more in evidence than usual, and the original material has been embroidered a bit, because the editor wants to make sure that the moral of the story is clear. His goal is to teach the lessons of history, instead of the bare facts; thus he dismisses King Omri with only a few lines and says, "Omri sinned against God more than any of his predecessors" (16:25), although by worldly standards Omri was actually one of the greatest kings of this era. (Indeed, Israel was known to Assyrians as the land of Omri for many years.) Readers who want ordinary historical information are referred to other books such as *Annals of the Kings of Israel* (16:20); but the other books, which presumably contained only ordinary history, have not survived.

Chapters 1–11 discuss the reign of Solomon, and Chapters 12–16 deal with the traumatic first years of the divided kingdom. Chapters 17–22 continue the divided history, interweaving it with a third strand, the story of Elijah.

It is not easy to describe events that are happening simultaneously in two or three different places, but the author of Kings makes the best of it by switching back and forth in an interesting way. King X of Israel, say, begins to reign in the mth year of King Y of Judah; then the reign of X is described, lasting n years; then the scene shifts to Judah, the clock is rolled back, and the story continues to advance in zigzag fashion. When the relative dates are put together they don't quite check out, but clues from extra-Biblical sources have made it possible to reconstruct a fairly accurate chronology.

The principal theme of this book is that the kings of Israel and Judah have broken their covenant with God, yet God remains surprisingly patient with his wayward people. There are also subsidiary themes; for example, we read of several cases where prophets are able to predict the future.

ONE DAY TWO PROSTITUTES CAME TO SOLOMON SHALL OF JUDGMENT AND STOOD BEFORE THE KING

1. Kings 3:16

1 Kings 3 : 16   Hermann Bongard

51

THE WISDOM OF SOLOMON was legendary, and in this story we find him at his wisest. Chapter 3 is an introduction to the biography of Solomon that occupies the next few chapters. In verse 9, which is part of a dream, Solomon asks God for the wisdom to rule with justice; in verses 12 and 13, God grants his request and includes riches and honor as well.

Verses 16–28 are a self-contained demonstration of Solomon's wisdom in action, and a fine example of courtroom dialog. The story concerns two women of ill repute, living in the same house, who became pregnant and gave birth; one of the two babies has died. Each woman claims to be the mother of the live child. Nobody else was present in their house (verse 18); therefore there is no evidence other than the words of the women themselves. Solomon is asked to resolve the dispute. His decision is to cut the live child in half, thereby treating both women equally (verse 25). The true mother soon reveals herself, by disclaiming the child so that it will not be harmed (verse 26).

1 KINGS 3:16
One day two prostitutes came to Solomon's hall of judgment and stood before the king.

Solomon is probably sitting on his throne during this scene (see 2:19), because the Hall of Judgment in his future palace will be called the Throne Room (7:7). People of all classes are allowed to appear before him, and there is nothing exceptional about this aspect of the story. For example, a woman is able to come to David with a problem in 2 Samuel 14:4; Absalom promises instant justice in 2 Samuel 15:4; five sisters appear before Moses and other leaders in Numbers 27:2. Tablets found at Ras Shamra tell of kings being personally accessible to widows, orphans, and other unfortunate people.

The "oldest profession" goes back at least to Genesis 34:31. According to Deuteronomy 22:21, a bride could be stoned to death unless she was provably a virgin. Yet professional adultery was not uncommon, and Proverbs 7:6–27 is an eloquent poem in which a father warns his son not to be seduced.

Harlotry was often associated with hostelry. One indication of this practice appears in the ancient Code of Hammurabi, which places restrictions on "female wine-sellers." The two women of our story live in the same house (verse 17), so they probably have a business like that of Rahab, who provided shelter for Joshua's spies in Jericho (Joshua 2:1, 6:25).

Although the Bible does not condone prostitution, it emphasizes that sins can be forgiven. Thus, Jesus says in Matthew 21:31–32 that prostitutes and tax-collectors are entering God's kingdom ahead of priests, because of their repentance and faith. Rahab herself is cited as an example of faith and good works in Hebrews 11:31 and James 2:25; she is listed as the mother of Boaz, hence an ancestor of Jesus, in Matthew 1:5.

When the Jewish historian Josephus retold this story in the first century A.D., he added another twist by assuming that the dead and the living child were both present in court. According to Josephus, Solomon ordered both babies to be bisected, so that each woman would receive half of each child. This makes the judgment curiously like the law of Exodus 21:35, which applies to cattle. (That law is fair for another reason: Dead cattle have monetary value.)

Similar stories have been found in many parts of the world. The version that comes closest to this Biblical account appears in the *Mahā-Ummagga-Jātaka*, one of the tales of the Buddha's former incarnations in India. Here the women who contend for a child are ordered to have a tug-of-war over it, one pulling by the hands and the other by the feet. When the child cries out in pain, the real mother—with her heart almost "ready to burst"—lets go. The image of a heart ready to burst, in this extract from Buddhist literature, is parallel to verse 26 of Solomon's story, which speaks of the mother's "emotions in ferment."

Since different versions of this tale have been found in many cultures, some people take verses 16–28 to be a legend, something like the story of George Washington and the cherry tree, rather than the record of an actual happening in Solomon's court. We can't expect the compiler of Kings to have authenticated all of his sources with the precision of a modern historian; but whether or not this incident truly occurred, the significance is the same: The story is a perfect characterization of the judicial qualities that Solomon was perceived to have, a blend of shrewdness and tact that sees through people's disguises. Since all citizens had equal right of access, Solomon's talent for administering justice was soon known throughout the land.

Solomon was also endowed with other types of wisdom, including the ability to compose poems and proverbs, as well as an unusual knowledge of plants and animals (4:32, 33). He was not, however, said to have excelled at mathematics, which was already highly developed in Mesopotamia. Perhaps that is why he spent too much money.

Verse 28 aptly points out that Solomon's wisdom came from God. Our fervent prayer, today as then, remains the same: "Please, God, endow our rulers with your own fair judgment" (Psalm 72:1).

THE SECOND BOOK OF KINGS completes a series of four books, beginning with 1 Samuel, that were called '1 Kingdoms' through '4 Kingdoms' in the first Greek and Latin translations of the Old Testament. The original Hebrew Bible had only two books in their place, called Samuel and Kings; but the Greek translators decided to chop them up, probably because Greek writing requires about twice as much space as vowel-less Hebrew. It would be nice to put 1 Kings and 2 Kings back together again, except that millions of reference works would then become obsolete.

This part of Kings is particularly valuable today because it helps us understand the background of the second half of the Old Testament. Chapter 1 completes the story of Elijah begun in 1 Kings; then Chapters 2–8 tell about Elijah's successor, Elisha. The combined history of Israel and Judah continues in Chapters 9–17, leading up to the demise of Israel. Finally comes the downfall of Judah in Chapters 18–25.

Each king is rated as to whether he did good or evil in God's sight. The combined scores after 400 years are 0–20 for Israel and 9–11 for Judah, showing a clear superiority for the kings of the south. However, the north had several great prophets. The continuity of David's line is stressed repeatedly; for example, in most cases the southern kings are said to be buried in the city of David, and the queen mother's name is given, but such information almost never appears for the northern kings. Clearly God has not annulled his promise of perpetuity to David's descendants (8:19, 20:6; 2 Samuel 7:16).

This book is part of a still larger unit, beginning with Deuteronomy, Joshua, and Judges, that is called the "Deuteronomic history" because it is a history of Israel imbued with the philosophy stated forcefully in the book of Deuteronomy: The people of Israel are expected to obey God's laws, especially with respect to the quality of worship. When they remain loyal, they are prosperous and happy; but when they fall away, they meet with disaster.

Many scholars think that a first edition of the book of Kings, and perhaps also of the entire Deuteronomic history, was put together during the reign of Josiah after a copy of the long-lost book of Deuteronomy was found in the Temple (see 22:8). According to this theory, 2 Kings ended approximately at 23:25; this made a happy and powerful ending to the entire story. Unfortunately, Josiah's reforms did not last, and Jerusalem soon lay in ruins. The final edition of 2 Kings, prepared during the Babylonian captivity, could end on an upbeat note only by mentioning the release of David's heir from prison (25:29).

Elisha declared,
Here is what GOD says
Pools of water will fill this dry riverbed.

2 Kings 3 : 16

Andrzej Kot

55

GOD PROVIDES WATER for allied armies who are making a retaliatory raid against Moab, in this illuminating snapshot of activity from the year 850 B.C.

Jehoram, the new king of Israel, has teamed up with Jehoshaphat, his older contemporary from Judah (verses 1 and 7). There was peace at that time between Israel and Judah. Indeed, Jehoshaphat had previously offered his services to Jehoram's father Ahab; Jehoshaphat's agreement in verse 7 echoes some of what he had said to Ahab in 1 Kings 22:4. Jehoshaphat had also cooperated with Jehoram's older brother Ahaziah in a shipbuilding venture at the gulf of Aqaba, south of Edom (2 Chronicles 20:36). Jehoshaphat's son, who was also named Jehoram, married the other Jehoram's sister Athaliah, and the two royal families remained close for several years (see 8:18, 25–29).

2 KINGS 3:16
Elisha declared, "Here is what God says: Pools of water will fill this dry riverbed."

Their opponent is Mesha, king of Moab (verse 4), whose name appears on a famous stone slab now in the Louvre museum. This massive piece of black basalt, known as Mesha's Stele, was discovered a few miles north of the Arnon River in 1868. It contains a long inscription that explains ancient history from Mesha's point of view, in a language almost indistinguishable from Biblical Hebrew. Mesha admits that Moab has been subservient to Israel's former King Omri, but he is proud of having struck back. He claims that his god Chemosh has helped him capture cities such as Nebo and Ataroth, which belonged to Reuben and Gad according to Numbers 32:34, 38. Thus Mesha's "rebellion" was more substantial than we might have guessed from verse 5.

Visitors to the Bunker Hill museum near Boston can read accounts of a battle as told by British soldiers to their parents back home, together with accounts of the same battle as told by their American adversaries. The two versions are very different; it becomes clear that facts are perceived quite differently by eyewitnesses on opposite sides. Similarly, Mesha's stone makes only an oblique reference to losses in southern Moab, as described in verse 25, and it is silent about the failure of his prior attack on Jehoshaphat reported in 2 Chronicles 20. On the other hand, the Bible records only one of Mesha's victories.

The armies of Jehoram and Jehoshaphat are joined in our story by those of the "king of Edom" (verse 9), who was really a deputy from Judah (8:20; 1 Kings 22:47). Edom is the territory south and southeast of the Dead Sea, hence south of Moab; the plan is to attack Moab from its relatively vulnerable southern flank. But the land is very dry, and the troops run out of water.

Jehoram blames Israel's God Jehovah for luring them into a trap (verse 10); no doubt he remembers the death of his father Ahab (1 Kings 22:20).

The site of this activity is almost surely the valley of the Zered River (Deuteronomy 2:13), which forms Moab's southern boundary. It flows westward, about 30 miles south of the Arnon. The armies have probably set up camp several miles upstream from where the Zered empties into the southern tip of the Dead Sea. The riverbed is dry.

What shall they do? Jehoshaphat suggests asking a prophet (verse 11, see also 1 Kings 22:7), and Elisha happens to be present. Elisha first spurns King Jehoram, whose parents have been devotees of Baal. Indeed, Jehoram's mother Jezebel—who is still alive (9:30)—once tried to kill all the prophets of Jehovah (1 Kings 18:13). But Elisha agrees to help Jehoshaphat (verse 14).

A musician is called in verse 15, so that Elisha can get into the mood to prophesy. This brings "the hand of God" upon him, as it has been on Elijah (1 Kings 18:46). Music is associated with prophetic excitation in 1 Samuel 10:5 and in 1 Chronicles 25:1, 3. We don't know what kind of music this was; it might have been sophisticated psalmody or it might have been simply a steady rhythmic swaying and chanting. An Arab historian has written about a leader called Kûkubury who became so ecstatic over religious music that he shed his clothes, as King Saul did in 1 Samuel 19:24. The prophets of Baal went even further, to self-mutilation (1 Kings 18:28). Elisha's request for music indicates that he was a more traditional prophet than his ascetic master Elijah.

Elisha's prophecy in verse 16 is somewhat cryptic, and it can be interpreted in two ways: Either the men should dig lots of artificial pools, or lots of pools will appear by themselves. Perhaps both meanings are intended. The modern name of the Zered canyon is Wadi el-Ḥesa, 'valley of sandy water-pits', and ground water can usually be obtained there by digging in the sand. But verse 17 makes it clear that something more than ordinary ground water is involved in this story. And indeed, a flash flood suddenly occurs in verse 20, filling the valley with water from a distant rainstorm and fulfilling the prophecy.

Flash floods are infrequent but not really uncommon in this part of the world, so verse 18 remarks that this miracle is just a "light thing" in God's eyes. Elisha predicts that God will also do much more: He will fatally confuse the Moabites. And this is just what happens in verse 23, when the enemy is fooled by the unusual appearance of water on the red sandstone, possibly because of strange-looking artificial pools. An Israelite victory follows (verse 24).

THE FIRST BOOK OF CHRONICLES is the first of four Biblical books written by a man whom scholars call the Chronicler. A distinctive style pervades these four books, which begin with a recapitulation of the history already given and carry it forward to important events that took place in Jerusalem after the Babylonian captivity. About half of the material in Chronicles covers the same ground as Samuel and Kings, but from a different perspective; there is also a lot of new information.

Chapters 1–9 contain genealogies that start with Adam and carry several branches through to the Chronicler's own time. This part of the book was evidently transcribed from source materials quite different from those used in the remaining sections. Chapters 10–21 introduce the main theme by retelling the story of David's empire; here we find cherished memories of the greatest moments in Israel's distant past. The concluding chapters, 22–29, tell about David's detailed preparations for a national shrine. We learn here that the great Temple was carefully planned long before Solomon took over the actual job of construction.

The sons of Levi, who were responsible for Israel's religious activities, are explicitly mentioned more than 100 times in the books of Chronicles, but only 4 times in the books of Samuel and Kings. Therefore the Chronicler was probably a Levite; perhaps, in fact, he was a cantor, because music and song are especially prominent here. Indeed, these books are by no means a mere chronicle of events that had been noted down long ago. Nowhere else in the Bible, except in the Psalms, do we get such a vivid picture of the joy that ancient Hebrews experienced in their regular worship of God in the Temple.

The Deuteronomic history in the preceding books of the Bible might be compared to a documentary movie in which archival newsreels have been tied together with a narrator's comments. In these terms the Chronicler's history, which was composed more than 150 years later, is more like a series of edifying sermons, which reflect on historic scenes that are depicted in stained-glass windows. Sometimes the Chronicler has access to more accurate data than the Deuteronomist had available, but he is not primarily interested in historical facts per se; he generally assumes that the reader already knows them. The Chronicler's real purpose is to derive an important practical lesson from history, namely that Israel's strength derives from spiritual power rather than from military might. These experiences imply that strong religious institutions will provide the best hope for the future.

1 CHRONICLES 3:16

The descendants
of JEHOIAKIM
were:

JECONIAH,
his son;

ZEDEKIAH,
his son.

1 Chronicles 3:16   Werner Schneider

GENEALOGIES look boring. It may be true that x begat y, and that y begat z, but so what? St. Paul himself complains of "endless genealogies" in 1 Timothy 1:4; he calls them "futile" in Titus 3:9. Yet my wife and I have spent many a pleasant day tracing our roots, exploring dusty archives in dozens of county courthouses across America and deciphering old church documents in Europe. We have met many other people who have been bitten by the same bug. There is something fascinating about discovering the relationships between people we never knew, but whose lives had a significant influence on our own; the continuity of history is quite striking when it applies directly to ourselves. Therefore the first nine chapters of 1 Chronicles must have been extremely popular with the many people whose great-great-grandfathers are listed there.

1 CHRONICLES 3:16
The descendants of Jehoiakim were: Jeconiah, his son; Zedekiah, his son.

In fact, a closer look at the Bible's genealogies shows that they aren't really as sterile as they might seem, even though such lists don't actually tie in with our own family trees. Chapter 3 of 1 Chronicles is a case in point. Its main purpose is to list the descendants of David, but it also sheds light on several other aspects of the Bible.

Verses 10–14 list the kings of Judah from Solomon to Josiah, in each case listing only the one son who succeeded to his father's throne. If we add the links from David to Solomon and from Josiah to Shallum, we can see that the Davidic dynasty was very impressive indeed: The crown passed regularly from father to son in an unbroken string extending through 18 generations, covering almost 400 years.

The pattern changes in verse 15, because three of Josiah's sons occupied the throne during the turbulent period just before the fall of Jerusalem. First came Shallum (Jeremiah 22:11), who ruled for only three months before being taken to Egypt; then his older brother Jehoiakim was installed as king for eleven years (2 Kings 23:34, 36). Jehoiakim's son Jeconiah was next; but after a three-month reign, he was taken to Babylon as a prisoner and replaced by his uncle Zedekiah, who repeated Jehoiakim's feat by lasting eleven years (2 Kings 24:8, 15, 17). Verse 15 also mentions Josiah's first-born son Johanan (the same name as 'John'), a person who is otherwise unknown.

The lists of names in Chapter 3 look very much like family history records from much more recent times that my wife and I have found in many parts of the world. Archives everywhere seem to be fragmentary, loosely organized,

60

ambiguous, and peppered with errors. Genealogists have to do a lot of detective work, piecing together scraps of information from many documents in order to assemble a clear picture. In this case the situation is complicated by the fact that kings of those days had a habit of changing their names: Shallum was also Jehoahaz; Jehoiakim was also Eliakim; Jeconiah was also Jehoiachin; Zedekiah was also Mattaniah (see 2 Kings 23:31, 34; 24:6, 17). Furthermore, Jeconiah was sometimes known as Coniah (see Jeremiah 22:24 and 24:1).

The Hebrew text of verse 6 contains two apparent scribal errors, if we compare it to the similar list in 14:5; 'Elishama' and 'Eliphelet' should be 'Elishua' and 'Elpelet'. A scribe has evidently inserted two names from verse 8 into verse 6 by mistake. Similarly, 'Pedaiah' in verse 19 should probably be 'Shealtiel', because Zerubbabel is called the son of Shealtiel in Ezra 3:2 and in ten other places. In this way we learn from the Bible that errors of copying can creep in.

Verse 16, which is our chief concern, has three possible interpretations, and Bible commentators are about equally divided as to which is most likely. (1) The Zedekiah in verse 16 might be King Zedekiah of verse 15. In this case the author is using 'son' in a broad sense to mean 'heir' or 'successor'; if we leave out the first part of verse 15, we get a complete list of the kings of Judah in verses 10–16. (2) The Zedekiah in verse 16 might be the second son of Jehoiakim. King Zedekiah was only two years older than King Jeconiah, and he is called Jeconiah's brother in 2 Chronicles 36:10, but the earlier data in 2 Kings 24:17 and Jeremiah 37:1 may be more trustworthy. Comparison of verse 16 with the style of other nearby verses (e.g., 2:31; 3:10) makes the second hypothesis improbable. (3) The Zedekiah in verse 16 might be a son of Jeconiah, named after his grand-uncle the king. Against this hypothesis is the fact that other sons of Jeconiah are listed in verses 17–18; but these are said to have been born in captivity, so it makes sense to treat them separately. I personally favor Hypothesis 3, but there's no way to be sure.

The genealogy of Jesus in Matthew 1:11–12 skips from Josiah to Jeconiah to Shealtiel, thereby losing Jehoiakim. Three other kings between Jehoshaphat and Jotham are missing in Matthew 1:8–9; scholars think that Matthew was perhaps working with a defective copy of 1 Chronicles 3.

The remaining verses of Chapter 3 read as if they extend to the Chronicler's own day. From these lists and other evidence it is reasonable to guess that Chronicles was written about 400 B.C.

THE SECOND BOOK OF CHRONICLES is the second half of what was originally a single book. It continues the story of 1 Chronicles at essentially the place where the parallel accounts in 1 Kings take over from those in 2 Samuel.

Chapters 1–9 review the reign of Solomon, and the remaining chapters (10–36) discuss the continuation of David's line in the kingdom of Judah. Only the southern half of Israel's divided monarchy is treated here. The people of Judah survived, because they remained faithful to God. Although the leaders of Judah were subsequently deported, many of their descendants (including the Chronicler himself) came back to settle again in Palestine. By comparison with the book of Kings, which was based on similar source materials, this account downplays the civil affairs of state and emphasizes rather the significance of Jerusalem as a religious center.

The books of Chronicles have often been unjustly neglected, perhaps because they originally appeared at the very end of the Hebrew Bible. Even after they were moved to their more appropriate present position by ancient Greek translators, they received the uninspiring name *Paraleipoménon*—'leftovers'—implying that they were merely intended to fill a few gaps in a story that had already been told. Bible scholars once doubted that the Chronicles contained any historical information of value, because these books were written so long after the events they describe. However, the balance of opinion is now changing; recent archaeological discoveries tend to confirm that the Chronicler drew his facts from authentic documents, not from legends or from a vivid imagination. In particular, he frequently quotes from prophets whose writings later became lost. The Chronicles therefore shed important light on a little-known period of Old Testament history.

Even more important, of course, is the Chronicler's spiritual message about the significance of worship. After many years of exile, the Israelites have come to a new understanding of what it means to be God's people. Now, as their religious institutions are being re-established, the Chronicler wants to reaffirm and clarify the ideals of the people who founded those institutions. He recalls the glorious moments when his ancestors were in tune with God and contrasts such periods with the dark days when they were not. The Chronicler doesn't write with the liveliness and wit we find elsewhere in the Bible, but his earnestness and evident enthusiasm combine to make an eloquent statement of his beliefs. Many verses of this book are in wide use today as antiphons in modern liturgies.

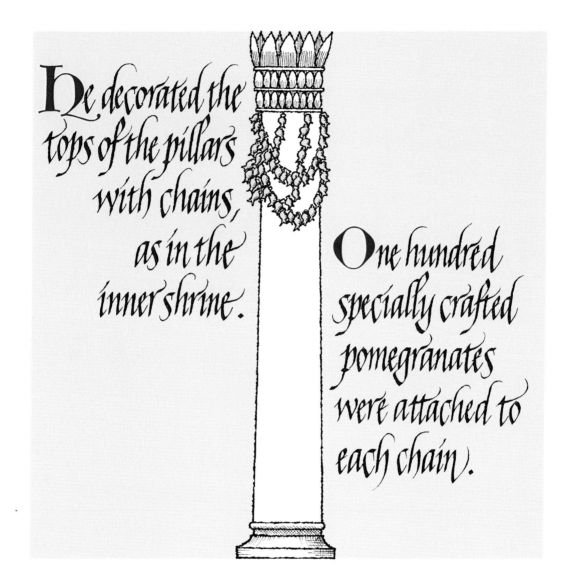

He decorated the tops of the pillars with chains, as in the inner shrine.

One hundred specially crafted pomegranates were attached to each chain.

2 Chronicles 3:16

Allen Q. Wong

LUXURIOUS DECORATIONS adorned every part of Solomon's Temple, including the two massive pillars that stood in front. Verses 15–17 discuss the fabrication of these two pillars, which are also described in 1 Kings 7:15–22, 2 Kings 25:16–17, and Jeremiah 52:21–23.

According to verse 15, the pillars were 35 cubits high; but the other three references all report a height of 18 cubits, so the figure in Chronicles must be based on a misunderstanding. The old cubits of Solomon's day (verse 3) were more than 20 inches long, hence the pillars were more than 30 feet tall.

The pillars were so impressive, they had names: Jachin and Boaz (verse 17). Nobody knows the exact significance of these words, but they were not uncommon as personal names (Genesis 46:10; Ruth 2:1; 1 Chronicles 24:17); therefore Solomon's pillars might have been named for prominent people, as Absalom's pillar was (2 Samuel 18:18). On the other hand, Jachin and Boaz might also stand for 'Stability' and 'Strength'.

2 CHRONICLES 3:16

He decorated the tops of the pillars with chains, as in the inner shrine. One hundred specially crafted pomegranates were attached to each chain.

Anybody who visits old ruins knows that ancient architects put special care into the capitals that sat on top of pillars or columns. Verse 16 describes the decoration on the capitals of Jachin and Boaz.

The standard Hebrew text of verse 16 has been miscopied somewhere along the line, because it reads, literally, '... chains in the inner shrine'. This cannot be right, since the inner shrine—also known as the 'oracle' or the 'holy of holies'—was in the rear of the Temple, far from these pillars. If we add one letter to the Hebrew, we get 'chains, *as* in the inner shrine'; and this makes sense, because chainwork was part of the inner decor (verse 5; 1 Kings 6:21). Alternatively, some commentators think that the word *debîyr* ('inner shrine') was originally *râbîd*, since 'd' and 'r' look very similar in Hebrew; this makes the phrase 'chains like a necklace'. In any case we know that there were chains, probably arranged as festoons, and that pomegranates hung on the chains.

Pomegranates made appropriate ornaments for the Temple, not only because of their intrinsic beauty but also because they appeared on the high priest's robe (Exodus 28:33). Four of the 100 pomegranates were attached to the capital, and the other 96 hung on the chains at the sides (Jeremiah 52:23); this suggests that the capitals were square. There were four long chains, two on Jachin and two on Boaz, making 400 pomegranates in all (4:13).

The pillars, capitals, chains, and pomegranates were all cast of bronze by Huram-abi, a master craftsman from Tyre (2:13). The total weight of bronze was said to be incalculable (4:18), but we can calculate the approximate weight of the pillars by using the fact that they were hollow cylinders, 18 cubits high, 12 cubits around, and 4 fingers thick (Jeremiah 52:21). The product of these dimensions, multiplied by a weight of 530 pounds per cubic foot of bronze, gives a total of about 40 tons for each pillar without its capital. The casting was done in the sand, between Succoth and Zarethan in Transjordan (4:17; 1 Kings 7:46); Solomon drafted non-Israeli laborers to haul the loads (2:18).

Freestanding pillars something like Jachin and Boaz were probably a common feature of Phœnician temples. For example, they are pictured in a sculpture from ancient Tyre and in old coins from Sidon. Bases of two freestanding stone pillars from about 300 years before Solomon's time have also been found in front of a temple excavated in the Galilean city of Hazor. The Tyrian example shows flames arising from fires atop the capitals; Solomon probably did not use this symbolism, because the Bible refers to fires only inside the sanctuary.

The pillars must have been well-known tourist attractions and centers of attention for a long time. For example, we're told that King Joash stood in front of either Jachin or Boaz at the time of his coronation, some 120 years after the Temple had been built (23:13). But finally, after about 375 years, the Chaldean forces of Nebuchadnezzar dismantled everything and carried the bronze to Babylon, pomegranates and all (2 Kings 25:13–17). The Temple was later restored, but the ceremonial pillars were never rebuilt.

How opulent should our churches be? When I first visited Vatican City, I was overwhelmed by the concentration of beautiful objects in one place. I marveled at Michelangelo's masterworks, which he had called "a shadow of the divine perfection," and I was glad to affirm that man's finest creations should be dedicated to God. On the other hand, I knew that the construction of St. Peter's basilica had been financed by questionable practices like the sale of indulgences; and I knew that millions of needy people in the world could make good use of this wealth. The proper balance between richness and austerity will always be a dilemma. We know that poverty will not disappear even if we abandon all finery (Matthew 26:11), and we also know that personal wealth has limited value (Luke 18:22). The ideal situation occurs when people willingly make sacrifices and devote their best efforts to the glory of God, their creator (Exodus 35:21–29; 1 Chronicles 29:9).

THE BOOK OF EZRA is a sequel to the Chronicles, written by the same author. It is named after a famous Hebrew scribe and priest who is sometimes called the father of Judaism because of his legendary religious reforms. Ezra, whose name means 'help', led a large group of Jews back to Palestine after they had been in captivity near Babylon. Several leading specialists of Old Testament history believe that Ezra himself was the Chronicler.

This book is our main source of information about activities in Jerusalem when various groups of exiles were returning. It was compiled from contemporary records that aren't always arranged in chronological order; the story sometimes jumps ahead in time and flashes back again, with little or no warning. This can be baffling to modern readers unless some of the main events of ancient history are kept in mind: Nebuchadnezzar's short-lived empire collapsed in 539 B.C., when Babylon was captured by Cyrus the Great of Persia. Cyrus ruled over a vast territory until 530; he was succeeded by Cambyses (530–522), Darius I (522–486), Xerxes I (486–465), Artaxerxes I (465–424), Xerxes II (424–423), Darius II (423–404), Artaxerxes II (404–358).

In Chapters 1–6, Cyrus allows Zerubbabel and others to lead some exiles back home. Worship resumes in Jerusalem, and the Temple is eventually rebuilt during the reign of Darius I. Ezra enters the picture in Chapters 7–10, at the time of Artaxerxes. (Scholars have argued endlessly about which Artaxerxes it was; more facts are necessary before a decision can be made. I'm betting on Artaxerxes I.)

Two sections of this book (verses 4:7 to 6:18 and 7:12 to 7:26) are written in Aramaic instead of Hebrew. They contain interesting quotations from court records, expressed in the diplomatic language of that day.

The Jewish people came back from Babylon with a better perspective. Their love for God deepened as they began to appreciate the unique spiritual gifts they had received. Unfortunately, they chose to safeguard the purity of their religion by deciding that Judaism was only for Jews; this book ends with the sad story of compulsory divorces in which more than 100 foreign wives were sent away with their children. Such drastic measures may have been the only way to keep the priceless Jewish heritage from melting into oblivion at that particular time, but it set a dangerous precedent. Isaiah 56:6–9 points out that God welcomes foreign proselytes; yet it took many years before people understood that true religion is a matter of the heart, not of race. Peter learned this lesson in Acts 10:35; Paul proclaims it forcefully in Galatians 3:28.

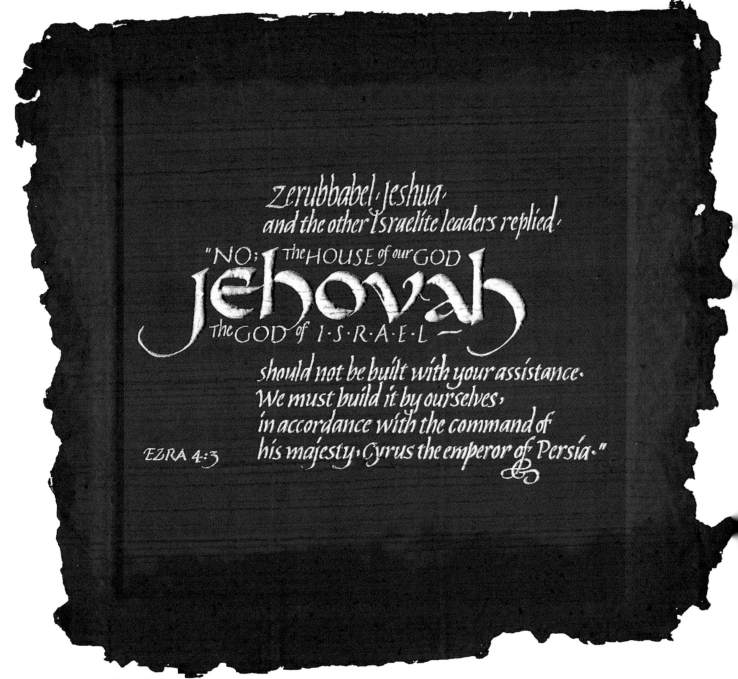

zerubbabel · Jeshua ·
and the other Israelite leaders replied ·
"NO; the HOUSE of our GOD
JEHOVAH
the GOD of I·S·R·A·E·L —

should not be built with your assistance ·
We must build it by ourselves ·
in accordance with the command of
EZRA 4:3   his majesty · Cyrus the emperor of Persia · "

Ezra 4 : 3   Derick Pao

A DECISIVE TURNING POINT in the history of Israel's religion was reached when the returning exiles refused to compromise with their new neighbors.

Let's look first at the cast of characters in this controversy. Zerubbabel, whose name means 'born in Babylon', is a Jewish prince, a grandson of King Jeconiah (1 Chronicles 3:19). Many scholars think his official Babylonian name was Sheshbazzar (see 1:8, 3:6, and 5:16), just as Daniel had the alternative name Belteshazzar (Daniel 1:7). His co-leader Jeshua is the chief priest, a descendant of David's priest Zadok (see 3:2 and 1 Chronicles 6:15). Jeshua is the Aramaic form of the Hebrew name Joshua, by which he is also known (Haggai 1:1; Zechariah 3:1). The other Israelite leaders are named in 2:2. Their opponents, the "adversaries of Judah and Benjamin" (4:1), can be called Samaritans, since Samaria was apparently their capital (4:10, 17).

EZRA 4:3

Zerubbabel, Jeshua, and the other Israelite leaders replied,

"No; the house of our God—Jehovah, the God of Israel—should not be built with your assistance. We must build it by ourselves, in accordance with the command of his majesty, Cyrus the emperor of Persia."

The returning Israelites, 50,000 strong (2:64–65), first set up a sacrificial altar (3:2); then they laid a foundation for the Temple, in a dramatic ceremony that mingled joy with tears (3:10–13). The next step was to build the Temple itself, and the Samaritans came forward with an offer of help (4:2). "Let's build together," they said, "since we and our ancestors have been offering sacrifices to your God for 150 years."

If I had been a member of Zerubbabel's group, I would probably have welcomed this gesture. I would have said, "Surely it's better to have help than to work alone, and to work *with* our neighbors instead of against them. By collaborating, we avoid the danger that they might build a rival shrine."

But my colleagues in this imagined dialog would have told me, "No! These people never really worshipped our God Jehovah; they merely added him to their pantheon of gods (2 Kings 17:24–41). They refused Hezekiah's invitation to celebrate the Passover (2 Chronicles 30:10). To join up with them would mean abandoning the purity of our religion. And it would cause more strife, not less, because we've never gotten along with Samaritans."

Being a Bible student, I'd reply, "Well, these people came later to Josiah's Passover, after he had destroyed their temples (2 Kings 23:19; 2 Chronicles 35:18); some of them even came to worship at Jerusalem after our Temple was destroyed (Jeremiah 41:5). Perhaps they seek Jehovah improperly, but the best way to correct their misunderstanding is to work with them and win them over with kindness. Let's not be selfish, intolerant, narrow-minded, ultra-orthodox, myopic, fanatical bigots; that will just drive them further away."

"Don, you forget that the people of God must be separate from the sinful world. A rotten apple spoils the whole barrel (Haggai 2:11–14). If our argument with the Samaritans were merely about a trivial matter of detail, it would naturally be best to forego our personal preferences for the sake of harmony. But a vital principle is at stake here, the very first of the Ten Commandments (Exodus 20:3). We exist on earth to uphold and testify to those laws, hence we must put our feet down firmly and walk apart from the crowd."

The Jews' actual reply to the Samaritans, in our key verse 4:3, avoids outright confrontation by relying on a technicality: "Much as we might value your aid, we must obey Cyrus's decree." Permission to rebuild had been granted only to the exiles (1:3). This response seems to have carried some weight, because the Samaritans hired lawyers to contest it in court (4:5).

A literal translation of 4:3 would say, 'It is not for you and for us to build...'. This Hebrew idiom is found frequently in the Bible; for example, Jesus says, 'What is there for me and for you' to his mother in John 2:4. The Israelites remain aloof by referring pointedly to 'our God', as the Samaritans had diplomatically referred to 'your God' in 4:2.

I don't agree with all the arguments that I have put into ancient mouths above, but I do think Zerubbabel and his friends came to the right decision. The Samaritans showed their true colors soon afterward (4:4); they had been no more sincere than Judas when he came to Jesus with a kiss (Luke 22:47; see Proverbs 27:6). Sometimes we must say No. St. Paul observes that light cannot commune with darkness, and God's Temple cannot tolerate idols (2 Corinthians 6:14–16). Some of the Samaritans were, in fact, converted (6:21). If the Israelites had enlarged the fold further at that time, their religion would probably have degenerated and disappeared into a swamp of indifference.

On the other hand, I greatly dislike religious factionalism that emphasizes being "holier than thou" in comparatively unimportant matters. Instead of wasting time defending the gates and arguing about the elusive borderline between good and evil, it is far better to concentrate on having a strong central fountain of nourishment. The Israelites wisely turned to the source in later years (Nehemiah 8:1–8).

THE BOOK OF NEHEMIAH is the second part of what was originally one large book of Ezra, just as Chronicles was originally a single book. This part was separated from the preceding chapters because it consists largely of the personal memoirs of Nehemiah, who was governor of Jerusalem and its environs about 75 years after the Temple was rebuilt.

Nehemiah is one of the most genial personalities in the Bible, and his writing gives this book a fresh, distinctive flavor. He was blessed with great administrative skills, and it is instructive to see how he solves the problems of his day. Although he is a man of sometimes violent emotions (1:4; 13:8, 25), his approach is primarily characterized by turning frequently to God in prayer (1:5–11; 4:9; 5:13; 6:9), because of his conviction that God is in control of events (2:8, 20; 5:9; 6:16). He also prays that God will remember his good works (5:19; 13:14, 22, 31). In later years he was credited with establishing a large religious library at Jerusalem (2 Maccabees 2:13, in the Apocrypha).

Chapters 1–7 tell of Nehemiah's first term of office, when he restored the city walls and introduced economic reforms. Chapters 8–10 resume the story of Ezra, which had left off in Ezra 10; that story now has a happy conclusion: Ezra inspires the community by teaching them the Law ('Torah') of Moses. Then Nehemiah returns in Chapters 11–13 to dedicate the walls and to institute religious reforms.

Verses 7:6–73 are almost identical to Ezra 2:1–70, yet these sections both appear in the Hebrew text of the original (combined) book of Ezra. An author does not intentionally write a book in which two chapters are virtually the same; therefore it is almost certain that somebody has inserted Nehemiah's memoirs into the Chronicler's original work. In fact, there once was a Hebrew manuscript in which Ezra 10 was immediately followed by Nehemiah 8; it was included in the ancient Greek translation of the Old Testament, and it is now known as the book of 1 Esdras. (That book, which is part of the Apocrypha, begins with a slightly modified version of the history in 2 Chronicles 35–36.)

This evidence of later editing has led to all sorts of debate about the true order of events. Some scholars maintain that Ezra lived at a later time than Nehemiah; this requires deleting Nehemiah's name from 8:9 and Ezra's name from 12:36. On the other hand, it is not really improbable that Ezra came first; the text does make sense as it stands. Ezra's strict racial policy probably led to unrest, and Nehemiah may have been asked to straighten things out and restore order.

Nehemiah the son of Azbuk,
leader of half the beth·zur district,
restored the next section of the wall,
from a point facing the tombs of David,
to the artificial pool and to the house of
Heroes.

Daniel Wolkowicz

VOLUNTEER WORK by a busy multitude is the subject of Nehemiah 3, which tells about the rebuilding of Jerusalem's walls. This chapter is especially tantalizing to archaeologists, since it is one of the few sources of information about the topography of ancient Jerusalem.

The city had been devastated by Nebuchadnezzar (2 Kings 25:9–10), and it was desolate at the time the Temple was being rebuilt 70 years later (Zechariah 2:4, 7:7). Now another 70 years have gone by and things are still in a terrible mess (2:17); the people mostly live elsewhere (7:4, 11:1).

Everybody pitches in to help, including priests (verse 1), Levites (verse 17), temple servants (verse 26), craftsmen and merchants (verse 8). Most of the helpers are townspeople from surrounding communities like Jericho (verse 2). The only apparent shirkers are some noblemen of Tekoa, who will not stoop so low (verse 5); but others from Tekoa do double duty (verse 27).

NEHEMIAH 3:16

Nehemiah the son of Azbuk, leader of half the Beth-zur district, restored the next section of the wall, from a point facing the tombs of David, to the artificial pool and to the House of Heroes.

At least forty teams worked simultaneously on different segments of Nehemiah's wall. Chapter 3 lists these portions systematically, beginning with the Sheep Gate in verse 1 and proceeding counterclockwise until returning again to the Sheep Gate in verse 32. The Sheep Gate was north of the Temple. Verses 4–14 describe the west wall, which passed through the location of today's Wailing Wall and continued to the tip of the City of David (verse 15), a narrow promontory lying south of the Temple Mount. The City of David, also known as Mount Zion (2 Samuel 5:7), is bounded by the relatively steep slopes of the Tyropœon Valley on the west and the Kidron Valley on the east.

Verse 16 talks about a section of the wall in the southeast corner, which is the responsibility of Nehemiah the son of Azbuk. (This is not the "real" Nehemiah, whose father was Hacaliah (1:1). Azbuk is not mentioned elsewhere in the Bible.) The Nehemiah of verse 16 is a local magistrate who has authority over half of the district surrounding Beth-zur, a city about 13 miles south of Jerusalem that once was fortified by Rehoboam (2 Chronicles 11:7). Excavations at Beth-zur have shown that it, like Jerusalem, was razed by Nebuchadnezzar and rebuilt in the Persian period.

The leader of the other half of Beth-zur isn't mentioned, although both halves of the nearby city of Keilah are accounted for (verses 17 and 18), and so are both halves of Jerusalem itself (verses 9 and 12). Moreover, some people are said to work on a second section, but no first section is listed (verses 19, 20; compare verses 4 and 21). This suggests that Chapter 3 is not a complete record of the work done.

Verse 15 helps us locate the terrain of verse 16, because it mentions the Fountain Gate, the Pool of Shelah, the royal garden (2 Kings 25:4), and a flight of steps. The Pool of Shelah, called Siloam in John 9:7, can still be visited. It lies at the end of a remarkable 1,750-foot tunnel that King Hezekiah constructed to protect his water supply when Jerusalem was under threat of siege (2 Chronicles 32:3, 30). This was Jerusalem's main water source, hence it was a good place for gardens and a Fountain Gate. Indeed, the ruins of an ancient gate, adjoining a steep flight of rock-cut steps leading down from the City of David, have been unearthed not far from the Pool of Siloam.

The man-made pool mentioned in verse 16 is not so easy to identify, because it has long since vanished. It may have been the reservoir mentioned in Isaiah 22:11, or it may be the "upper pool" mentioned in Isaiah 7:3.

The tombs of David (1 Kings 2:10; 2 Chronicles 32:33) might have included several imposing sepulchres now visible on the southeast slope of the City of David. A vaulted tunnel more than 50 feet long and 13 feet high has been found in one of these. Most of the archaeological evidence here was unfortunately destroyed by quarrying operations in Roman times.

I suspect that the House of Heroes was a monument of some sort to commemorate illustrious warriors of the past. Pilgrims to Jerusalem might have passed by such a monument on their way up to the Temple, after seeing the royal gardens and cemeteries. Nehemiah was particularly interested in the preservation of gravesites (2:5), and the tomb of David could evidently still be visited in Christ's day (Acts 2:29). However, most of the commentators on verse 16 think that the House of Heroes was merely an old barracks that had been used by David's "mighty men" (2 Samuel 23:8).

The work on the wall was completed quickly, in only 52 days (6:15). Everybody realized that it had been done with God's help (6:16). This was not just the fortification of an ordinary city; Jerusalem was holy ground, destined to become a great religious capital.

The willing workers of Nehemiah's day have inspired many other groups of people through the ages. And there still is an abundance of work to be done; thus we can join them joyfully, saying, "Let us rise up and build!" (2:18).

THE BOOK OF ESTHER tells the story of a beautiful young Jewish woman who becomes queen of Persia and saves her people, with the help of her cousin Mordecai. The villain of the piece is Haman, whose private grudge against Mordecai develops into a scheme to exterminate all Jews everywhere. At the end the tables are turned and Haman becomes a victim of his own plot. The action takes place about 480 B.C., during the reign of Xerxes I (1:1).

This story contains many fanciful details and other characteristic traits of folklore. But it is also imbued with accurate local color, confirmed by recent excavations. Persian archives mention an official named Mardukâ who was fairly prominent under Xerxes, and many Jewish people had risen to responsible positions in later years of Persian rule. Therefore most scholars think that the story has a genuine historical basis, which has been generously embellished with literary devices to enhance its suspense and dramatic irony.

The book of Esther is decidedly secular; God is not mentioned once. Indeed, the author seems to have taken pains to downplay all traces of religious conviction. The heroine and hero are patriotic, unselfish, and brave, but we are not told the source of their strength. There is no mention of prayer, sacrifice, love, or mercy; instead we find intrigue, chauvinism, hatred, revenge, and savagery. Esther marries an uncircumcised man and presumably eats nonkosher food. Moreover, her name and the names of Mordecai and Haman are remarkably like those of the pagan gods Ishtar, Marduk, and Humman.

Why, then, is Esther included in the Bible? This book is ideally suited to be read during the festival of Purim, an annual commemoration of Haman's downfall that has been a refuge and hope to Jewish people for many centuries. Haman threw dice to determine the fateful day of doom, and the Persian word *purim* means 'dice' (3:7, 9:24). Purim is a time of revelry, an unholy feast when anything goes, analogous to Mardi Gras and Carnival. (The Talmud specifically allows people to drink on this day until they can't tell the difference between "Blessed be Mordecai" and "Cursed be Haman.") As the Esther scroll is read, the children in the synagogue twirl terrific noisemakers called "groggers" whenever Haman's name is mentioned. Burlesque merrymaking like this provides an antidote to excessive piety, a kind of safety valve that lets loose with fun after a year's worth of pent-up irritations.

On balance, I'm glad that the Bible contains a refreshing variety of materials that reflect all sides of life. A nationalistic book, like a patriotic hymn, helps us understand human nature.

When Mordecai heard the news,
he tore his clothes
into shreds,

wrapped himself in coarse burlap,
covered himself with ashes,
and walked into the middle
of the city, wailing
loudly and bitterly.

Esther 4 : 1   Fritz Eberhardt

75

RITUALIZED MOURNING is an art form in the Near East. Mordecai's actions in this verse not only express his deep, overwhelming grief, they also help him recover from a severe shock. He does four things, each of which has parallels in many other parts of the Bible: He rips his clothes; he puts on an uncomfortable sack; he applies ashes; and he cries aloud.

Clothes were especially precious things in those days. To tear them meant to renounce the world and its pleasures, to say "I can't go on like this," to make a radical re-evaluation of priorities. Reuben and Jacob did it in Genesis 37:29 and 34; Ahab did it in 1 Kings 21:27; Hezekiah and his cabinet did it in 2 Kings 18:37 and 19:1; Job did it in Job 1:20; the high priest at Christ's trial did it in Mark 14:63; Paul and Barnabas did it in Acts 14:14. Ezra ripped his clothing and also tore his hair (Ezra 9:3). Messengers of woe arrived with their clothes torn and with dirt on their heads (1 Samuel 4:12; 2 Samuel 1:2). The Bible's most graphic portrayal of this act is perhaps the one given in 2 Samuel 1:11, where David "took hold of his clothes and ripped them."

ESTHER 4:1

When Mordecai heard the news, he tore his clothes into shreds, wrapped himself in coarse burlap, covered himself with ashes, and walked into the middle of the city, wailing loudly and bitterly.

Torn-up robes are often discarded in these incidents and replaced by sackcloth, which is the exact opposite of fine rich clothing (Isaiah 3:24). The Hebrew word for sackcloth is *saq*; it's the same word that is used for a container in Leviticus 11:32 and Joshua 9:4. Grain and money were put into such sacks in Genesis 42:25, 27, 35. We don't know exactly what sackcloth was made of, but evidently it was coarse and scratchy, like today's burlap. Some think that a *saq* was made of camel hair or goat hair, because Isaiah is said to have worn sackcloth (Isaiah 20:2) and other prophets were attired in hair shirts (2 Kings 1:8; Zechariah 13:4; Matthew 3:4).

In early accounts of anguish, people are said to have put dust on their heads (Joshua 7:6; Job 2:12). Later, we read that Tamar applied ashes (2 Samuel 13:19), and this is presumably what Mordecai did in our verse 4:1. Another common practice was to lie down and wallow in an ash heap (4:3; Jeremiah 6:26; Ezekiel 27:30; Jonah 3:6; Luke 10:13).

The fourth component of Mordecai's lamentation is to wail loudly and bitterly. This is also a factor in many of the other instances already cited. Moreover, Ezra 3:13 says that cries of sorrow by some people could not be distinguished from other people's shouts of joy. Isaiah 15:3 speaks of grieving Moabites who "howl from the housetops and from the squares." Mordecai does his howling in the middle of the city, which in this case is Susa (3:15). Susa was about 250 miles east of Babylon, and today its ruins lie in southwestern Iran near the border with Iraq. The palace complex, which lies between Susa and a nearby river, has recently been excavated.

These customs were not specifically Jewish; they were also characteristic among Persians. For example, the Greek historian Herodotus describes a very similar scene that took place when the people of Susa heard about the defeat of Xerxes in Greece: "So sore was their dismay, that they all with one accord rent their garments, and cried aloud, and wept and wailed without stint" (*Herodotus* 8:99). Even today the traditions have not changed much: Ken Follett's *Wings of Eagles* tells of an incident in January 1979, when scores of women in chadors were wailing loudly in front of an Iranian jail where their relatives were imprisoned.

Jews everywhere went into mourning shortly after Mordecai did (4:3). Why? Because Haman had convinced Xerxes that Jewish people were unassimilable (3:8); putting them to death would solve the problem and reap financial rewards (3:9, 11). Here we see the deplorable roots of anti-Semitism.

The Greek and Latin translations of 4:1 add a sentence that tells what Mordecai supposedly shouted: "An innocent people is condemned to death!" For thousands of years the nonconformist ways of Jewish people, loyal to their God and to each other, have been misunderstood. Millions of people have been murdered just because they were Jewish, members of a condemned race.

Mordecai has secret sources of information inside the palace (2:22), so he knows exactly what is going on (4:7). We notice that he doesn't initiate guerrilla action or adopt terrorist tactics. He works through public opinion by calling attention to the injustice of the decree. This approach succeeds in getting his message across.

There is a deep contrast between 4:1 and the preceding verse, 3:15, where Xerxes and his courtier are relaxing and rejoicing in the palace. They sit comfortably without a care in the world, a picture of nonchalance; all reminders of misery and bitterness are banned from these precincts, kept outside the palace gates (4:2). What a tragedy it is that rulers are so insulated from the consequences of their decrees! We must sometimes wail loudly and bitterly before they will take notice and begin to understand.

THE BOOK OF JOB is one of the world's treasures. Alfred Tennyson called it the greatest poem ever written; Thomas Carlyle called it the greatest of all literary works. These may be exaggerations, but I know it's the only book of the Bible that I was required to study in college. On the other hand I must confess that I got little out of this book until later, when I was able to read it in modern translation and when I had experienced more of life.

Chapters 1 and 2 present an ancient folk tale, in prose. This establishes a framework for the poem that follows, in which Job, a wise and perfect man, suffers total disaster. God is testing his faith, but Job doesn't know this. Job's lament in Chapter 3 leads to a series of three dialogs (Chapters 4–14, 15–21, 22–27) in each of which his friends expound the conventional wisdom that goodness is rewarded and evil is punished. Job refutes their arguments, knowing that his pain is undeserved; but they insist that divine justice is simple and clear. Chapter 28 is sort of an intermission; it's an independent poem that extols the virtues of wisdom. Then comes Job's soliloquy (Chapters 29–31) in which he states his case. Chapters 32–37 contain remarks of Elihu; these are probably the work of a later author, the first of countless theologians who have been inspired to write a commentary on Job. God himself speaks in Chapters 38–41, mostly by asking new questions. The epilog (Chapter 42) returns to the folk tale, presenting a simple and happy ending that seems to negate much of what has gone before.

The author of this poem is a profound philosopher with a superb command of language and an exquisite sense of natural beauty. But the astonishing thing about the book of Job is that everyone who reads it comes to a somewhat different conclusion. Job makes us vividly aware of the paradoxes in one of life's ultimate questions—why do we suffer pain?—but he doesn't solve the problem. He merely demonstrates that there are no easy answers.

This is similar to one of the principal discoveries of computer science, namely that some problems are inherently so complex that they can't possibly be solved in a finite number of steps. We must learn to face the fact that an intellectual approach will not lead to an understanding of the cosmos; we can't transcend our limitations. Yet we should keep trying. We should question authority and be aware that the traditional wisdom of religious orthodoxy might be mistaken. This book says that after an honest search, like Job's, we'll learn to trust God's fairness—even though some good men suffer, even though some wicked men prosper, even though religion itself remains a mystery.

Why wasn't I stillborn,
hidden away?
a child who never saw
the light
of day?

JOB 3:16

Job 3 : 16   Luigi Cesare Maletto

DEPRESSION strikes everybody at some time or other, and Job has more than ample reason to be depressed when he begins his lament in Chapter 3. His possessions are gone (1:15–17); his children are dead (1:19); he has a terrible disease (2:7); his friends barely recognize him (2:12). He sits with them in silence for an entire week (2:13).

Now the patient Job of the prolog (Chapters 1–2) becomes the passionate Job of the dialogs (Chapters 3–31). He begins, in verses 3–10, by cursing the day of his birth, wishing that it were blotted out from history. (Similar sentiments are voiced in Jeremiah 20:14–18, but there is no special reason to believe that either author borrowed from the other.)

Knowing that the fact of his birth cannot be erased, Job begins to wonder why he couldn't have died right after being born (verse 11). What was the point of being held on his mother's knees and nursed at her breasts (verse 12)? In fact, why wasn't he born dead (verse 16)?

JOB 3:16
Why wasn't I stillborn, hidden away?
a child who never saw the light of day?

The Bible doesn't say much about miscarriages, but we can assume from verse 16 that stillborn babies were quickly hidden away. Psalm 58:8 expresses the hope that evil rulers do no more harm than if they had been born dead. Ecclesiastes 6:3 says that it's better to be stillborn than to live a long life without happiness. Otherwise there are only two references to the deaths of babies in peacetime: David and Bathsheba's first son died because of David's sin (2 Samuel 12:14, 18); a prostitute's baby died accidentally (1 Kings 3:19).

Infant mortality was evidently very high, because archaeologists have found hundreds of examples of tiny skeletons buried in womb-like clay pots. For example, nearly every home excavated in Hazor had several such infant burials under the packed-earth floors.

Job's wife has planted the idea of death in his mind (2:9), and he now begins to ponder the subject. Death is the great leveller. Rich men and poor men, great and small, all sleep placidly. Dead malefactors sin no more. Dead laborers toil no more (verses 13–19).

Job's 'Why?' in verses 11 and 12 is rhetorical, but in verse 20 he begins to ask questions that demand answers. Why should people's lives be prolonged when they are in misery, when they seek death as others seek priceless treasure (verses 20–22)? We notice that suicide and euthanasia are not options for Job. He doesn't try to sidestep God's will, but he does insist on knowing why.

One of the key issues in the debate over abortion concerns whether or not a fetus really exists as a human being before birth. Verse 16, in its context, seems to say that stillborn children have souls that join those of people who were born alive. Yet there's a similar passage in 10:18–19, which says that going directly from womb to tomb is tantamount to nonexistence. Since Job speaks in anguish, neither verse gives unambiguous advice.

The New English Bible moves verse 16 so that it falls between verses 12 and 13; other translators suggest moving it between 11 and 12. It does make better sense in these positions, especially because verse 13 ("for then I would lie in peace") works better, and verse 17 follows nicely after verse 15. The Hebrew text of Job is thought to contain numerous scribal errors; this accounts for a relatively large number of footnotes in most translations. Other instances of apparently misplaced verses occur later. For example, many scholars think that Chapters 24–27 have been thoroughly scrambled. On the other hand, others argue for leaving verse 16 in its place, as an afterthought of the poet.

Verse 16 is a typical "distich" of Hebrew poetry, in which an idea is expressed in two different ways. Our English translation happens to rhyme, but this is just a lucky accident; the Hebrew original has rhymes of sense rather than rhymes of sound.

There also are larger units of sense. For example, if we move verse 16 as suggested, Job's lament falls into seven "strophes" of three or four verses each (3–6; 7–10; 11, 12, 16; 13–15; 17–19; 20–23; 24–26). Chapter 4, by contrast, divides naturally into 5-verse groups (2–6; 7–11; 12–16; 17–21).

The author is fascinated by light. In verse 9, Job wishes his birthday had not come to light, nor seen the "eyelids of dawn." Verse 16 refers to absence of light. Verses 20 and 23 challenge light's continuance. Light will not be mentioned again until Chapter 12, but it will be considered 28 more times before the book ends.

When my father died, I was deeply grieved in a way that's hard to describe. For example, weeks went by before I could sing without choking up. Finally I came to feel comfortable about the fact that I too will die, and I resumed my normal life. So far I have never yet wished that I were dead or unborn, but I have known many elderly people who have expressed precisely the sentiments of verse 21. When the day comes that I no longer feel at home in this world, I hope that I can attain the relationship with God that Job reached in the later chapters of this book.

THE BOOK OF PSALMS is the Bible's hymnal. It is a magnificent anthology of religious poetry, containing 150 eloquent prayers and praises composed during many centuries of public and private worship in Israel. The prophetical books of the Bible can be regarded as the words of God addressed to men and women, and the historical books as the words of people addressed to each other; in these terms, the psalms are our words addressed to God.

Christians esteem this book more than any other in the Old Testament. Indeed, printed editions of the New Testament often include the Psalms as well. Although many of these poems are three thousand years old, they continue to inspire people as if they were new, since they express human emotions that are timeless and universal.

One of the nice things about the Psalms is that they're easy to find. Turn to the middle of any Bible, and chances are good that you'll be looking at a psalm. This works because Psalm 117 is the middle chapter of the Bible. (By coincidence, it's also the shortest.) Since there are lots of psalms, there's a margin for error in case you don't open to the exact midpoint.

The Psalms in their present form were evidently brought together from separate hymnbooks, each of which was itself a compilation of earlier collections. Most of the psalms ascribed to David occur near the beginning, and 72:20 says "Here ends the prayers of David." The doxologies in 41:13, 72:18–19, 89:52, and 106:48 probably mark the ends of former groupings. A few other patterns can be noticed among the titles of individual psalms; for example, the collections of Asaph (50, 73–83) and Korah (42–49, 84–88) refer to Levites responsible for the Temple entrance and its music (1 Chronicles 9:19, 16:5). The "Songs of Ascents" (120–134) were probably sung by pilgrims to Jerusalem or by Levites on the Temple steps. God is almost always addressed by the Hebrew name 'Yahweh' except in Psalms 42–83, where he is more frequently called 'Elohim'. Psalms 53 and 70 are almost identical with Psalms 14 and 40:13–17 except for changes in God's names. Psalm 108 is essentially the same as 57:7–11 followed by 60:5–12.

About half of the psalms are joyful hymns of praise and thanksgiving; many of the others are poignant lamentations. In between we can find just about every human emotion, including (unfortunately) the wish for revenge. Some statements, like the reference to baby-bashing in 137:9, seem to have no constructive purpose. But the great psalms more than compensate for those whose tone is not so uplifting.

I'll lay me down in peace, and go to sleep; for you alone, O God, my safety keep.

سلام

εἰρήνη

שלום

PACE

frieden

МИР

síolċáin

शांति

paz

paix

Psalm 4 : 8

Kris Holmes

83

SHALOM means safety, security, welfare, health, wholeness, prosperity, integrity, tranquillity, contentment, friendship, peace. It's a common Hebrew greeting, corresponding to the Arabic word *salaam*. 'Shalom' is now entering the English language, like the Hawaiian word 'aloha'. David named two of his sons Absalom ('father of peace') and Solomon ('peaceful'). God desires *shâlôm* for us (35:27). People who love God's law have great *shâlôm* (119:165). Psalm 4:8 associates *shâlôm* with refreshing sleep.

St. Augustine writes in his *Confessions* 9:4 that the book of Psalms greatly "inflamed him" toward God when he was a young man, and that he was especially stirred by Psalm 4. He paraphrases 4:8 by saying, "In you, O God, is the rest that forgets all troubles, since there is nobody else but you."

PSALM 4:8
I'll lay me down in peace, and go to sleep;
for you alone, O God, my safety keep.

The word 'alone' in 4:8 can be understood in two ways: Either God alone keeps us in safety; or God keeps us alone, in safety. Both interpretations are possible (see Deuteronomy 32:12 and 33:28). But the most recent translations all prefer the first alternative, which fits the context better.

Poetry is extremely difficult to translate, and each verse of Psalm 4 has multiple meanings. Scholars had hoped that new data about Canaanite languages, provided by discoveries of extensive ancient libraries at Ugarit and elsewhere, would clarify the interpretation of disputed passages. But in fact, the new discoveries have made the difficulties worse, by demonstrating the existence of additional archaic grammatical forms that make the Hebrew text even more ambiguous than previously believed. There used to be thousands of ways to interpret Psalm 4; now there are millions! For example, 4:8 contains a word *yachdāv* that means 'simultaneously'; the poet lies down and goes to sleep at once. But an old Canaanite dialect is now known to open up the possibility that the poet sleeps "in the peace of God's face" instead. This interpretation forms an interesting counterpart to the "light of God's face" in 4:6. I think the traditional interpretation of 4:8 is probably what the psalmist had in mind, but new renderings of 4:1 and 4:3 seem to improve on the old.

There will probably never be a consensus about the exact meaning of Psalm 4; no two commentators agree, because so many interpretations are possible. But the general outlines are clear: Influential people are casting aspersions on the worship of Yahweh, who has not answered their pleas for material goods. The psalmist remains faithful, and this brings joy (4:7) and peace (4:8).

84

Since sleep is mentioned in both 4:4 and 4:8, Psalm 4 is often regarded as an evening prayer. Franz Delitzsch has compared 4:8 to a cradle song, sung by a trusting child; the psalm "dies away softly and seems to fall asleep itself."

Martin Luther was especially fond of Psalm 4:8. His preface to *Burial Hymns* recommends it as an appropriate epitaph for gravestone inscriptions. Like all Catholic monks, he knew the words well as the antiphon *In pace in id ipsum* that is traditionally chanted on the morning before Easter. During a historic conference at Augsburg in 1530, when he feared his life was in danger, Luther wrote a famous letter to the prominent composer Ludwig Senfl: "This melody has delighted me ever since I was a boy, and it does so even more now that I understand the words." He suggested that Senfl might want to prepare a polyphonic arrangement. Senfl apparently did so, although the music has been lost; several months later, Luther sent him a chest of books in gratitude.

Music was, in fact, associated with psalms from the beginning. Psalm 4 is the first of 55 psalms whose title gives instructions to a 'choirmaster'; in this case stringed instruments are also indicated. Psalm 5, similarly, calls for accompaniment by flutes. The word 'psalm' itself, Greek *psalmós*, appears in 57 titles of the Septuagint translation beginning with Psalm 3; it comes from a Greek root meaning to twang on a string. The Israelites had a variety of instruments containing from three to twelve strings, often called 'lyres', 'harps', and 'psalteries' in English translations. These were joined on festive occasions by trumpets, trombones, and cymbals (1 Chronicles 16:5–6; Psalm 150).

Why is the poet at peace? Because he knows, somehow, that God listens to his call (4:3); and because God gives him great joy (4:7). How much better this is than the restless anxiety of those who don't share his faith! He can feel at peace even in wartime (27:3). When he lies down, no one can make him afraid (3:5; Job 11:19).

My wife Jill has illustrated this concept beautifully on page 147 of her book *Banners Without Words*. A sleeping figure at the bottom of her design is small and vulnerable, yet protected by the gentle hand of God. God's hand appears as a quilted outline, subtly visible in the sky above. We are reminded of Jesus, who slept peacefully in the midst of a storm (Matthew 8:24).

Psalm 4 encourages us to value spiritual things over material things, as in Matthew 6:33, and to maintain our confidence in times of criticism and controversy. We can safely leave tomorrow's issues in God's hands, as we fall asleep in the *shâlôm* that he provides.

THE BOOK OF PROVERBS is an anthology of astute observations, containing the distilled wisdom of many generations. The maxims in this book deal with basic aspects of everyday life: family relationships, business dealings, etiquette, self-control, respect for others. Here we have a work of religious humanism, a practical guide for living in harmony with God's will. This book has no plot, but there is an interesting cast of characters: farmers, lawyers, merchants, craftsmen, kings, courtiers, students, teachers, dropouts, gangleaders, drunkards, travelers, husbands, wives, children, in fact everyone.

Almost all of the proverbs appear as couplets, in accordance with the conventions of Hebrew poetry. "A soft answer turns anger away; a harsh reply intensifies it" (15:1). "Pride precedes destruction; arrogance leads to downfall" (16:18). Nowadays we shorten our proverbs into one-liners. Some people think that the two-line form was a teaching device, whereby students would call out the second part after the instructor said the first. But it's not clear how this would work in cases like 19:5 and 19:9, which have identical beginnings.

Chapters 1–9 form a poetic prolog that sets the context for the proverbs that follow. This excellent introduction was probably added by the unknown editor who brought this book into its final form. Chapters 10–31 contain the proverbs themselves. Like the psalms, they appear in almost totally random order, with subheadings to indicate the sources of different groups. The main collection, "proverbs of Solomon," runs from 10:1 to 22:16; another group of Solomon's proverbs, "copied by men of Hezekiah," fills Chapters 25–29. The sayings of other sages are introduced by subheadings in 22:17, 24:23, 30:1, and 31:1. An ancient Egyptian document called the *Instruction of Amen-em-ope* is so similar to the thirty proverbs in 22:17–24:22 that it clearly shares a common source with this part of the book.

King Solomon was a learned man who is said to have composed 3,000 proverbs (1 Kings 4:32). The 500 or so maxims ascribed to him in this book do not have a consistent style, so it is unlikely that he wrote all of them exactly in the form that has come down to us. However, many of these sayings are expressed in the archaic language of Solomon's day, so it is quite probable that the whole collection bears the stamp of his personality, even more than *Webster's Dictionary* retains the original spirit of Noah Webster.

Wry touches of humor (e.g., 20:14) make this book entertaining as well as instructive. But proverbs are best savored in small doses. Trying to read a hundred of them at once is like hurrying through the Louvre museum.

Proverbs 3 : 16

WISDOM :

*Long life is in
her right hand,
And her
left hand holds
riches and honor.*

Proverbs 3 : 16   Susie Taylor

87

WISDOM is personified as a woman in the opening chapters of Proverbs (1:20–33, 8:1–36). Indeed, if we speak of 'wisdom' in languages whose nouns have gender—Hebrew *chokmâh*, Greek *sophía*, Latin *sapientia*, French *sagesse*, German *Weisheit*, Russian *mudrost'*—we use a feminine word in each case. It's dangerous to speculate about why this is so, and the femaleness of wisdom is not crucial to the meaning of Proverbs 3:16; Semitic and Indo-European languages ascribe feminine gender to all abstract qualities, including 'stupidity' and 'virility'. Yet the personification here isn't just grammatical. Several proverbs have also been credited to a wise woman (31:1); the male-dominated ancient world did not consider wisdom to be an exclusively masculine trait.

Wisdom means knowledge, understanding, sound judgment, skill in living; it's a combination of ethics and intelligence. Wisdom is something that human beings never fully attain (Job 28:12–13, 23), but it is an

PROVERBS 3:16
Wisdom: Long life is in her right hand,
and her left hand holds riches and honor.

ideal worth striving for. Indeed, the main point of verses 13–18 is that wisdom is more valuable than anything else on earth. It has a greater yield than silver and gold; it gives more pleasure than jewels; it bestows long life, riches, and honor, the world's most sought-after blessings.

An old Jewish parable tells of a king who asked his counselor to name a gift, and the man reasoned as follows: "If I ask for silver and gold, I'll receive silver and gold; but if I ask for his daughter, I'll receive his daughter, plus silver and gold" (*Midrash Rabbah Song of Songs* 1:1.9). The moral is that it's best to go to the source. Similarly, God was pleased when Solomon prayed for wisdom, so he granted wealth, honor, and long life as well (1 Kings 3:10–14).

Some commentators say that verse 16 gives equal weight to 'right' and 'left': Wisdom lavishly distributes her gifts with both hands. A symmetrical balance between right and left is consistent with patterns of Hebrew poetry (see, for example, Genesis 13:9 and Isaiah 9:20). But a majority of the scholars who have written about this verse think that the gift of long life, which is associated here with the right hand, takes precedence over the gifts of the left hand, although the latter are not undesirable. The right hand has been associated with special honor since ancient times; see, for example, Genesis 48:14; Psalm 16:8; Matthew 25:33. The left hand is inferior in Ecclesiastes 10:2.

Long life is perhaps the Old Testament's most cherished ideal. It is promised as a consequence of honoring one's parents (Exodus 20:12) and

88

of loving God (Deuteronomy 30:20). Some scholars think that ancient historians adjusted the ages of Israel's patriarchs in order to reflect their relative virtue. Although verses 2 and 16 seem to say that wisdom conveys long life, Job 12:12 presents the other side of the coin by observing that you need many years of experience before you can acquire wisdom. Longevity and wisdom form a feedback loop.

Riches and honor are nice companions of wisdom (8:18), but we are foolish to trust in them (11:28), since they do not last forever (27:24). Riches should be shared with the poor (14:31, 22:9).

The figures of speech in verse 16 may contain echoes of Egyptian mythology, since Ma'at and other goddesses of Egypt are often depicted with an ankh (the symbol of life) in their right hand and a papyrus scepter in their left.

The Greek Septuagint translation of the Old Testament, which was made in Egypt about 200 B.C., appends two additional lines to verse 16: "Out of her mouth proceeds virtue, and she carries law and mercy on her tongue." This may be a lost couplet of the original Hebrew text, but it does not really fit the context very well. Bible scholars generally agree that the Greek translator or some earlier Hebrew editor added these words in order to keep verse 16 from sounding too materialistic. The additions may have been inspired by similar phrases in 31:26 and Isaiah 45:23.

From one point of view, verse 16 simply states that a prudent person tends to stay healthy, and that a good education leads to wealth and esteem. But the message is really more profound, when we examine the context, because wisdom is by no means a purely secular thing that we acquire apart from God. On the contrary, the book of Proverbs repeatedly states that a reverence for God is the first principle, the very root and foundation of wisdom (1:7, 9:10, 15:33; see also Psalm 111:10 and Job 28:28).

I think it's tragic that scientific advances have caused many people to imagine that they know it all, and that God is irrelevant or nonexistent. The fact is that everything we learn reveals more things that we do not understand. The message of Isaiah 29:13–14, that wisdom decays when our hearts are far from God, is even more true today than when it was first spoken. St. Paul puts human wisdom in its place when he remarks that God's 'foolishness' ranks above man's best attempts at understanding (1 Corinthians 1:25). Reverence for God comes naturally if we are honest about how little we know. Humility, not conceit, is what really leads to long life, riches, and honor (22:4).

THE BOOK OF ECCLESIASTES is an essay or sermon that discusses the emptiness and transience of earthly goals. It was written by a philosopher who adopted the Hebrew pen-name *Qôheleth*; in Greek translation his name is *Ecclésiastes*, and in English it has been rendered 'Preacher', 'Teacher', 'Gatherer', 'Academic', 'Philosopher', or 'Discussion Group Leader'.

Qoheleth is an independent thinker who takes an intellectual approach to religion. He observes that, from a rational standpoint, our struggles to achieve success might well be useless. "Let's be realistic," he says. "Things aren't so simple as the Proverbs seem to imply. It's foolish to make sweeping generalizations or sharp distinctions, since nothing is actually black or white; we must learn to deal with shades of gray. Most of life is uncertain, except for the fact that it will end with death."

Ecclesiastes is an enigmatic and fascinating book whose purpose is to raise more questions than it answers. It probes standard assertions and shows their limitations. The author makes false starts and states things ironically, in order to create a mood; then he steps back and rejects everything as a vain delusion. Since he cannot prove anything to be good in an absolute sense, he concludes only that some things are relatively better than others.

The Hebrew is often difficult to translate, since many rare words and constructions are used. Therefore it is sometimes as difficult for us to be sure about Qoheleth's intentions as it was for Qoheleth to be sure about God's.

The author adopts a common literary custom of his time and speaks as if he were King Solomon. This identifies him as a person qualified to comment on the Proverbs, and gives him a chance to point out that the good old days were no better than the present.

The message of Ecclesiastes is disconcerting to people who want simple answers to the complex problems of life. But it provides an important counterweight to the dangers of smug assurance, since empty hopes·can cause people to descend into despair when trouble strikes. Qoheleth warns us not to set our sights too high; other parts of the Bible tell us not to set them too low. We must face life's restrictions with open eyes. We must be prepared for difficulties and death.

Yet Qoheleth concludes that we can savor life itself, because God gives us many joys each day. Indeed, the process of living is itself a pleasure, when we practice moderation; this is what we have been designed to do. Walking can be more fun than reaching a destination.

90

I have also noticed something else under the SVN

IN THE PLACES WHERE JUSTICE OUGHT TO BE, THERE IS WICKEDNESS

IN THE PLACES WHERE VIRTUE OUGHT TO BE THERE IS WICKEDNESS

Ecclesiastes 3 : 16

Sheila Waters

EVERYTHING UNDER THE SUN is tarnished. In every walk of life we can find people who do their jobs poorly. Malpractice suits against poor doctors are sometimes argued by dishonest lawyers. The university at which I work has extremely high standards for admitting students and appointing faculty members, yet our students and teachers sometimes prove to be incompetent. No filter has ever been devised that lets only the good people through. When we contemplate human society, we cannot help but share Qoheleth's disappointment and distress. Indeed, even when I look closely at the artificial world of computer programming, I never see a system that is completely free of "bugs."

The author of Ecclesiastes is a keen observer of life. His picturesque phrase "under the sun" is an especially appropriate way to describe the Near-Eastern world in which he lived. In Chapters 1 and 2 he has explored the limits of wisdom and wine, of projects and possessions; nothing has proved to be really satisfying. Success in one area has always led to problems in another. Chapter 3 begins with Qoheleth's famous poem about opposite forces in life—birth and death, weeping and laughing, war and peace, each in its own time. Although we cannot penetrate the inscrutable mysteries of God (verse 11), Qoheleth observes that God has given us precious gifts of food, drink, and the ability to enjoy our work (verse 13). God is in control of everything (verse 15).

ECCLESIASTES 3:16

I have also noticed something else
   under the sun:
  in the places where justice ought to be,
   there is wickedness;
  in the places where virtue ought to be,
   there is wickedness.

This upbeat theme dissolves in verse 16, when Qoheleth remembers the existence of evil. How can we trust God's goodness if we find corruption everywhere? Even in the courts of justice, where good and evil are supposed to be sharply distinguished, it turns out that might makes right. Bribery is a continuing problem (Exodus 18:21; 2 Chronicles 19:6; Proverbs 17:23).

Verse 16 also speaks of places where virtue ought to be; these are probably the religious institutions of Qoheleth's day (see 9:2 and Deuteronomy 19:17). Thus, both civic and religious leaders are tainted. Wickedness abounds in both palace and temple (see Jeremiah 23:11). Qoheleth mentions wickedness twice, for effect, just as he says "there is no one to comfort them" twice in 4:1.

Chapters 1 and 2 of this book are written from King Solomon's perspective, but it is hard to imagine Solomon writing verse 16 of Chapter 3. A powerful monarch cannot be a disinterested observer of corruption in his own administration; he must try to reform the system. Yet the author of Ecclesiastes is apparently content to urge patience and acquiescence. We cannot use this argument to prove conclusively that Solomon did not write Ecclesiastes, because we know that God himself—who is much more powerful than Solomon ever was—has not eliminated vice. Solomon, in 1 Kings 8:46, knows that everyone is fallible, just as Qoheleth does (7:20); can it be that a wise ruler will tolerate a certain amount of wickedness (7:16–17)?

Verse 16 states a problem, and the following verses comment on it. Qoheleth presents the conflicting thoughts that occur to him as he broods about the venality of judges and priests. He has an original method of argumentation, which has been compared to counterpoint in music. This unique style has confused many interpreters, who have suggested that verse 17 was added by someone who edited Qoheleth's original words. But the prevailing opinion among today's Bible scholars is that the book of Ecclesiastes is almost entirely the work of a single author.

Qoheleth in verse 17 temporarily latches onto the comforting thought that God will judge people himself, in his own good time, just as there is a time for everything else (verses 1–8). Human lives are too short to ensure justice in earthly terms, so it is best to leave this to God. But verse 18 introduces a more pessimistic alternative: Perhaps God is trying to demonstrate to us that we are no better than beasts, in spite of our supposed intelligence.

Certainly we are going to die, just as animals do (verse 19). We came from dust and will return to dust (verse 20). Furthermore, it's debatable whether human souls are intrinsically different from those of other creatures; who knows what will really happen (verse 21)? We must confess much ignorance about the sequel to death. On the other hand, if we really are like animals, we can at least learn from them the simple, tranquil pleasures of each passing moment (verse 22; see also 5:18, 9:7–9; Matthew 6:26–34).

The philosophy of Qoheleth does not pretend to be complete; it is, after all, only one small part of the Bible. But the words of Ecclesiastes certainly provide a hungry mind with food for thought, and I'm sure that Qoheleth wants us to relish our personal quests for understanding just as we enjoy exercising our other God-given abilities.

Let us therefore bask under the sun and continue our study, even though reading does involve some effort (12:12).

THE SONG OF SOLOMON, also known as Canticles or the Song of Songs, is a rhapsody about the mutual love of a man and a woman. It extols God's gifts of physical beauty and sensual pleasure. It affirms that attraction between sexes is healthy and natural.

This book has the flavor of folk poetry; it breathes the pure atmosphere of the countryside. It may have been written by a woman who lived during Solomon's reign or shortly thereafter. The title in 1:1 was probably added much later, at a time when Solomon was assumed to be the author.

Most of the verses of this Song are spoken by a woman to her lover or vice versa. There is no special structure to the shifting pattern of images; but the poem is easier to follow if the existing chapter divisions are ignored, and if the verses are broken into stanzas just before 2:8, 3:6, 5:2, 6:4, and 8:5.

Human sexuality is a strong passion quite unlike our other instincts. It affects our thought processes, our social structures, and our language to such an extent that it must be treated delicately. Therefore it is not surprising that the Song of Solomon has been given more distinct interpretations, per word of text, than any other book of the Bible.

Many pious expositors have treated Canticles as an allegory or parable, which illustrates the mutual love between God and Israel, or between Christ and the Church, or between God and individual believers. The most detailed interpretation of this kind was worked out by St. Bernard and his 12th-century followers, who expressed their conclusions in an eloquent series of 253 sermons. People throughout the centuries who have had intimate experiences of divine love have looked at the Song and said, "Yes! It's like this!"

From about 100 A.D. to 1800 A.D., allegorical interpretations were adopted by almost everybody, because human sexuality was considered too beastly to deserve a hallowed place in the Bible. The leaders of both Judaism and Christianity squelched anyone who dared to suggest that Solomon's Song spoke directly of earthly love. For example, the Westminster Assembly Bible of 1651 reported that some readers "had lower conceptions of it, and received it as an hot carnall pamphlet.... This blasphemy hath perished."

But all of the allegorical interpretations have turned out to be quite arbitrary. Almost any preconceived notion can be cast in allegory form, because the sexual metaphor is so versatile. The allegories tell us something about their interpreters, but not about the Song of Songs. By looking at the plain meaning of the text, we are able to appreciate this book in its original sense.

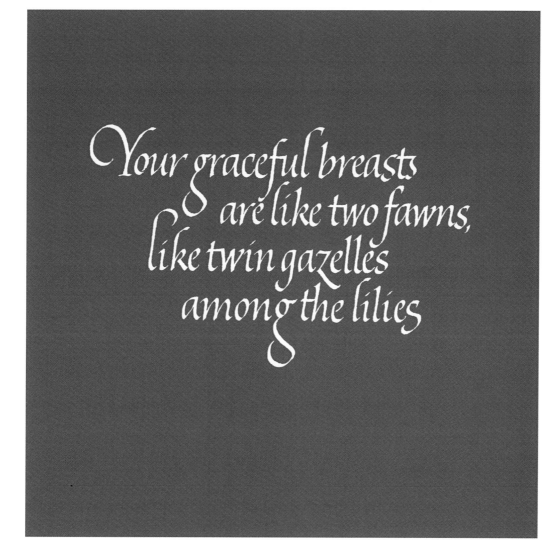

Song of Solomon 4 : 5

Bent Rohde

95

THE HUMAN BODY is delightful to behold. "How beautiful you are, my darling!" (1:15, 4:1). In verses 4:1–7, a man praises the charms of his beloved, and she does the same for him in 5:10–16. These songlets are examples of an ancient type of love poem called a *wasf*, in which a beloved's body is praised part by part, often making use of extravagant and far-fetched metaphors. For example, an Egyptian papyrus from about 1250 B.C. contains a fragment of a wasf that says, "my sister's mouth is a lotus; her breasts are mandrakes." Wasf songs appear several times in the *Thousand and One Nights*, and they are still popular in modern Arab poetry. A 19th-century wasf includes this line: "Her bosom is like polished marble tablets, as ships bring them to Sidon; like pomegranates topped with piles of glittering jewels."

SONG OF SOLOMON 4:5
Your graceful breasts are like two fawns,
like twin gazelles among the lilies.

A woman's breasts are perhaps the most appealing aspects of her body, from a man's point of view. Western culture has become overly obsessed with this symbol of female sexuality, but even in Bible times a voluptuous bosom was an object of special attraction for the male (see Proverbs 5:19; Ezekiel 23:3). I can remember reading Ezekiel 23 with great interest but little understanding, when I was a student in eighth grade.

Verse 4:5 compares a beloved's breasts to twin fawns, perfectly matched. Gazelles are well-known symbols of gentle beauty and charm. The simile in this verse is not meant to be anatomically exact, but it might be suggested by the graceful motion of gazelles as they frolic and play. Gazelles are also metaphors for the man (2:9, 17; 8:14).

The lilies in 4:5 are called lotus blooms by some recent translators. Their function in this metaphor has been given several different interpretations. For example, some commentators see them as a garland covering most of the woman's breasts. Others see them as simply completing the pastoral image of gazelles, since Near-Eastern art frequently depicts gazelles browsing among lotus plants, and since the scent of flowers adds a sweet freshness to the scene. Verse 7:3 repeats 4:5 without mention of lilies; so some people think that the lilies in 4:5 are superfluous, included perhaps to make the verse end like 2:16 (since 4:6 begins like 2:17). Still another interpretation proceeds by comparison with 5:13, where lilies represent the man's lips. This implies that lotus-lilies are red in hue; they may therefore represent the nipples of the beloved or the kisses of her lover (see 1:2, 13).

96

More fanciful metaphors about a shapely bosom appear later in the Song, when breasts are compared to date clusters (7:7) and towers (8:10).

Allegorical explanations of 4:5 began with Hippolytus of Rome, about 200 A.D., who said that the two breasts represent the Old and New Covenants. The Targum on Canticles, a Jewish interpretation that was written in Aramaic about 650 A.D., compared them instead to two promised redeemers, a Messiah son of David and a Messiah son of Ephraim; the twin gazelles were said to be like Moses and Aaron. A 12th-century Cistercian abbot, John of Ford, interpreted the beloved's breasts as allegories of mercy and truth. Rabbi Tamakh in the 14th century compared them to the king and high priest, who are being praised for living in harmony, i.e., grazing together. The 17th-century Weimar Bible says that breasts represent the sacraments of Baptism and Communion, because 1 John 5:8 associates water and blood with the Spirit, while 1 Peter 2:2 encourages us to seek the "pure spiritual milk." Finally in the 19th century, the breasts were identified with faith and love—because Paul speaks of the "breastplate of faith and love" in 1 Thessalonians 5:8. Considerable ingenuity and imagination have clearly gone into these interpretations, and we can get valuable insights into spiritual mysteries by seriously contemplating such metaphors. But the diverse allegory theories do not provide a reliable guide to the true meaning and intention of the original verse 4:5.

Commentators from the Victorian era had this to say: "All is natural to an Eastern imagination, which revels in eulogium that to our colder taste would seem extravagant.... Had these verses no other meaning than this literal one, we cannot think they would have found a place in the Holy Scriptures. Therefore we take them as setting forth, under their rich Oriental colouring, the blessed truth that, in the sight of their Lord, his people are without blemish."

The 20th century approach, exemplified by Marcia Falk's recent translation, is simple and direct: "Your breasts—twin fawns in fields of flowers."

Genesis 2:25 speaks of the first husband and wife, in the idyllic Garden of Eden. They were naked yet not ashamed. However, after eating forbidden fruit, they felt the need to conceal their bodies (Genesis 3:7). I think the Song of Solomon is in the Bible so that we can learn to balance the evils of lust and adultery with the blessings of wholesome desire and fulfillment. Let us thank God for pulchritude, both male and female! Let us not be ashamed of the natural attraction that a man and a woman feel for each other. It is part of God's magnificent creation.

THE BOOK OF ISAIAH is the first and greatest of the prophetical books that appear at the close of the Old Testament. These books record words of God that were communicated to prophets—to people who were specially called to relay God's messages to their contemporaries.

Isaiah lived in Jerusalem, about 750–700 B.C. It was a pivotal time in his nation's history, during which the northern kingdom of Israel was wiped out by Assyrian aggression while his own southern kingdom barely survived.

Isaiah spoke boldly about the decadence he saw everywhere. He denounced his countrymen's pride and their callous oppression of the poor. He was a patriotic statesman who counseled against foreign alliances that would lead people even further from God. His advice wasn't heeded until the time of Hezekiah, but he wrote it down so that important lessons could be learned later (8:16).

This book contains Isaiah's prophecies together with interpretations and supplementary materials that were added by later commentators. Chapters 40–66 are often called Deutero-Isaiah because they have a distinctly different flavor, and because they are addressed to the Jewish exiles in Babylon some 150 years after Isaiah's time. The anonymous author of these later verses is the supreme poet of the Bible; he speaks in modulated, lyrical, contemplative cadences of unsurpassed beauty. Isaiah's words in Chapters 1–39 have their own eloquent style, but these earlier verses are more abrupt and terse, often cryptic.

Many separate elements have been brought together in this book. Roughly speaking, there are prophecies addressed to Isaiah's contemporaries in Chapters 1–12; prophecies addressed to other nations in Chapters 13–23; prophecies addressed to Samaria and Jerusalem in Chapters 28–33. Chapters 36–39 are historical narratives almost identical to 2 Kings 18–20. Chapters 40–55 contain a poem of promise for Babylonian captives, the Book of Consolation. Chapters 56–66 speak primarily to former exiles who have returned to Jerusalem. In between are an "apocalypse" (Chapters 24–27) and a "little apocalypse" (Chapters 34–35), which look ahead to the end of the world.

Some people are disturbed by the idea of a book with multiple authors, as if editorial contributions might perhaps be spurious or non-authentic. But the entire book of Isaiah as we now have it was chosen to be part of the Bible, and indeed, it is an especially beloved part. Several themes give unity to this book in spite of its diverse authorship: the fresh, vivid imagery; the emphasis on God as the Holy One of Israel, awesome and transcendent, governing all; the promise of a Messiah who will establish a kingdom of peace and justice.

God says:

"The women of this city
are so haughty! They strut around
with heads held high,
flirting with their eyes;
they mince along with dainty steps
jingling with their feet."

Isaiah 3:16   Donald Jackson

99

THE PROUD WOMEN of Jerusalem are denounced in these words of God to Isaiah. Here they strut, opulently dressed, while other people live in abject poverty. The 'women of this city' mentioned in verse 16 are, literally, the 'daughters of Zion'; Zion was the hill on which the palace stood, so it was probably the site of pretentious houses. Isaiah himself is probably a member of the upper classes, because he has easy access to kings and other notables (7:3, 8:2, 22:15, 37:6). The reign of King Uzziah has brought prosperity (2:7). But the rich people have nothing to be proud of (2:11), because they have gained their wealth by exploiting the poor (verses 14 and 15).

Isaiah has been painting a grim picture of his nation's depravity, and in verse 16 he turns to the worst feature of all: Even the women, society's last bastion of goodness, have lost their integrity. Hence he foresees doom. The women will be humiliated and ravaged (verses 17 and 24).

ISAIAH 3:16

God says:

"The women of this city are so haughty!
They strut around with heads held high,
* flirting with their eyes;*
they mince along with dainty steps,
* jingling with their feet."*

Verses 18–23 go on to dramatize the vanity and extravagance of rich women's apparel. These verses present an extensive catalog of female finery that was available at Isaiah's time, twenty-one items in all.

Pride is hateful to God, and Isaiah repeatedly decries it (13:11, 14:13, 25:11, 26:5, 28:1, etc.); proud women are castigated again in 32:9–13. Verse 16 mentions stretched-out necks as a symptom of pride, and this image occurs also in Psalm 75:5. Elsewhere we find condemnations of haughty eyes (Psalms 18:27, 101:5; Proverbs 6:17).

Two of the Hebrew words in verse 16 have an uncertain meaning, because they don't occur elsewhere in the Bible. The women's eyes are said to be *m^{e}saqq^{e}rôth*, which is usually understood as 'ogling' or 'glancing wantonly' (see Genesis 39:7). Other interpreters imagine the women 'glancing coyly' to see if they are being noticed. Another plausible explanation is that *m^{e}saqq^{e}rôth* means 'with painted eyes', since it is similar to an Arabic word for 'paint', and since Near-Eastern women have long been known for their eye makeup (see 2 Kings 9:30; Jeremiah 4:30; Ezekiel 23:40).

The other mysterious Hebrew word is *ṭâphôph*, which sounds so much like shuffling feet it is thought to mean 'mincing along'. A third word, *'akaç*, appears only here and in verse 18; it almost surely denotes ankle bracelets, metal rings that make a jingling noise. Archaeologists have learned that such bangles were used in Egypt as early as 1900 B.C.

Some female names in the Old Testament are apparently connected with ornamentation. For example, Caleb's daughter Achsah (Judges 1:12) probably got her name from the Hebrew word for ankle bracelets. Job's daughter Keren-happuch (Job 42:14) was named, literally, 'horn of eye-shadow'.

Verse 16 has an interesting connection with American literature. One of Edgar Allan Poe's editors objected to a line in *The Raven* that refers to "seraphim whose foot-falls tinkled on the tufted floor." But Poe replied that he was thinking of the daughters of Zion in Isaiah 3:16! Evidently he knew the Bible rather well, although not well enough to prove his point; the women of this passage are not at all the seraphim of 6:2.

The words 'God says' at the beginning of this verse are a trademark of prophecy. Similar constructions are found throughout the prophetical books; indeed, Biblical prophecy means 'forthtelling' God's will, not 'foretelling' the future. Isaiah has received a divine message, which he is putting into poetic form. Sometimes Isaiah has God speak in the first person, 'I' (verse 4), but verse 17 uses a third-person construction. This inconsistency is common in prophetic writings, which have a distinctive style.

The message of Isaiah 3:16 has a parallel in verse 24:31 of the Koran: "Tell the believing women to lower their eyes and be modest ... and let them not stamp their feet so as to reveal hidden ornaments they wear."

Should we conclude from these verses that women—and men—are to abandon elegant clothes? No; the clothes are not being attacked here. Finery is just a symptom, not the disease. Pride is the root of the problem. Pride is rightly mentioned first.

Some religious groups restrict their members to very modest clothing. But this prohibition does not cure the people of pride, which can still be exhibited in many ways. God surely does not object to bright colors, unless he made a mistake when he created birds and flowers.

Gaudy and/or immodest clothing is another story. The recommendations for simple dress in 1 Timothy 2:9–10 and 1 Peter 3:3–4 are primarily directed against the overly flamboyant garments worn by prostitutes to attract attention. These verses also point out the superiority of spiritual raiment to physical attire. Earthly beauty is only skin deep, and we might well ask: "How should we adorn ourselves so as to be most attractive to God?"

THE BOOK OF JEREMIAH is an anthology of writings by and about one of Israel's greatest prophets. Jeremiah was born at a time when his nation badly needed prophecy, just when it was about to enter its gravest crisis. His long career spanned the chaotic period during which Jerusalem and the kingdom of Judah fell into Babylonian hands and a long captivity began.

Jeremiah pulled no punches as he denounced the deviant religious practices of his day, but his urgent appeals were spoken more in sorrow than in anger. The messages he relayed from God fell mostly on deaf ears, yet he could not keep silent (20:9). His life was a dismal failure by the standards of his countrymen; he was lonely (15:17), persecuted (20:2), imprisoned (32:2). But he ultimately became recognized as the most significant person of his time. His words have proved to be instructive, comforting, and inspiring to all subsequent generations who have studied them.

This book contains many short prophecies, in both prose and poetry, mixed with biographical narratives. Like the Psalms and Proverbs, it consists of individual items that have been juxtaposed with little or no apparent order. Many sections have been carefully dated, but the dates are not in sequence; if we want a chronological account of Jeremiah's activities, we must read 45:1 before 36:9, then 24:1, then 49:34, 51:59, 39:1, 32:1, 39:2, 43:8, and 46:13. There are many repeated passages; for example, 6:13–15, 6:22–24, 16:14–15, and 23:19–20 are almost identical to 8:10–12, 50:41–43, 23:7–8, and 30:23–24. We clearly shouldn't expect to read this book like a novel.

Yet there is some structure to the grand disarray here, since items are often grouped by topic. Most of Jeremiah's prophecies appear in three sections: Chapters 1–25 are primarily messages of judgment, and Chapters 30–33 of hope, for Jeremiah's own people; Chapters 46–51 are addressed to foreign nations. The remaining chapters contain historical records, which often supplement the accounts found in 2 Kings and 2 Chronicles. For example, Chapter 29 is Jeremiah's letter to the first group of Babylonian captives. Chapter 36 tells how the first draft of this book was written, destroyed, and written again. In Chapters 43–44, Jeremiah is forced to flee to Egypt.

Of special interest are Jeremiah's "confessions" in which he cries out to God in anguish about his innermost feelings. (See, for example, 11:18–12:6; 15:10–11, 15–21; 17:14–18; 18:18–23; 20:7–18.) Here we learn of the intense personal communion with God that has endeared Jeremiah to the hearts of the countless people who have shared these emotions.

God declares that
there will come a time
when you return and repopulate
the
land.
THE ARK
Then nobody
OF THE
will speak
COVENANT
People
any more
won't think
about
OF THE LORD."
about it;
they won't remember it;
they won't
need it;
they won't
make another.

Jeremiah 3 : 16   Claude Dieterich

THE ARK OF THE COVENANT played a significant role during Israel's early history. It was a small box, about $4' \times 2' \times 2'$ overall, made of acacia wood and overlaid with gold both inside and out (Exodus 25:10). Two stone tablets, containing the original Ten Commandments of God's covenant with Israel, were kept inside (Deuteronomy 10:5; 1 Kings 8:9); hence the name 'Ark of the Covenant of the Lord'. Modern Bible translations sometimes call it the 'Covenant Box', because the Hebrew word that has traditionally been rendered 'ark' in this context actually signifies a box or chest-like container. Money could be kept in such an 'ark' (2 Kings 12:9), and Joseph was buried in one (Genesis 50:26). A boat-like shape is not implied; indeed, Noah's 'Ark' of Genesis 7 corresponds to a completely different Hebrew word.

JEREMIAH 3:16

God declares that there will come a time when you return and repopulate the land. Then nobody will speak any more about "The Ark of the Covenant of the Lord." People won't think about it; they won't remember it; they won't need it; they won't make another.

Atop the Ark of the Covenant was a solid gold lid, sometimes called the 'mercy seat' (see Exodus 25:17), above which God spoke to Moses (Exodus 25:22; Numbers 7:89). It was adorned with a pair of golden cherubim, which were originally part of the lid (Exodus 25:19) but greatly enlarged when the Ark was installed in Solomon's Temple (1 Kings 6:23–28). These cherubim were probably shaped like the winged sphinxes that archaeologists have found buried with royal thrones in Canaan.

The Ark was fitted with rings through which carrying poles could be inserted (Exodus 25:14). It was frequently carried into battle (Numbers 10:33; Joshua 6:8), where it represented God's presence on Israel's side (1 Samuel 4:3). It symbolized God's leadership when the Israelites crossed the Jordan (Joshua 3:11). However, most of the time it resided in the inner sanctuary of the Temple; the 'Holy of Holies' (Exodus 26:33; 1 Kings 8:6), where it had special significance in the annual Day of Atonement ritual (Leviticus 16:15).

The Israelites frequently imagined that God was enthroned between the cherubim (2 Kings 19:15; Psalms 80:1, 99:1, 132:7–8). However, the Ark was not worshipped as an idol, like the images of Canaanite gods were (10:3–5); the Israelites regarded it in somewhat the same way as Christians now associate God's presence with bread and wine in the sacrament of the Eucharist.

The second part of verse 16 seems at first to be a lament about the future decline of religion: What could be worse than forgetting about the Ark of the

104

Covenant? But the context makes it clear that Jeremiah is actually speaking words of consolation. He is announcing God's promise of a happy future when the present crises will be forgotten. And he does this in a characteristically provocative way, by pointing out that an enlightened future, with no Ark of the Covenant, will actually be better than the glorious times of the past.

The first part of verse 16 promises that the Israelites will repopulate the land; literally, it says they will 'be fruitful and multiply', using the same Hebrew words as in the story of creation (Genesis 1:22). This expression appears also in 23:3 and in Ezekiel 36:11, where similar predictions are made.

The Bible doesn't tell us explicitly when the Ark of the Covenant disappeared. Many people think Manasseh removed it when he installed an image of Asherah (2 Kings 21:7); Manasseh's successor, Josiah, spoke of putting the Ark into the Temple (2 Chronicles 35:3). But some interpreters believe that Josiah was merely making a reference to history and saying, "Levites have other duties in today's Temple because they no longer need to carry the Ark as they did in Solomon's day." Therefore it is not certain that the Ark was included in Josiah's reforms. No Ark is mentioned in the list of valuable items plundered from the Temple in the final Babylonian conquest (52:17–23). The most likely explanation is that Nebuchadnezzar looted it on his earlier rampage, since 2 Kings 24:13 says that Solomon's golden objects were all destroyed at that time. Many years later a legend sprang up, reported in 2 Maccabees 2:5, that Jeremiah hid the Ark in a cave on Mount Nebo; but verse 16 makes it clear that Jeremiah would not have wanted to do any such thing.

The Ark is lost. But its absence need not be regretted, since it has served its purpose. In God's plan for the future, everyone will have knowledge and understanding (verse 15). The entire city of Jerusalem, not just the mercy seat, will be God's throne (verse 17). In other words, God will live inside his people; the city as a whole will be filled with glory. The consciousness of God's presence will be so widespread that the old Ark will be utterly unimportant. The law will be in people's hearts (31:33), so it need not be kept in a holy Box. Moreover, the Ark's exclusiveness, as a symbol of separation from other nations, will vanish; people from everywhere will gather in Jerusalem (verse 17).

The prediction of verse 16 was soon fulfilled: Ezra and Nehemiah made no mention of the Ark when they restored the Temple after the exile, and the people grew in knowledge and understanding. We realize now that we ourselves are God's inner sanctuary (1 Corinthians 3:16).

THE BOOK OF LAMENTATIONS is a set of five solemn elegies especially suitable for individual or group reading in times of sorrow. The first, second, and fourth of these poems are specifically concerned with the destruction of Jerusalem, and the fifth discusses the aftermath of that disaster. The third is a more general, personal prayer.

Jeremiah composed a funeral song, now lost, for King Josiah (2 Chronicles 35:25), and he often spoke of mourning (for example, in Jeremiah 9:10, 20). Therefore it is not surprising that many people have regarded him as the author of these lamentations. Indeed, our English word 'jeremiad' is derived from the traditional association of Jeremiah with outbursts of sorrow. But Lamentations 2 and 4 have less in common with Jeremiah than they do with Ezekiel, and 63 of the 66 verses in Lamentations 3 use expressions that do not appear anywhere in the long book of Jeremiah. It is most likely that the unnamed authors of Lamentations were among the gifted men or women of Israel who contributed anonymous poems to the book of Psalms.

Jewish people read this book annually on the Ninth of Ab, a solemn festival named for the fifth month in their ancient calendar. On the ninth day of Ab, in 70 A.D., Roman soldiers destroyed the Second Temple in Jerusalem. This took place almost exactly 655 years to the day after the Babylonians had sacked the First Temple, on either the seventh of Ab (2 Kings 25:8) or the tenth (Jeremiah 52:12). Thus the ninth of Ab became the Pearl Harbor Day of Judaism. A commemorative fast during the fifth month was instituted during the exile (Zechariah 7:3), and it has continued ever since. On the evening before the Ninth of Ab, darkened synagogues fill with worshippers who touch ashes to their foreheads and use candles to follow the Hebrew text of Lamentations, as the dirges over Jerusalem are chanted. The mood is similar to that of Black Friday in Christian churches, when portions of Lamentations are part of the traditional liturgy. ·

Lamentations 2 and 4 can also be read as history. They present a vivid account of siege, famine, humiliation, and slaughter, followed by a political and religious vacuum, evidently written by an eyewitness of those events.

The poems gain effectiveness by frequent contrasts between the new situation and the old: "How lonely is she now, the city that once teemed with people!" (1:1). But the main theme of Lamentations is not doom and gloom. The bottom line in all these poems is an affirmation of faith in God's continuing power, mercy, and justice.

He ground my teeth in gravel, trampling me in dust and ashes.

LAMENTATIONS 3:16

Lamentations 3 : 16

Georgia Deaver

AN ACROSTIC is a poem in which each verse begins with a predetermined letter of the alphabet. The first four chapters of Lamentations are Hebrew acrostics that run through the entire alphabet in sequence. For example, in Chapter 3, verses 1–3 all begin with Aleph; verses 4–6 all begin with Beth; verses 7–9 with Gimel; and so on until verses 64–66, which all begin with Tav, the 22nd and final Hebrew letter.

The Bible contains ten alphabetic poems besides those in Lamentations, namely Psalms 9–10, 25, 34, 37, 111, 112, 119, 145; Proverbs 31:10–31 (the poem about a perfect woman); and Nahum 1:2–8 (which stops after the first 11 letters). The supreme example of this genre is Psalm 119, the famous poem that contains 22×8 carefully crafted verses in praise of God's law. Only Lamentations 3 approaches that psalm in complexity of construction.

The acrostic nature of these poems is usually lost in translation, although Ronald Knox was able to find excellent English equivalents when he translated the Bible a generation ago. The New Jerusalem Bible (1985) uses English alphabetical order in its translation of Psalm 25. Our translation of Lamentations 3:16 begins with 'V' because the sixth letter of Hebrew is Vav (also called Waw); this is the letter that appears at the beginning of verses 16–18. If the scheme used for verse 16 is adopted for verses 17 and 18, we might render them as follows: "Villainy destroyed the peace I long for; memories of joy soon vanished. Very soon my life will be concluded; all my hope in God seems wasted." On the other hand, if we prefer to use the sixth letter of the English alphabet, verse 16 could begin with the word 'Ferociously'.

Songs of lamentation were often taught to groups of people (see 2 Samuel 1:18; Jeremiah 9:20), so the alphabetic idea may have been devised as an aid to memory. But this is probably not the real reason, because Lamentations 2–4 reverse the standard alphabetical order of Ayin and Pe that is found in Chapter 1 and in all of the other acrostic psalms. Comparatively few people in ancient Israel could read and write, so alphabetical order was not as helpful for memorization then as it is now.

Perhaps the alphabet was used to give a sense of completeness: "Everything has been said, from Aleph to Tav," that is, from A to Z. But the primary reason for constructing an alphabetic psalm was probably the same as Shakespeare's motivation for writing sonnets according to definite rules: A restricted form stimulates creativity and provides structure that enhances the beauty of a poem. The conscious artistry of Lamentations is the poet's offering of his or her best work to God.

Alphabetic psalms have proved to be useful in another way that their authors probably did not foresee: We can easily spot errors in acrostics that have repeatedly been copied and recopied. For example, all of the Hebrew manuscripts of Psalm 145 known to Bible scholars before 1947 lacked the verse corresponding to the letter Nun, yet the ancient Greek translation did have a suitable verse in the right place. The Hebrew verse had apparently been dropped by mistake. Then an old copy of Psalm 145 was found in one of the Dead Sea Scrolls, and sure enough, the missing Hebrew verse was there! Perhaps similar corrections will someday be found for the alphabetic anomalies in Psalm 25:5 and 18, in Nahum 1:4, and in several parts of Psalm 10.

Very few Hebrew words begin with Vav. Indeed, none of the Solomonic proverbs collected in Proverbs 10:1–22:16 start with this letter. The scarcity of such words may account for the lack of a Vav verse in Psalm 34. In English we might have similar troubles with X. Yet there is no great difficulty in constructing completely alphabetical Hebrew psalms, because Vav by itself can be prefixed to other words; it's a connective that means 'and', 'also', 'then'.

Verse 16's message is, of course, much more important than its contrived medium of expression. The author of this powerful lamentation uses the opening verses to describe his intense sufferings. He is being trampled, forced to lick the dust. Similar imagery can be found in verse 34, and in other poems (Job 30:19; Psalms 7:5, 72:9; Isaiah 3:15). The stones in verse 16 might also refer to adulterated food, continuing the metaphor of verse 15 (see Exodus 32:20; Psalm 102:9; Proverbs 20:17; Matthew 7:9). Jewish observance of the Ninth of Ab often includes the eating of an egg sprinkled with gritty ashes.

The unnamed source of these agonies, the 'he' in verse 16, is none other than God himself. This is clear from verse 1, since the "rod of his wrath" is a common Biblical metaphor for God's chastening hand (2 Samuel 7:14; Job 9:34, 21:9; Psalm 89:32; Isaiah 10:5), and from verse 37, which points to God as controller of all. (See also 1:13–15 and 2:1–8.) The psalmist's grief turns to hope when he realizes that God has not run out of mercy (verse 22). Indeed, mercy is renewed every morning (verse 23). God afflicts, but he also has compassion (verse 32). And he heals (Exodus 15:26; Psalm 103:3; Isaiah 30:26).

THE BOOK OF EZEKIEL is a collection of prose and poetry written by a great prophet who lived among the exiles during the early years of Israel's captivity in Babylon. Ezekiel was a priest (1:3) who was deported from Jerusalem with King Jehoiachin in 597 B.C., eleven years before the kingdom of Judah finally collapsed (see 2 Kings 24:15). He is not mentioned in other books of the Bible, but it is clear that he was a major spiritual figure during this time of crisis. Leaders of the exile community came regularly to his house (8:1, 14:1, 20:1), to hear the spiritual messages he had received.

The first half of this book, Chapters 1–24, contains prophecies that were made before the fall of Jerusalem. At this time many people were still predicting that the exile would be short-lived and that the city would be spared (see 13:10 and Jeremiah 28:3–4). But Ezekiel pointed out the certainty and the necessity of Jerusalem's destruction, because of the people's great wickedness. Chapters 25–32 contain eloquent warnings to Egypt, Phœnicia, and other nearby nations. Chapters 33–39 give consolation and hope for the future, when the scattered Israelites will be invigorated and reunited. Finally, Chapters 40–48 envision a system of ideal worship by ideal people in an ideal Temple.

Ezekiel's passionate prophecies and fiery oratory are filled with vivid word pictures, sometimes magnificent, sometimes harsh. He often speaks in parables; God repeatedly asks him to perform bizarre symbolic actions that convey important messages. Ezekiel has sublime visions of the overwhelming transcendence and majesty of God—a God who is unspeakably holy, glorious, and just. In these ecstatic revelations, Ezekiel is virtually transported to other locales.

The Hebrew text of this book was rather badly damaged in ancient times, and modern translators often have to guess at the original forms of phrases that no longer make sense. At one time scholars doubted the authenticity of many passages, and there was widespread speculation that much of this material had been composed in Palestine long after Ezekiel's death; but further study has tended to confirm the essential unity of authorship and the straightforward conclusion that this book was written in Babylonia before 560 B.C.

Personal responsibility is one of Ezekiel's major themes. God always addresses him directly, using the name 'Son of man', i.e., 'Mortal'. Ezekiel is responsible for transmitting God's words, and his hearers are individually responsible for acting on them. The key refrain of this book, repeated some 75 times beginning in 6:7, is "they shall know that I am Jehovah." Indeed, knowledge of our God, who is constantly with us (34:30), should be our chief goal.

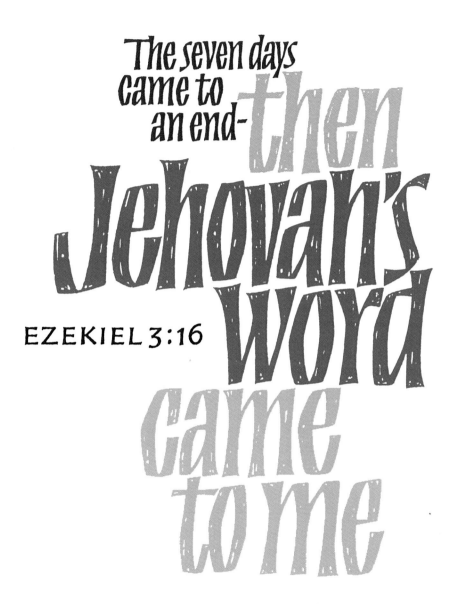

The seven days came to an end— then Jehovah's word came to me

EZEKIEL 3:16

Ezekiel 3:16

Michael Harvey

111

EZEKIEL WAS DUMBFOUNDED by a tremendous vision in which God commissioned him to be a prophet (1:4–3:13). He came to a colony of exiled Israelites and sat stupefied among them in a state of shock for seven days (verse 15).

Many explanations have been offered for the significance of Ezekiel's seven-day prostration, because seven is a number that symbolizes God's covenant with Israel. Job's friends sat in silence with him for seven days (Job 2:13); seven days of mourning were sometimes observed (Genesis 50:10; 1 Samuel 31:13); the rite of ordination for priests lasted seven days (Exodus 29:35; Leviticus 8:33). It is plausible to suppose that Ezekiel's first vision and the one that followed in verse 16 both took place on the sabbath day.

We can well imagine why Ezekiel was dazed by his experience. In the first place, the vision itself was quite powerful, and we can compare Ezekiel's reactions to those of Gideon, Daniel, and Paul in similar circumstances (Judges 6:22; Daniel 8:27; Acts 9:9). In the second place, Ezekiel's whole life was being transformed by God's call. We are reminded of Moses saying "Please send somebody else" (Exodus 4:13), Isaiah saying "Woe is me" (Isaiah 6:5), and Jeremiah saying "I'm too young" (Jeremiah 1:6). What a terrible thing it would be if God were to appear to me and tell me that I should spend the rest of my life as his messenger. I already have so many other things I want to accomplish before I die!

EZEKIEL 3:16

The seven days came to an end—
then Jehovah's word came to me.

Verse 14 says that Ezekiel felt bitter and angry. His indignation may have been a reflection of God's own sentiments (verses 3–5); Ezra was similarly overcome with grief and rage when he learned of his colleagues' corruption (Ezra 9:3). But I think Ezekiel was simply dismayed by the new duties that were being imposed on him. A similar ambiguity is found in Jeremiah 15:17.

The site of this action, Tel Abib (verse 15), probably got its name from the ancient Akkadian *til abûbi,* which signifies a mound abandoned after the great flood. A Hebrew variant of this name, Tel Aviv ('hill of springtime'), was adopted in 1910 by the city that has now become the largest in Israel.

"Jehovah's word came to me." This phrase occurs almost 50 times in the book of Ezekiel, and it is also used to describe the experiences of many other prophets (see 1 Samuel 15:10; 1 Kings 18:1; Isaiah 38:4; Jeremiah 42:7). The word here translated 'came' is an emphatic form of the verb 'to be'; it means, more fully, 'came into existence'.

112

Our English word 'Jehovah' has a peculiar derivation. Ancient Hebrew was written entirely without vowels, and God's divine name was originally spelled with four consonants, 'YHWH'. About 100 years after Ezekiel's time, devout Jews decided to stop pronouncing this name aloud, for fear of profaning it; they substituted the word Adonai ('Lord') instead. Another thousand years went by, and a system of "points" was invented, by which Hebrew vowels could be indicated together with the consonants. Scribes of the Masoretic sect, who had been entrusted with the task of preserving the sacred texts, added vowel points to the entire Old Testament, and when they came to 'YHWH' they inserted the vowels of 'Adonai' as a guide to pronunciation. Christian translators in the fourteenth century, unaware of this history, began to read the sacred name as 'Jehovah', mixing the consonants and vowels of two words.

In fact, the Masoretic vowel pointing is sometimes 'Jehovih' instead of 'Jehovah'. This occurs when a nearby word is already 'Adonai', in which case 'Elohim' (with its different vowels) is to be read. 'Jehovih' occurs more often in the book of Ezekiel than elsewhere in the Bible; in Chapter 3 it is found in verses 11 and 27, while 'Jehovah' occurs in verses 12, 14, 16, 22, and 23.

Today's Bible scholars almost unanimously prefer the name 'Yahweh', which better reflects the ancient Hebrew pronunciation, to 'Jehovah', which has been called a "morphological monstrosity." However, I've tended to avoid the name 'Yahweh' in this book, because it still sounds too academic. English has many words whose etymology is based on ancient misunderstandings; if I were to avoid all of them, I'd be left with a severely limited vocabulary. Thus I'm quite content to continue using the time-honored name 'Jehovah', at least until more poets have written inspiring hymns addressed to Yahweh.

The Masoretic Hebrew text of verse 16 contains a curious blank space between phrases. Literally, it reads 'And there came the end of seven days (space) and there came the word of Jehovah to me'. Such spaces are common at the ends of verses, where they indicate the end of a section or paragraph, but they are relatively infrequent in mid-verse. Scholars have not been able to agree on what (if anything) such spaces signify. Seventy-two instances of this phenomenon are known to appear in ancient manuscripts, mostly in the book of Samuel. Two of these exceptional verses (2 Samuel 7:4 and 1 Kings 13:20) have exactly the same structure as Ezekiel 3:16. For example, 2 Samuel 7:4 reads, "Nighttime came—then Jehovah's word came to Nathan."

May we always be ready to receive and to recognize Jehovah's words to us.

THE BOOK OF DANIEL tells of a Jewish exile leader whose faith became legendary. This book is quite different from the books of prophecy that precede and follow it in English Bibles, because its protagonist, Daniel, doesn't exhort his contemporaries with divine messages; he is a wise man rather than a prophet. Therefore the location of this book in Hebrew Bibles, where it appears between Esther and Ezra, is more consistent with its content.

Chapters 1–6 contain six independent stories about Daniel and his friends. The remaining chapters, 7–12, contain four dream-visions about future events. These two quite different sections are tied together by a similar outlook and by the fact that much of the text—from the middle of verse 2:4 to the end of Chapter 7—is written in Aramaic instead of Hebrew. Linguistic studies suggest that the entire book of Daniel, except perhaps the prayer in 9:4–20, was originally composed in Aramaic, which was the common language throughout the Middle East for many centuries. But nobody has thought of a simple reason why only the beginning and ending were subsequently translated into Hebrew.

This book was probably the last part of the Old Testament to be put into writing. Most scholars agree that it was written about 165 B.C., during a particularly terrifying time of tragic persecution in Jerusalem, although the stories in Chapters 1–6 are evidently based on oral traditions from Daniel's day. Many of the historical details in the early chapters incorporate misconceptions of later years. Chapter 11 contains an extremely precise account of Palestinian history in the 3rd and 2nd centuries B.C.

The author was inspired to convey urgent messages to his countrymen in a particularly effective way. First he recalled stories about powerful monarchs of bygone days who had tried to destroy the Jewish religion; then he presented episodes of world history from a religious perspective, by imagining visions that might have come to Nebuchadnezzar and Daniel. The author made his points vividly by saying 'I, Nebuchadnezzar' (4:34) and 'I, Daniel' (7:28), without expecting his readers to believe that these words were actually penned by Nebuchadnezzar or Daniel. This style of "apocalyptic literature" became very popular from the 2nd century B.C. to the 2nd century A.D.

The book of Daniel encourages us to be unswerving in our devotion to God, who is sovereign over all, who is guiding history in a mysterious but ultimately fair manner. Although people in all times and places feel helpless in the face of tyranny, this book emphasizes that the world is not out of control; we can always rely on God, whose kingdom will last forever.

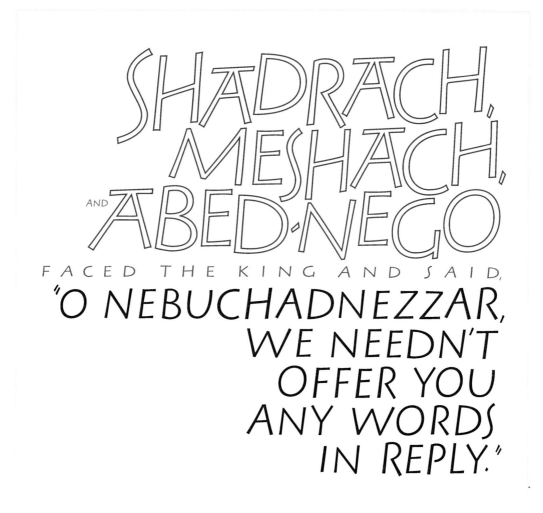

SHADRACH, MESHACH, AND ABED-NEGO FACED THE KING AND SAID, "O NEBUCHADNEZZAR, WE NEEDN'T OFFER YOU ANY WORDS IN REPLY."

Daniel 3 : 16

Sumner Stone

115

THE AFFIRMATION OF FAITH made by three stalwart young Jews in this passage has been called the key to understanding the entire book of Daniel. These men were in imminent danger of death in a fiery furnace; yet they maintained an absolute loyalty to God. They refused to compromise their integrity.

Shadrach, Meshach, and Abed-nego were members of the Jewish nobility who were brought to Babylon for service in Nebuchadnezzar's palace (1:3–4). At that time they were given Babylonian names in place of their Hebrew names Hananiah, Mishael, and Azariah (1:7). Many years went by before these Babylonian names were written down in Aramaic and Hebrew, so it is difficult to reconstruct their original spelling and pronunciation. 'Abed-nego' was probably *Abdi-Nabû*, 'servant of Nebo'; 'Shadrach' and 'Meshach' were perhaps related to the name of the god Aku. We can imagine that Hananiah, Mishael, and Azariah hated

DANIEL 3:16
Shadrach, Meshach, and Abed-nego faced the king and said, "O Nebuchadnezzar, we needn't offer you any words in reply."

to be called by names based on Babylonian mythology. Throughout Chapters 1–3, these three men act in concert. However, Azariah/Abed-nego may have been more vocal than the others, since an eloquent "Prayer of Azariah" appears as one of the additions to the book of Daniel in the Apocrypha.

Nebuchadnezzar's real name was *Nabû-kudurri-uṣur*, and this was evidently quite a jawbreaker for the Jews because the Old Testament has several different ways to transliterate it. Ezekiel calls him 'Nebuchadrezzar' (see Ezekiel 26:7, 29:18–19, 30:10); Jeremiah is inconsistent but uses 'Nebuchadrezzar' more than three-fourths of the time (see, e.g., Jeremiah 29:3, 21); Daniel and other books all use the less correct form 'Nebuchadnezzar'.

In the story of Chapter 3, Nebuchadnezzar has set up a huge golden image (verse 1). He commands everyone to worship this idol or to face immediate death by fire (verse 7). Shadrach, Meshach, and Abed-nego refuse to prostrate themselves, and they are brought before the king for a dramatic confrontation (verse 13). Nebuchadnezzar asks if they really have disobeyed his orders (verse 14), and he gives them another chance. He taunts them by asking rhetorically, "Who is the god that can save you from a white-hot furnace?" (verse 15; see 2 Kings 18:35).

Shadrach, Meshach, and Abed-nego reply without hesitating or flinching. They say there is no need to argue the matter; actions will speak louder than

116

words. They believe that the God they serve is able to rescue them, if any god can (verse 17). Moreover, even if God does not choose to save them in this instance, they still will never stoop to worship a golden image (verse 18). Nebuchadnezzar's vast power is not enough to crush their spirits.

Similar incidents are mentioned in 1:8, when Daniel steadfastly refuses to eat nonkosher food, and in 6:10, when he continues to pray daily in defiance of royal orders. These examples of nonviolent resistance have become an inspiration to oppressed people everywhere. We can rely on God to help us when we are doing the right thing.

Of course it's often difficult to decide where to draw the line. When is stubbornness a virtue? Confrontation is not always better than compromise; we must be able to get along with many types of people in this world. But when we are called to take a stand on vital matters of principle, we cannot back down without losing our very souls.

According to the punctuation in the Aramaic text of verse 16, Shadrach and his friends address the king simply as 'Nebuchadnezzar', without a royal title. This is a serious breach of etiquette, which would have been insulting to an oriental potentate. However, punctuation marks were not added to the text until long after it was written, so we need not assume that the young men replied arrogantly and disrespectfully. Normal courtesies are observed in verses 17 and 18 and everywhere else in the book of Daniel, although the Jews consistently maintain their pride and independence (see 5:17).

Some commentators say that Shadrach, Meshach, and Abed-nego were not afraid. But I think they were plenty afraid; faith overcame their fear. Surely Nebuchadnezzar's threat was real. For example, Jeremiah 29:22 speaks of two exiles who were burnt to death for other reasons at about this time.

If I myself had been faced with this situation, I'm afraid I wouldn't have measured up to the task; I'm no martyr. I would probably have thought, "This king hasn't really asked me to renounce my God, only to bend my knee briefly to a lifeless idol. Surely I can do more good for my countrymen if I stay alive and work quietly behind the scenes for their liberation."

But the three young men knew that such rationalizations are weak. Like Peter and the other apostles in Acts 4:19 and 5:29, they knew that it was better to obey God rather than men. Martin Luther must have had this episode in mind when he declared, "I cannot and will not recant anything, for to act against conscience is neither right nor safe. God help me! Amen."

THE BOOK OF HOSEA is the first of twelve short collections of prophecies that appear at the end of the Old Testament. These twelve books formed a single scroll in the ancient Hebrew scriptures; but we can understand them better if we keep them separate, because each of these so-called minor prophets had a distinctive, major mission.

Hosea was one of the earliest prophets whose sayings have been preserved, and he is the only such prophet who was a native of northern Israel. His words had a profound influence on Jeremiah and other prophets who followed. He prophesied during the turbulent years at the end of Jeroboam II's reign, about 750 B.C.; this was a time of bitter infighting between political factions, as several kings were assassinated in rapid succession (2 Kings 15:8–13). Hosea's nation was destined to be obliterated by Assyrian forces about 25 years later.

The first three chapters tell of Hosea's marriage to a woman who has affairs with other men. This unhappy experience gives Hosea a special insight into God's relationship with Israel, which he sees as analogous to his own situation. Hosea understands how God, the outraged partner, has become heartbroken by the people's attitude; he perceives how Israel has totally misunderstood God's love. Yet he knows from his own experience that God's love doesn't quit, and that the relationship might be repaired if Israel would come back.

The remaining eleven chapters contain miscellaneous messages that Hosea addresses to the people. The main theme of these messages is stated immediately (4:1): There is no integrity, no faithful love, and no knowledge of God in the land. Hosea condemns Israel's false worship of the true God, and her true worship of false gods. He denounces political intrigues and the politicians who crave power rather than justice. He decries the people's faith in armaments and alliances. Although disaster is imminent, he calls Israel to repentance, since there still is hope for reconciliation and renewal.

Hosea's impassioned pleas are expressed in a unique style that has baffled many translators. He often chooses to remain tantalizingly enigmatic about details; he names no names of the contemporaries he speaks against, and he makes fragmentary allusions and oblique references to things we can no longer decipher. Commentators have called many passages "maddeningly difficult to grasp," and different translations often disagree on details. Chapter 5 has been interpreted by one scholar as an account of a war between Israel and Judah, while another scholar sees it as a poem about a harvest festival. Yet Hosea's main messages come through.

Orgies with old wine and new wine
are making my people lose their wits.

Hosea 4 : 11   Steven Skaggs

SELF-INDULGENCE in sensual pleasures is no way to worship God. Israel's religion had declined drastically as it incorporated more and more pagan practices, and Hosea realized that a radical reformation was necessary. The fertility cults of Canaan featured licentious rituals involving male and female prostitutes (see Exodus 34:16 and Deuteronomy 23:17); such ceremonial copulation was evidently practiced under shady trees near the altars (4:13; 2 Kings 16:4, 17:10). The rites were supposed to engender bountiful crops and to symbolize unity between the god Baal, the goddess Asherah, and the people.

These bacchanalias were more exciting than the offering of sacrifices to Jehovah, who is neither male nor female; so the Israelites had begun to change their notion of Jehovah. Pottery from about Hosea's time has recently been discovered in the Sinai desert bearing pictures that we would consider pornographic today, accompanied by the motto 'May you be blessed by Jehovah and by his consort Asherah'. Many pictures and descriptions of orgiastic rituals have been found in Mesopotamia. The depths of degradation into which the Jews had fallen are documented by the detailed account of Josiah's reforms in 2 Kings 23:4–24. Such debauchery is what the Bible sometimes refers to euphemistically as "serving other gods."

HOSEA 4:11
Orgies with old wine and new wine are making my people lose their wits.

Since Chapter 3 of Hosea has only 5 verses, the 3:16 verse of Hosea is 4:11. This verse has been treated in a variety of ways in different translations of the Bible, because the underlying Hebrew is difficult to understand. The traditional form of the text as arranged by Masoretic scribes begins verse 11 with the word $z^e n\hat{u}th$ (promiscuity, orgies), and verse 10 ends literally with something like 'Jehovah they-left-off to-attend-to'.

Many translators put $z^e n\hat{u}th$ into verse 10, which then becomes 'they forsook Jehovah for orgies'; otherwise that verse means, 'they stopped giving attention to Jehovah'. (The latter is a rarer construction grammatically; but Hosea uses the verb 'tend to' in the same way, without a direct object, in 12:12.) The Masoretic text also has 'my people' at the beginning of verse 12, but both verses 11 and 12 seem to improve if this is moved to verse 11.

A further complication is that the verb in verse 11 is singular. Some people think that the implied subject is the errant priest who is mentioned in 4:4, 6, and 9; another possibility is that the verb is singular because it goes with the abstract notion of orgies and wine, i.e., debauchery. A third alternative puts

120

'orgies and old wine and new wine' into the sentence of verse 10, then says 'It makes my people lose their wits'. In any case Hosea's main point is the same: Something is very wrong with religious festivities that feature sex and alcohol.

A literal translation of the Hebrew would say that the orgies and wine are 'taking away my people's heart'. The heart was considered the seat of under-standing (see, for example, Proverbs 23:12 and Isaiah 6:10), and it also was thought to contain a person's psyche or conscience (1 Samuel 25:31; 1 Kings 8:61; Proverbs 20:9). In Psalm 104:15 we read that "wine gladdens the heart." Hosea is primarily concerned that the Israelites have no knowledge of God (4:1, 6), so his reference to the heart in this passage probably corresponds to what we would call the brain.

Hosea mentions both old wine and new wine here—both vintage wine and *vin nouveau*. (The Hebrew words are quite distinct.) Abuses of old wine in religious ceremonies are mentioned again in 9:4 and in Amos 2:8; Isaiah also speaks of "the drunkards of Ephraim, overcome with wine; ... priest and prophet reel and stagger" (Isaiah 28:1, 3, 7). Similarly, new wine could be abused, especially at the wild harvest festivals (7:14, 9:1–2).

The Bible contains many warnings about inebriation and alcoholism (for example, in Proverbs 23:29–35; Isaiah 5:11; Habakkuk 2:5; Ephesians 5:18). To avoid such problems, the Rechabites abstained from wine (Jeremiah 35:8), and the Nazirites wouldn't even eat fresh grapes or raisins (Numbers 6:3). On the other hand, the Bible does not condemn the moderate use of wine, which is said to be good for the stomach (1 Timothy 5:23). Jesus helped with the wine at a wedding (John 2:9) and remarked that people who have been drinking old wine don't like to switch to new (Luke 5:39). Although new wine can be intoxicating (Acts 2:13), it "cheers both gods and men" (Judges 9:13). Isaiah 62:9 speaks favorably of new wine being quaffed in God's sanctuary.

Hosea says that God is especially concerned about mindless drunkenness. If Hosea were speaking today he would no doubt also condemn the excessive use of narcotics. What could be more displeasing to God than frenzied cultic rituals at which people are governed only by their baser instincts and carried away by a spirit of promiscuity (4:12, 18)?

Hosea's third child was symbolically named Lo-Ammi, 'Not-My-People' (1:9). Yet God continues to refer to the Israelites as 'my people', here and in 4:6. In spite of the disasters that are about to occur, God has a parental love for his people (11:1, 8) and calls on them to turn back from their apostasy.

THE BOOK OF JOEL is a poetic prophecy about the Day of Jehovah, when all nations will be judged. It begins with a vivid account of a natural disaster, which causes the Israelites to think seriously about ultimate questions concerning their relationship with God. It is a timeless message, appropriate for all people who are in deep distress.

'Joel' is a fairly common name, which occurs more than a dozen times in the Old Testament; it means 'Jehovah is God'. The 'Jo-' at the beginning is familiar in names like Joshua ('Jehovah is salvation') and Johanan/John ('Jehovah shows favor'); the '-el' at the end is even more familiar, in names like Israel ('ruling as God'), Ishmael ('heard by God'), Michael ('Who is like God?'), and so on. Another common ending, '-iah', refers to Jehovah just as 'Jo-' does at the beginning; thus 'Elijah' is something like 'Joel' with the syllables reversed. On the other hand, we cannot always predict a valid Hebrew derivation from the English form of a name; neither 'Joseph' nor 'Rachel' come from 'Jo-' or '-el'. Ancient Semitic names are not yet well understood. For example, the recent excavations of cuneiform tablets at Ebla have surprised scholars by revealing that names such as Israiah, Ishmaiah, and Michaiah already were used along with Israel, Ishmael, and Michael more than 500 years before the time of Abraham.

Nothing is known about Joel except his name and his poem. It seems most likely that he wrote these words in Jerusalem about 400 B.C., but definite proof is lacking. Joel was evidently quite familiar with the rest of the Old Testament, because he quotes from it frequently. (For example, 2:2, 6, 13, 17, 28, and 32 can be compared to Zephaniah 1:15, Nahum 2:10, Exodus 34:6, Psalm 79:10, Ezekiel 39:29, and Obadiah 17.) Joel also seems to expect his readers to be familiar with certain Bible passages to which he gives a new twist; for example, 2:3 is essentially the reverse of Isaiah 51:3 and Ezekiel 36:35. This book was probably composed to be read at worship services on special occasions, just as liturgies today are literary collages, skillfully fashioned from a series of related Biblical phrases.

The first chapters describe a devastating invasion of locusts, which has destroyed all the crops. Joel sees this plague as a forewarning of God's future visitation (1:1–2:11); he calls for true repentance before fertility can be restored (2:12–27). The remaining verses, from 2:28 to 3:21, speak of the last days, when God's Spirit will be poured out upon all people. Special portents on the earth and in the sky will accompany God's ultimate judgment.

On that Day

GOD WILL ROAR
FROM MOUNT ZION;
HIS VOICE WILL THUNDER
FROM JERUSALEM.
THE HEAVENS
AND THE EARTH
WILL TREMBLE AND
QUAKE.   BUT
GOD WILL BE A SHELTER
FOR HIS PEOPLE,
A MIGHTY FORTRESS
FOR THE ISRAELITES.

Joel 3:16

Joel 3:16   Friedrich Peter

123

A FINAL DAY OF JUDGMENT is mentioned frequently by the Old Testament prophets, who call it the Day of Jehovah. (See, for example, 1:15, which is essentially a quotation from Isaiah 13:6 and Ezekiel 30:2–3.) In the New Testament this forthcoming event is called the Day of our Lord Jesus Christ (1 Corinthians 1:8). It is to be the inescapable day when all accounts are finally settled.

Our study of Joel 3:16 and its context will make frequent references to other parts of the Old Testament, because this verse is an excellent example of the way in which Joel combines themes and phrases from many parts of Scripture. Incidentally, the Hebrew Bible and some English versions call this verse 4:16 instead of 3:16, because they divide Chapter 2 into two separate chapters. We shall stay with the verse numbering that is used in the majority of English translations.

JOEL 3:16

On that day, God will roar from Mount Zion;
his voice will thunder from Jerusalem.
The heavens and the earth
will tremble and quake.
But God will be a shelter for his people,
a mighty fortress for the Israelites.

Verse 16 begins by quoting verbatim from Amos 1:2: "God roars from Zion, and thunders from Jerusalem." From Mount Zion, which is the so-called City of David just south of the Temple in Jerusalem or perhaps the Temple Mount itself, God pronounces judgment on the vast throngs in the valley below (see verse 14), just as a lion roars when it has captured its prey. Jeremiah 25:30 uses the same imagery, and Amos 3:8 points out that a lion's roar instills fear. Yet Hosea 11:10 speaks of the Jews returning home when they hear God's roar.

The opening words of verse 16 were originally spoken by Amos two years before a memorable earthquake took place (Amos 1:1). Thunder and earthquakes are often associated with special manifestations of God's presence (see, for example, Psalms 18:7, 13 and 68:8). Isaiah 13:13 says that the earth will shake and the heavens will tremble on the Day of Jehovah. People in those days believed that the earth was supported by massive pillars (Job 9:6), established by God at the time of creation (1 Samuel 2:8; Job 38:6; Psalm 104:5; Proverbs 8:29). On the day of judgment the earth will totter, but God will keep its pillars from toppling (Psalm 75:3).

Old Testament cosmology likewise regarded the heavens above the earth as being supported by shakable pillars (Job 26:11). It is interesting to note that the Hebrew word for heaven or sky is always *shâmayim*, 'two heavens' or

124

'two skies'; the singular form *shâmeh* never appears in the Bible. Similarly, the word for water (verse 18) always has the dual form *mayim*, 'two waters'. People of Joel's day imagined that the sky was filled with a hierarchy of heavens; Deuteronomy 10:14, 1 Kings 8:27, and Nehemiah 9:6 refer to 'heavens of heavens', meaning the highest heaven. In the apocalyptic literature that was popular for several centuries before and after the time of Christ, we can find references to systems of either 3, 7, 10, or 72 heavens. St. Paul speaks of the 'third heaven' in 2 Corinthians 12:2.

Joel has set the stage for the Day of Jehovah by mentioning that the sun, moon, and stars have lost their brilliance (verse 15; see also 2:31). Such portents had already been foretold in Amos 5:20 and 8:9; in Isaiah 13:10; in Zephaniah 1:15; in Jeremiah 4:28; and in Ezekiel 32:7. These well-known signs are repeated in the New Testament (Matthew 24:29; Mark 13:24; Revelation 6:12). We can easily imagine how Joel, when swarms of locusts have darkened the sky (2:10), is able to see the resulting devastation as an ominous warning about the universal Day that is destined to come.

But the tone changes in the last part of verse 16, from outbursts of violence to a promise of peace: God is and will be a shelter and a fortress for his people. Here Joel picks up a theme that is often expressed in the psalms.

The Bible uses six different words to describe this aspect of divine mercy. God is said in various places to be his people's shelter (Hebrew *machăçeh*), their fortress (*mâ'ôwz*), their stronghold (*mâtsûwd*), their high tower (*misgâb*), their strength (*'ôwz*), and their escape (*mânôwç*). Psalm 31:2–3 calls God a fortress and stronghold; 2 Samuel 22:3 calls him a stronghold, high tower, and escape; Psalm 59:16 mentions high tower, strength, and escape; Jeremiah 16:19 speaks of fortress, strength, and escape; Psalm 91:2 mentions shelter and stronghold; in Psalm 46:1 God is shelter and strength. Now Joel 3:16 reinforces the idea by introducing yet another combination: shelter and fortress.

Wickedness will be punished (verse 19). But the people who have been faithful to God have nothing to fear from this awesome judgment, because everyone who continues to invoke God's name sincerely will survive as part of a remnant on Mount Zion (see 2:32; Obadiah 17; Romans 10:13). Zion is characterized as a stronghold in 1 Chronicles 11:5; it will also be God's permanent dwelling place (verse 21). New wine and milk will flow from the mountains (verse 18, see Amos 9:13); and "You will know that I am Jehovah, your God" (verse 17, see Ezekiel 38:23).

THE BOOK OF AMOS is the oldest known collection of recorded prophecies. Amos was prominent a few years before Hosea, who was prominent a few years before Micah and Isaiah. This was a time of great prosperity in Israel, but it was also a time of great corruption. Amos has often been called the prophet of social justice, because he courageously proclaimed God's indignation about the exploitation of the poor. His poetic prophecies have a distinctive, energetic style, with strong structural patterns reminiscent of folk songs. They speak plainly to members of affluent societies in every age.

Amos was a sheep-farmer from Tekoa (1:1), a village on the outskirts of the desert about 12 miles south of Jerusalem (see 2 Chronicles 20:20). God called him to prophesy to the people of the northern kingdom (7:15). As an outsider, he had no trouble seeing the rottenness underneath the glitter, the emptiness of spirit behind the fullness of pride. He predicted natural disasters followed by political disasters; and indeed, the northern kingdom was destroyed within forty years.

Chapters 1 and 2 begin with an indictment of the neighboring nations; then they hit home by pointing out that Israel is no better. Chapters 3–6 contain three messages beginning with 'Listen to this' (3:1, 4:1, 5:1), followed by several words of 'Woe' (5:18, 6:1). Chapters 7–9 give accounts of several visions, into which have been inserted a historical section in prose (7:10–17) and another 'Listen to this' (8:4–14).

The poems of Amos resonate with the rugged austerity and discipline of the desert where he had lived. They draw a great variety of metaphors from nature; for example, Amos hopes to see justice "roll down like water" (5:24). There is also some interesting word-play in Hebrew, as when summer fruit (*qayits*) symbolizes the end (*qêts*) of Israel (8:2).

God asks Amos to denounce the oppression of weak people (2:6–7, 4:1, 5:11, 8:4) and the travesties of justice involving rampant bribery (5:12) and fraud (8:5). Religious decay is shown to be the root of these social crimes; Amos points out that the empty rituals enacted at Israel's shrines are actually hateful to God (5:21).

Verse 3:10 says it all: "They don't know how to do what is right."

These uncomfortable truths are too much for the people of northern Israel, and the high priest tells Amos to go back home (7:10, 12). But in 3:8 Amos exclaims, "The lion has roared; who can help but be afraid? God has spoken; who can help but prophesy?"

126

LISTEN TO THIS
You fat cows
of Bashan,
You women who live
on the hill of Samaria:
YOU, WHO SQUEEZE
THE POWERLESS
AND CRUSH THE
AMOS 4:1   PENNILESS;
You, who order
your husbands to bring
lots of drinks!

Amos 4 : 1   Peter Fraterdeus

THE PAMPERED LADIES OF HIGH SOCIETY share the guilt of their husbands, when they make extravagant demands that increase the unfair pressure on people of lower classes. In previous verses God has condemned predatory rich men for violence and robbery (3:10); he says that their fancy summer houses and winter houses will be destroyed (3:15). Now in verse 4:1 he addresses the wives and finds them equally at fault. This passage can fruitfully be compared with Isaiah's condemnation of female vanity (Isaiah 3:16–4:1 and 32:9–15) and with Jeremiah's rebuke of idolatrous women (Jeremiah 44:18–23).

The area of Bashan was famous for its fertile pasturelands and prize cattle (see Deuteronomy 32:14; Psalm 22:12; Isaiah 33:9; Ezekiel 39:18; Micah 7:14; Nahum 1:4). It lies just east of the Jordan and north of Gilead. The western part of this region is now known as the Golan Heights (see Joshua 20:8). Samaria was the capital of northern Israel (see 1 Kings 16:24 and 2 Kings 14:23), which spanned a large territory including Bashan at the time of this prophecy.

AMOS 4:1
Listen to this, you fat cows of Bashan,
  you women who live on the hill of Samaria:
You, who squeeze the powerless
    and crush the penniless;
you, who order your husbands
    to bring lots of drinks!

Fashionable women of Amos's day may have been flattered to be addressed as cows of Bashan, since thoroughbred cows were admired as symbols of wealth and beauty. But Amos mocks their opulence and sees these cows of Bashan with a herdsman's eyes. Like a troop of cattle, he says, they go trampling over whatever gets in their way. Luxury has made them into beasts, living only for their own gratification.

Cows also represented fertility in Canaanite mythology. The women addressed in 4:1 may therefore have imagined themselves as consorts of God in the cult rituals of 4:4.

The innocent victims of the rich and powerful are the poor and weak, whose plight is examined further in 8:4–6. Penniless people are implicitly called righteous in 2:6 and 5:12. God's covenant with Israel specifically warns against perversions of justice based on a person's inability to pay (Exodus 23:6). The poor and needy are to be objects of generosity, not of oppression (Deuteronomy 15:11 and 24:14). Yet the women in 4:1 are accused of bearing down on the lower classes and crushing them; the illegality and immorality of such actions are clearly indicated in 1 Samuel 12:4, where the same Hebrew words appear.

128

Amos doesn't say that the women themselves are crushing the penniless; they do it indirectly, by calling for drinks from their husbands (literally, from the 'lords' of the people being crushed). Amos contrasts these human lords with the divine Lord, Jehovah, in 4:2. God himself is speaking and "swearing by his holiness" that dire consequences follow from such disregard for his will.

Verse 4:2 makes it clear that the husbands are being accused here as well as their wives. It uses the typical parallel form of Hebrew poetry to say that days will come upon 'you men' when 'you men' will be dragged away with hooks, and when the last of 'you women' will be dragged off like fish. (This difference in the gender of pronouns, 'you men' instead of 'you women', is often lost in English translation, but it is definitely present in the original Hebrew text.) Verse 4:3 is aimed entirely at women once again; then both sexes are addressed in 4:4 and the following verses. The imagery in 4:2 and 4:3 probably refers to the Assyrian practice of leading captives by hooks in their noses (see 2 Chronicles 33:11); archaeologists have found illustrations of such nose hooks on relief carvings from this era. We also can visualize fatted cattle being led by nose rings, on their way to be slaughtered.

The prosperous people of Samaria undoubtedly think that their wealth is a blessing from God. They love to make ostentatious thank-offerings at the altar (4:5). They feel secure (6:1); they have lives of ease and luxury (6:4–6). Yet God has an entirely different view. He sees that the love of money has corrupted their hearts (3:10). He detests their pride (6:8).

This situation has always been one of the great dilemmas: Success often spoils the people who achieve it. Jeremiah spoke eloquently about the problem of wealth (Jeremiah 9:23–24 and 22:13–17). Jesus said that a rich person can enter the kingdom of God only with extreme difficulty (Luke 6:24 and 18:25).

Since Amos came from an austere country background, we might suspect that his outbursts against rich people reflect a farmer's native distrust of city slickers and their sumptuous life style. But if we read carefully we can see that he is not condemning wealth per se. He is condemning ill-gotten gains. Riches should be acquired honestly, not by extortion. Furthermore, 4:1 implies that those who have riches should not simply indulge themselves; they should show kindness and justice to the powerless and penniless (see, for example, 5:14).

People who are prosperous today need to realize that Amos's messages are as relevant as ever. If we ignore God's will as the people of Samaria did, won't we be just as wrong as they?

THE BOOK OF JONAH provides an amusing and instructive change of pace from the conventional books of prophecy that surround it. The strong, fanciful language of this skillfully crafted story has helped to make it one of the most popular books of the Bible. All of the characters in this book are admirable—the sailors, the king and people of Nineveh, even the animals—*except* for Jonah, who is the only Israelite in the picture. Jonah is the anti-hero; his foibles help us to understand our own faults. The hero and chief character is God himself, whose universal love and compassion extend to Israel's enemies as well as to her recalcitrant prophets. Jewish people traditionally read this book on Yom Kippur, the annual Day of Atonement.

Jonah's name is the same as the Hebrew word for 'dove', the bird that Noah once sent on a mission (Genesis 8:8–12). Doves were famous for their cries of mourning (Isaiah 38:14, 59:11) and for their tendency to be a bit silly (Hosea 7:11).

In Chapters 1 and 2, God calls Jonah to Nineveh, but Jonah boards a ship and heads the other way. After a storm and a ride inside a large sea creature, he finds himself back home. This episode may be a symbolic reference to Israel's captivity (see Jeremiah 51:34, 44). God calls Jonah again in Chapter 3, and this time Jonah obeys orders. The people of Nineveh hear his prophecy of imminent destruction, and they resolve to change their wicked ways; therefore God changes his mind about destroying the city. This leads to Chapter 4, which presents the main point of the book: Jonah is angry that his prophecy didn't come true, but God teaches him a lesson about divine justice and mercy by demonstrating the absurdity of his prejudices.

Jonah was a prophet who counseled King Jeroboam II during the time of northern Israel's great expansion, shortly before the era of Amos and Hosea (see 1:1 and 2 Kings 14:25). Nineveh was destined to become the capital of Assyria (modern Iraq) about 75 years later. The Book of Jonah was probably not written until 400 years or so after Jonah's death, judging by its style and its allusions to other parts of the Bible.

In the New Testament, Jesus commends the Ninevites of this story for their repentance, comparing them favorably to the obstinate and hypocritical religious leaders of his day (Matthew 12:41).

This book reminds us that there are many people waiting to learn more about God. It closes appropriately with a question: Isn't God right to be concerned about the multitudes who know very little about him?

THEN GOD MADE A PLANT
וימן יי אלהים קיקיון
SPRING UP OVER JONAH'S HEAD,
ויעל מעל ליונה
TO GIVE HIM SOME SHADE
להיות צל על־ראשו
AND TO CALM HIM DOWN.
להציל לו מרעתו
THIS PLANT MADE JONAH VERY HAPPY.
וישמח יונה על ־הקיקיון שמחה גדולה

Jonah 4 : 6   Lili Cassel Wronker

JONAH IS SULKING. The wicked people of Nineveh, who deserve to be punished, have now renounced their misdeeds (3:5,8), and God has rescinded his threat to destroy their city (3:10; see Jeremiah 18:7–8 and Ezekiel 18:21). Jonah's thoughts are like those of the workers in a parable of Jesus, who complain that they slave all day in the hot sun only to receive the same wages as the latecomers (Matthew 20:12). Why should these Gentiles—these uncircumcised pagans who know little or nothing of the law of Moses, these people whose ancestors committed atrocities during their wars with Israel—be eligible for God's mercy?

But God says, "Stay cool, man!" He causes a plant to grow quickly so that there will be additional shade for Jonah's head, as Jonah sits in the sun and waits for Nineveh to fall.

JONAH 4:6

Then God made a plant spring up over Jonah's head, to give him some shade and to calm him down.
This plant made Jonah very happy.

The Hebrew phrase in verse 4:6 is somewhat unusual; it means, literally, 'God measured out a plant'. The same words are used in 1:17 with respect to a sea creature, in 4:7 with respect to a worm, and in 4:8 with respect to the wind. We might imagine God as a scientist who is making careful measurements while overseeing and nurturing the laboratory of life, giving each part of nature a signal to go ahead when the time is right.

The plant mentioned here, whose Hebrew name is *qîyqâyôwn*, is almost certainly the castor-oil plant, also called 'palma Christi', which is common in tropical Asia and Africa. *Herodotus* 2:94 remarks that this plant grows wild in Greece and is called 'kiki' in Egypt. However, the ancient translators of the Septuagint (the Greek Bible of Jesus's day) chose the Greek word for 'gourd plant' as their rendition of *qîyqâyôwn*, probably because desert dwellers commonly plant calabash gourds next to their temporary shelters in order to produce shade quickly.

This discrepancy between the Greek and Hebrew versions of Jonah 4:6 led to a protracted controversy in 400 A.D., when St. Jerome prepared a Latin translation called the Vulgate. Jerome was working with the Hebrew text of the Old Testament, so he knew that 'gourd' was incorrect; but there was no Latin equivalent of *qîyqâyôwn*. Therefore he used the word for 'ivy'. When a bishop in northwestern Libya read this verse in the new translation, it caused an uproar, because the people had been hearing and singing about Jonah's gourd plant for many generations. St. Augustine wrote to Jerome: "I do not want your translation read in the churches, for fear of upsetting the flock of Christ with a great scandal by publishing something new, something contrary to the authority of the Septuagint—which their ears and hearts are accustomed to hear, and which was accepted by the Apostles. Even if that shrub in Jonah is neither ivy nor gourd, . . . I think the Septuagint translators said 'gourd' because they knew it was like a gourd." Jerome, who knew that this was only one of thousands of places where the Septuagint deviates from the Hebrew, replied by defending his scholarship, and he was later vindicated; but he also made some unwise remarks about 'gourd-heads'.

Castor-oil plants have been known to grow more than 13 feet tall in 90 days. But the plant of Jonah 4:6 was supernatural; it grew even faster than that. God sent it as a pacifier to relieve Jonah's misery, literally 'to deliver him from evil'. The Hebrew word for 'evil', used also at the end of 4:2 and twice in 3:10, can also signify 'discomfort'; hence the words of 4:6 have a double meaning. We learn later that God's real purpose is not simply to give Jonah temporary relief from distress, but rather to give him an object lesson that will permanently deliver him from his evil attitude.

In 4:6, Jonah is very happy to see the plant. He literally 'rejoices with great joy'. The plant is a pleasant diversion; its leaves provide refreshing, green protection from the desert sun. Such little delights of nature always improve our spirits.

Then in verse 4:7, God ignites a spark of compassion in Jonah's heart by making the plant wither away. Jonah now has an inkling of the destruction he had wished on the Ninevites. We learn in 4:10 that Jonah is genuinely sorry to see the plant die.

And this leads to the climax of the story, in verse 4:11, when Jonah is asked to forget his self-pity and to consider God's point of view. Surely the people and animals of Nineveh—God's own creatures—mean much more to God than a short-lived plant can possibly mean to Jonah. After all, Jonah hasn't even helped the plant to grow. How can Jonah, who has received a gift like this from God, legitimately begrudge others a share of God's mercy?

This is a lesson for all time, because there are always people who want to limit divine favors to a select few. There are always people who are more interested in the destruction of their enemies than in the improvement of their own souls—much less the improvement of their enemies' souls.

THE BOOK OF MICAH contains the passionate prophecies of a man who fearlessly championed the causes of his underprivileged countrymen. Micah, like Isaiah, lived at the critical time between 725 and 700 B.C. when the northern kingdom of Israel fell to the Assyrians and the southern kingdom nearly capitulated. Thus he flourished shortly after the time of Hosea. Unlike the false prophets of his day (2:6, 3:5), Micah dared to denounce the corrupt merchants, judges, landowners, and priests who were abusing their powers. And he got results: King Hezekiah listened to him and instituted reforms that were credited with saving Jerusalem (see Jeremiah 26:18–19).

Micah was born in Moresheth (1:1), in the foothills about halfway between Jerusalem and Gaza. This fertile region is now the site of a kibbutz called Bét Guvrin. The spirit of the countryside permeates Micah's prophecies, providing an interesting counterpoint to what Isaiah was saying at about the same time. Isaiah was an aristocrat, a confidant of kings, who lived in Jerusalem; Micah was a provincial who associated with commoners and lived on the land. God's messages need to be expressed from a variety of different perspectives.

Chapters 1–3 predict imminent disaster in Samaria, Jerusalem, and the outlying villages, because of rampant crime. Chapters 4–5 contrast this with a vision of hope and cheer for the future. Another indictment of the Israelites appears in Chapter 6 and the opening verses of Chapter 7; the remainder of Chapter 7 contains another promise of reconciliation and renewal.

The Hebrew original does not expressly associate all of this material with Micah. A single book containing prophecies from many different eras was later broken into twelve parts, at the twelve places where names of prophets were given: Hosea, ..., Jonah, Micah, Nahum, ..., Malachi. Since some of the authors may not have been named in the original book, there has been considerable scholarly debate about whether portions of Chapters 4–7 came from one or more anonymous prophets of a later period. The material of 7:8–20 was probably written during the exile or shortly thereafter.

One particularly noteworthy passage is Micah's description of the energy and strength he feels when filled with God's Spirit (3:8). Another is his beautiful summary of true religion: to deal fairly, to love steadfastly, and to walk humbly before God (6:8).

The prophecies in this book were evidently well known at the time of Jesus, because the New Testament contains two references to the statement in 5:2 that Israel's Messiah would come from Bethlehem (Matthew 2:6; John 7:42).

People will dwell in the shade
of their own grape vines,
and their own fig trees;
nobody will make them afraid.
For God Almighty has made this decree.

Micah 4:4

Micah 4 : 4   Tim Girvin

PERSONAL PROSPERITY AND SECURITY are part of everyone's dream for the future. What could be more satisfying than fruit, shade, and the leisure to enjoy them? Indeed, the king of Assyria was promising Micah's contemporaries an opportunity to eat from their own vines and fig trees (2 Kings 18:31). Micah 4:4 paints an idyllic picture of a Palestinian countryside in which everybody can relax and enjoy the fruits of their own labors, sitting in the open rather than in a protected enclave.

This was a radical idea in Micah's day, and it still is a radical notion today, because of the context in the preceding verses. Micah 4:3 is the classic call for disarmament. The prophet foresees a day when nations will change their swords into farm implements, when they will no longer learn how to make war.

MICAH 4:4
People will dwell in the shade
 of their own grape vines
 and their own fig trees;
  nobody will make them afraid.
For God Almighty has made this decree.

How is this possible? Today's conventional wisdom tells us that we should convert natural resources continually into armaments, so that we will have a deterrent to war. Somehow we are supposed to feel more and more secure as we add more and more missiles to our nuclear stockpiles. But the truth is that we get more and more worried as the armaments increase.

The alternative world implanted by Micah 4:4 into Israel's consciousness needs no weapons, because everybody's priorities have changed. People of many nations—not just Jews, as in Hosea 2:18—have come to Jerusalem to learn God's ways (4:2; see Luke 24:47). When people's appetites for excess wealth are brought under control, arms are no longer necessary to maintain inequities of the status quo. When people understand God's will, they'll be content with a fair share; they will respect the rights of others, instead of seizing property (2:2).

"Nobody will make them afraid." This is a common Old Testament idiom (Leviticus 26:6; Job 11:19; Jeremiah 30:10; Ezekiel 34:28, 39:26; Nahum 2:11; Zephaniah 3:13). We can perhaps understand it best if we observe how it is applied in reverse to animals in Deuteronomy 28:26 and Isaiah 17:2.

The words of Micah 4:1–3 are almost identical to those of Isaiah 2:2–4, and this has caused much speculation. Some scholars say that Isaiah is quoting Micah, while others say that Micah is quoting Isaiah; still others think that both are quoting an earlier prophet. A fourth possibility is that the material was added many years later. The saying was evidently so popular that it was preserved in two different collections, which eventually became part of the Bible. (Several psalms and proverbs now appear twice, for similar reasons.)

Some people think that Micah did not write 4:1–4 because 4:4 refers to God Almighty, literally 'Yahweh Sabaoth', 'Jehovah of Hosts'. This phrase is very common in the prophecies of Isaiah, Jeremiah, Amos, Haggai, and Zechariah, but it appears only this once in the book of Micah. The argument is not conclusive, however, because Micah may well have chosen to use the phrase for special effect in 4:4; indeed, 'Yahweh Sabaoth' emphasizes that God's heavenly armies (hosts) have made earthly armies obsolete.

"God has made this decree": literally, 'the mouth of the Lord has spoken'. This phrase, familiar from a song in Handel's *Messiah*, can be found also in Isaiah 1:20, 40:5, and 58:14. It underscores the divine inspiration of the preceding passage. Here it might also refer to the fact that peace flows from God's words of instruction and justice in 4:2 and 4:3 (see James 3:17).

The people of Israel had been able to dwell safely under their own vines and fig trees during Solomon's reign (1 Kings 4:25). But this security was achieved at the expense of their neighbors, and enforced by a vast apparatus of tax collectors and soldiers (1 Kings 4:21, 26). It could not be sustained.

Perhaps it is naïve to hope that human nature will ever change to the extent that, some day, nobody will need to be restrained by force. Yet when we realize that governments typically allocate about one third of their budgets for weapons, it becomes clear that arms merchants are leading us down a terrible path. Much of what we read in newspapers or see on television consciously or unconsciously foments hatred and distrust of foreigners. Surely we will be better off if we try instead to promote understanding, friendship, and interdependence among people of all nations, by loving everyone as God does.

Martin Luther King, Jr., summarized the situation beautifully when he quoted Isaiah 11:6 and Micah 4:4 while accepting the Nobel Peace Prize in 1964: "I believe that what self-centered men have torn down, men other-centered can build up. I still believe that one day mankind will bow before the altars of God and be crowned triumphant over war and bloodshed, and nonviolent redemptive goodwill will proclaim the law of the land. 'And the lion and the lamb shall lie down together and every man shall sit under his own vine and fig tree and none shall be afraid.' I still believe that we shall overcome."

THE BOOK OF NAHUM celebrates the fall of Nineveh, the capital city from which Assyrian kings had long dominated the ancient world. Ashurbanipal had sacked Thebes, the Egyptian capital, in 663 B.C. (see 3:8); now, fifty years later, the tide had turned. It was the destroyer's turn to be destroyed.

Nahum means 'comforted'; his name is akin to Menahem, 'comforter', and to Nehemiah, 'comforted by Jehovah'. The Galilean city of Capernaum, where Jesus often ministered (Mark 1:21), means 'village of Nahum'; but most scholars think that Nahum lived southwest of Jerusalem, near Micah's birthplace.

This book is generally ranked as one of the literary high points of the Bible. Nahum's matchless poetic style pulsates with brilliant images. He relishes each detail yet maintains a swift pace. Deftly painted pictures flash before our eyes with photographic realism as we hear the rumbling of chariots and the galloping of horses.

Some commentators also place this book among the Bible's theological low points. We find here no condemnation of Israel, only hatred and vengeance for her arch-enemy (1:2). There is no trace of Jesus's call to pray for our persecutors (Matthew 5:44); there is only gloating over Nineveh's ruin (3:19).

But we cannot expect a short, 47-verse poem to be a complete theological treatise. On the contrary, this book would be far less effective if its message were diluted. We have here a strong statement about how those who take the sword will perish by the sword (Matthew 26:52).

Chapter 1 opens with a statement of theological principles: God is good (1:7) and slow to anger (1:3), but has the power to punish evil (1:4–6). Chapters 2 and 3 are songs about the forthcoming siege of Nineveh and her imminent destruction. Hurrah! At last the cruel tyrants are getting what they deserve!

The Assyrians were not all bad. For example, we know that they were patrons of magnificent literature and art. But their military machine was one of the most brutal in history. Archaeologists have uncovered miles of sculpted walls depicting their savagery; for example, prisoners were often impaled or covered with burning tar. Assyria's neighbors had been crushed for many generations and forced to pay heavy tribute in order to survive. Thus Nahum and his contemporaries had little to hope for except Assyria's downfall.

This book makes us painfully aware of the thoughts of people who are being pushed around by rich nations today. Surely there are many who would exult if, say, Moscow or Washington, D.C., were wiped out tomorrow. World powers are hated, and they fall, because lasting kingdoms cannot be founded on force.

Nahum 3:16

Your merchants outnumbered the stars in the sky. Grubworms strip, then off they fly.

Nahum 3 : 16   Gunnlaugur SE Briem

COMMERCE is generally controlled by agents of whatever government is dominant. Therefore we can be sure that hordes of merchants set up shop in the wake of Assyria's armies, as more and more nations became subservient to Assyrian authority. Ezekiel 27:12–25 gives a detailed description of the merchandise of Tyre, about 50 years after Nahum's time; the situation was probably very similar in countries that lay further inland.

"Merchants as numerous as the stars." This is a familiar idiom for a vast multitude (see, for example, Genesis 15:5 and 22:17; Deuteronomy 1:10). Nahum loves overlays of figurative language, so he combines this expression with another metaphor for multitudes, the image of young locusts or grubworms (see Judges 6:5; Jeremiah 46:23 and 51:14). He has already introduced this metaphor in verse 15, which states that the defenders of Nineveh won't be able to save the city even if they become as numerous as grubworms, as locusts.

NAHUM 3:16
*Your merchants outnumbered the stars
   in the sky.
Grubworms strip, then off they fly.*

The Bible contains nine different Hebrew words for locusts and similar insects, calling them cutters, swarmers, lickers, ravagers, diggers, crushers, leapers, clouders, or creakers. Joel 1:4 refers to the first four of these: "What the cutters left, the swarmers ate; what the swarmers left, the lickers ate; what the lickers left, the ravagers ate." Leviticus 11:22 says that swarmers, crushers, leapers, and clouders are kosher food (see Matthew 3:4). Swarmers, whose name is related to the Hebrew word for increasing and multiplying, are evidently the most common; these are the locusts mentioned at the end of verse 15 and the beginning of verse 17. Lickers are probably young locusts in the larva or pupa stage; these are the grubworms mentioned in verses 15 and 16. Diggers are mentioned in the second part of verse 17, where they are compared to huddling Assyrian bureaucrats who will flee when the sun comes out. Creakers are mentioned only in Deuteronomy 28:42.

Verse 16 says that grubworms 'strip', and this word has two meanings in Hebrew just as it does in English. It can mean to shed clothing, as in Leviticus 16:23 and Song of Solomon 5:3; or it can mean to plunder, as in 1 Samuel 23:27. Both senses are combined in 1 Samuel 31:8 and 2 Samuel 23:10. And both of these meanings are appropriate in connection with grubworms; because grubworms devour everything in sight and then they moult, leaving their nymph-skin behind.

140

Ancient Hebrew poetry is no easier to interpret than modern English poetry, so we cannot be sure exactly what Nahum had in mind; but he may well have intended both of these meanings. Archives from Assyria indicate that the merchants and scribes often had Aramean names, indicating a Syrian ancestry; by contrast, pure-blooded Assyrians seemed to prefer military adventures to the more settled life of industry and trade. Therefore most businessmen probably had no great love for Assyria as such; they would go wherever the gold was. Since there was much booty in Nineveh, there were plenty of wheelers and dealers keeping the money in circulation. We can easily imagine that carpetbaggers would milk the Assyrian economy for whatever they could get, just as locusts devour all vegetation in their vicinity.

The ravages of locusts and other *orthoptera* are dramatic indeed (Exodus 10:15). Americans are familiar with the story of the cricket plague encountered by Brigham Young's Mormon pioneers in Salt Lake City, and with the catastrophic invasion of grasshoppers experienced by Laura Ingalls Wilder in Minnesota prairie country, *On the Banks of Plum Creek*. Travelers to the Middle East have repeatedly described massive migrations of locusts, which are said to march in devastating armies up to 50 miles wide. Thus it is likely that Nahum's hearers knew of grubworms as plunderers.

Grubworms also fly away, after shedding the membranous sheath that they no longer need when they emerge from the pupa stage. Nahum is saying that Nineveh has innumerable traders, but that when the city is about to fall they will suddenly sprout wings and flee for greener pastures elsewhere. This abandonment of the capital is central to Nahum's point, for in verse 17 he emphasizes that government officials will also leave the doomed city in the lurch. Verse 2:8 compares this exodus to the bursting of a dam. And indeed, history records that the collapse of Nineveh and of all Assyria was amazingly swift and amazingly complete; after a coalition of conquering armies had left the scene, Nineveh was nothing more than a ghost town.

Verse 16 has a parallel in Ezekiel 27:36, where tradesmen scorn the fallen city of Tyre. There is also a similar passage in Revelation 18:11, 15, 23; but in this case the merchants observing the demise of Babylon seem to have more sympathy for the fallen metropolis.

The central message of verse 16 and the surrounding verses is that Nineveh's position is truly hopeless. A society has no future when it is so corrupt and so shallow that it doesn't even command the loyalty of its leading citizens.

THE BOOK OF HABAKKUK confronts one of the most fundamental paradoxes of religion, the fact that good people often seem to suffer more than bad people do. How can this be God's will?

Chapters 1 and 2 are essentially a dialog in which the prophet alternately speaks to God as a representative of the people, then to the people as a representative of God. He asks questions that children often ask their parents: "How long will it be?" (1:2) and "Why?" (1:13). Habakkuk wants to know when lawlessness and injustice will end, and God replies that foreign conquerors will discipline the evildoers. But then Habakkuk respectfully demands to know why the people of Judah should be punished by invaders who are even more wicked than they. Doesn't this cause unnecessary cruelty? God replies that, in the long run, proud oppressors are overthrown, but good people survive because of their faithfulness (2:4). Indeed, everybody hates the greedy conquerors, who are doomed to suffer five 'woes' (2:6, 9, 12, 15, 19).

Chapter 3 is Habakkuk's prayer, which was evidently intended to be sung in temple rituals because it is accompanied by instructions just like those that appear with many of the psalms. It begins by extolling God's awesome power, and it ends by affirming that God is the source of strength and joy. This poem, which later became the popular canticle *Domine Audivi* in Christian liturgies, forms an appropriate conclusion to the questions raised in Chapter 1.

We know almost nothing about Habakkuk himself; even his name, Hebrew *Chăbuqqûwq*, is an enigma. There is a Hebrew verb *châbaq* that means 'to embrace' (see Ecclesiastes 3:5), so some have called him the Embracer. Saint Jerome said that this was appropriate because he wrestled with God; Martin Luther said it was appropriate because he supported people just as we embrace someone who is crying. On the other hand, *chabbaququ* is an ancient Semitic word for a fragrant herb, and many people consider that to be the source of Habakkuk's name. The reference to Chaldeans (Babylonians) in 1:6 makes it likely that Habakkuk prophesied at the time when Nebuchadnezzar was about to carry the Jews into captivity, about 600 B.C. This would make him a contemporary of Jeremiah, who asked God the same questions (Jeremiah 12:1–4).

Although this book of prophecy is only 56 verses long, many of its verses have become well known. For example, Mary quotes 3:18 in her *Magnificat* (Luke 1:47); Paul quotes 1:5 in an early sermon (Acts 13:41). Verse 2:4 is featured in several New Testament epistles (Romans 1:17; Galatians 3:11; Hebrews 10:38).

I heard this
and my body quaked,
my pale lips quivered at the sound.
My bones began to totter,
and I shook in terror where I stood.
I calmly wait for days
to come
when plunderers will meet with grief.

HABAKKUK 3:16

Habakkuk 3:16   Karlgeorg Hoefer

VIOLENT EMOTIONS accompany personal encounters with God. Jeremiah reports "shaking bones" and a drunken feeling (Jeremiah 23:9); Ezekiel lies awestruck for a week (Ezekiel 3:15); Daniel is overcome, unnerved (Daniel 8:27, 10:16). In this passage Habakkuk, likewise, is shaken up. He has just seen a vision of God's supernatural majesty (verses 3–15). There was dazzling light (verse 4); nature and nations were terrified (verse 6); bolts of lightning shot forth like arrows (verses 9 and 11); God trampled the earth and the sea in anger (verses 12 and 15).

Now the vision is over, and verse 16 harks back to verse 2: "I heard this, Jehovah, and I am totally in awe of your deeds." The vision was not just visual; it was auditory as well. Habakkuk has been deeply moved.

HABAKKUK 3:16

I heard this and my body quaked;
* my pale lips quivered at the sound.*
My bones began to totter, and
* I shook in terror where I stood.*
I calmly wait for days to come
* when plunderers will meet with grief.*

The first part of verse 16 says that the speaker's body quaked; some translators say that his heart pounded. The Hebrew words refer literally to his belly, as if he has experienced a sharp tightening in the pit of his stomach. Symbolically, his innermost self has been stirred.

His lips also "quivered"; the Hebrew verb in this phrase is used elsewhere to refer to ears that "tingle" at devastating news (1 Samuel 3:11; 2 Kings 21:12). The prophet did not have control of his lips.

Furthermore, Habakkuk's bones began to totter. Bones are the most solid parts of our bodies, yet they sometimes feel as if they've turned to mush. This phrase is a familiar Hebrew idiom; Proverbs 14:30 says that a tranquil mind makes our flesh lively, but "passion makes our bones rot." (See also Proverbs 12:4.) The opposite situation is described in Isaiah 66:14: "Your heart will be joyful and your bones will spring back like grass."

The poet "shook in terror." The Hebrew words at this point are difficult to understand, but they seem to mean that Habakkuk's legs could not go straight when he tried to walk. We have here a complete picture of physical as well as mental agitation.

Suddenly the mood changes, as the poet realizes the consequences of what he has just heard and seen. Aha! There's no need to worry about the people who are going to attack and plunder the country, because God is in control! These people will get what they deserve. "I calmly wait"; the Hebrew verb

144

here means to be settled down, in repose. As in Chapter 2, such peacefulness is contrasted with the fate that awaits the unscrupulous invading forces.

This explanation of verse 16 agrees with virtually all modern translations; yet we should note that the Hebrew words in the latter part of the verse have led to considerable debate, because they are ambiguous and hard to interpret. We can see here some of the difficulties that confront Bible translators when ancient texts accumulate errors during centuries of copying. Habakkuk 3 is a particularly instructive case, because a special translation of just this chapter was made into Greek by Hebrew scholars long ago. The so-called Barberini Codex in the Vatican library contains a Greek version of Chapter 3 that is quite independent of other Greek translations such as the Septuagint. The two Greek versions imply that two distinct Hebrew versions of Habakkuk were probably in circulation in different parts of the world. Several portions of Habakkuk 3 are unintelligible in the standard Masoretic Hebrew text, especially verse 14, and these ancient Greek translations give clues that help to reconstruct the original words. But the clues are inconsistent and choices need to be made. Verses 3–15 are written in an archaic style that makes many references to ancient Semitic mythology, and it may be that some editors or scribes decided to expurgate the names of false gods from the original poem. Or perhaps Habakkuk made statements that somebody felt were too subtle or misleading. We don't understand why, but we do know that original texts have not always been perfectly preserved. Extant manuscripts of the Bible often present puzzles whose solutions will probably never be known for sure.

There are other possible ways to understand verse 16: The speaker may be terrified by the impending threat of invasion by Nebuchadnezzar's armies, not by the vision that has just been described. (See Isaiah 21:3 and Jeremiah 4:19 for examples of similar anguish felt by other prophets.) The end of verse 16 may be the poet's prayer that he might find rest when calamity strikes his nation. However, the interpretation given earlier fits much better with the rest of the book of Habakkuk.

Indeed, verses 17 and 18 underline the speaker's faith and affirm the tranquillity at the end of verse 16. We see here that a true believer does not praise God only when times are good. This is the testimony of a person who trusts in God regardless of the circumstances, a person who can actually rejoice in the midst of famine and devastation. The prophet's initial suspicion of God's weakness, voiced in Chapter 1, has become a quiet confidence in God's power.

THE BOOK OF ZEPHANIAH was the first written prophecy to break a 60-year period of silence following the era of Micah and Isaiah. Zephaniah was soon followed, in turn, by Nahum, Habakkuk, and Jeremiah. Once again it was time to convey urgent messages from God to the people of Jerusalem, who had all but abandoned the religion of their ancestors. King Josiah—who turned out to be Judah's last good king—was on the throne, and there was reason to hope that a religious reformation might be possible.

Verse 1:1 traces Zephaniah's ancestry back four generations to Hezekiah. This may well be the Hezekiah who was Judah's second-to-last good king, because no other prophet has been given nearly such a long genealogy. It's not unlikely that Zephaniah's father Cushi (a great-grandson of King Hezekiah) was about the same age as Josiah's father Amon (a not-so-great grandson of King Hezekiah), because the chronological data in 2 Kings tells us that Amon was born when Hezekiah would have been 76 years old. Moreover, the message of Zephaniah is quite consistent with an assumed princely status as second-cousin-once-removed from the king.

Verse 1:2 plunges immediately into the main theme of this book, the Day of Jehovah when wickedness will be utterly destroyed. Chapter 1, which decries all kinds of false religion, concludes with a poem that inspired the famous medieval hymn *Dies Iræ*, "Day of Wrath and Day of Mourning." This chapter has been called a prophecy of anti-creation, since it reverses some of the statements of Genesis 1. Chapter 2 opens with a call to repentance, then predicts doom for foreign nations. Chapter 3 reiterates Jerusalem's guilt, but closes with the promise of a bright future for a remnant of the faithful. In essence, it promises an end to the curse of Babel in Genesis 11.

Zephaniah's forceful, articulate poetry is steeped in the traditions of former prophets, so he probably helped with the reforms that Josiah carried out when the book of Deuteronomy was discovered in the Temple (2 Kings 22:8). Indeed, the catalog of heathen practices outlawed by Josiah in 2 Kings 23:4–13 corresponds well with the evils that are condemned in Zephaniah 1.

Bible scholars used to think that the last half of Zephaniah 3 was contributed by a later editor, because prophets of doom were not supposed to have any cheery words to say. Similar hypotheses were put forward about the hopeful promises found in other books of prophecy. But current studies of ancient practice tend to confirm the unity of these compositions, except for occasional verses like 3:19–20 that may have been added during the exile.

On that day,
JERUSALEM
will hear
these words : Zephaniah 3:16

Zion, do not fear!
Don't let your hands hang limp!

THE GREAT DAY OF JEHOVAH will be a day of judgment when the nations of the world will be assembled for trial, and the earth as we know it will be destroyed (3:8). Micah and Isaiah have spoken of a time when God will rule from Mount Zion, the site of his Temple in Jerusalem (Micah 4:1, 7; Isaiah 2:2, 4:3; see also Isaiah 24:23 and 52:7). Proud people will be gone, but some humble folk will remain (verses 11–13); a new era of great joy will begin.

Zephaniah's hymn to Zion, which begins in verse 14, follows the general outline of "enthronement psalms" such as Psalms 95–99, which were traditionally sung at New Year's festivals. The opening words of verse 16—'On that day'—connect this hymn to the day of Jehovah mentioned in verses 8 and 11.

A message will be proclaimed in Jerusalem: "Do not fear! Don't let your hands droop!" We aren't told who will be the source of this saying. Perhaps God himself will speak the words, either directly or through his prophets; or perhaps the people

ZEPHANIAH 3:16
On that day, Jerusalem will hear these words:
Zion, do not fear!
Don't let your hands hang limp!

themselves will be applauding their new situation and spontaneously congratulating each other, because they are no longer threatened by enemies either inside or outside of the city.

The metaphor of slack hands versus strong hands appears frequently in the Old Testament, and it occurs at least once in the New Testament (Hebrews 12:12), so it must have been a common Hebrew idiom. For example, the words found in Zephaniah 3:16 appear also in Joshua 10:6, when the Gibeonites ask Joshua not to relax his hands from them, i.e., not to desert them. In another story, God tells an avenging angel to relax his hand before destroying Jerusalem (2 Samuel 24:16). Limp hands are usually associated with a loss of courage; for example, 2 Samuel 17:2 says that David was tired and 'weak-handed', and the latter term is usually translated 'discouraged'. (See also Jeremiah 6:24, 38:4, 50:43.) Weak hands are sometimes associated with weak knees (Job 4:3–4; Isaiah 35:3; Ezekiel 7:17, 21:7). The most significant passage related to Zephaniah 3:16 is perhaps Isaiah 13:7, which also speaks about the day of Jehovah: Here we read that "all hands will droop, all hearts will melt."

The opposite of drooping hands is a pair of hands that are strong and steady (Judges 7:11; 2 Samuel 2:7, 16:21; Ezekiel 22:14). Zechariah 8:13 says, "Fear not! Let your hands be strong." We are reminded also of hands that are uplifted in prayer (1 Timothy 2:8).

148

Verse 16 is, incidentally, of interest to scholars of Biblical Hebrew grammar, because it combines a masculine plural verb (to slacken) with a feminine noun (hands). The same construction is found also in a few other places (2 Samuel 4:1; 2 Chronicles 15:7; Nehemiah 6:9).

There is another possible and plausible way to interpret the Hebrew words of verse 16, but this alternative rendering has not been adopted by any modern translators because it is foreign to our present way of thinking. The words might mean: "On that day, Jerusalem will be called 'Fear-not'; Zion will be 'Not-of-limp-hands'." Similar prophecies give other names to the future Jerusalem: 'City-of-righteousness' and 'Faithful-city' (Isaiah 1:26); 'My-delight-is-in-her' (Isaiah 62:4, see also 2 Kings 21:1); 'Sought-after' and 'City-not-forsaken' (Isaiah 62:12); 'Throne-of-Jehovah' (Jeremiah 3:17); 'Jehovah-our-righteousness' (Jeremiah 33:16); 'Jehovah-is-there' (Ezekiel 48:35); 'City-of-truth' (Zechariah 8:3).

Why are the inhabitants of Jerusalem to be free of fear? Verses 15 and 17 explain that God will be right there in their midst, reigning as their king. In fact, the New Testament tells us that we need no longer speak of this event in the future tense; John the Baptist and Jesus proclaimed that "the kingdom of God is at hand" (Matthew 3:2, 4:17, 10:7; Mark 1:15). Jesus spoke continually about the kingdom of God, saying that it is within us or in our midst (Luke 17:21). "God is my light, my salvation; whom shall I fear?" (Psalm 27:1). "If God be for us, who can be against us?" (Romans 8:31).

Visitors to Hawaii nowadays are encouraged to "hang loose" instead of being "up tight," and it is interesting to ponder the relation between these modern idioms and the ancient notion of slack hands. Surely today's beach bums are not encumbered by fear; so they are in accord with verse 16's first injunction, not to be afraid. But Zephaniah is definitely not recommending a life of total euphoria and relaxation, especially when matters of religion are concerned. He severely censures the evils of religious complacency and indifference (1:6, 12). His metaphor of strong hands suggests rather a society in which people work and play with energy and confidence.

The human joy in verses 14–16 is matched in verse 17 by divine joy: God himself rejoices, like a parent who has just rescued a child. There is joy in heaven when a sinner repents (Luke 15:7). Here we have one of Zephaniah's great insights, a confirmation of God's persistent love for humanity, a picture of our God actually bursting into happy song.

THE BOOK OF ZECHARIAH, together with the short Book of Haggai that immediately precedes it, contains the first prophecies addressed to the Jewish people after their return from exile in Babylon. The theme now is restoration and rebuilding, not crime and punishment. These books should be read in conjunction with the first part of Ezra, which discusses the historical background; according to Ezra 5:1 and 6:14, Haggai and Zechariah were instrumental in getting the Temple rebuilt. The prophecies are precisely dated to a period between August of 520 B.C. and November of 518 B.C. (see Haggai 1:1; 2:1, 10, 20; Zechariah 1:1, 7; 7:1).

The first six chapters of Zechariah are devoted primarily to a series of eight visions, which are interpreted by an angel who indicates their significance for Zechariah's hearers. Jewish people read Chapter 4 regularly on the sabbath of Chanukah ('Dedication'), an annual Festival of Lights to commemorate the rededication of the Temple in 165 B.C. Chapter 7 discusses fasting and the fundamental purpose of worship. Chapter 8 contains ten predictions of a glorious future, each of which is introduced with the phrase 'God Almighty says this'.

Chapters 9–14 are quite different in character from the first eight, and they have in fact been given separate titles (9:1, 12:1) with no indication of an author's name. There seems to be little doubt that these chapters were written by somebody else besides Zechariah, but there is lots of doubt about when they were written and about how to interpret them. Some people think they come from the northern kingdom of Israel at the time of Isaiah or even earlier; some think they may have been added to the Bible as late as 100 B.C.; some think they represent ancient prophecies that were subject to periodic revision for use in Temple services; some think they are apocalyptic writing from the turbulent era that produced the book of Daniel. Nobody knows for sure, and it is clear from the variety of opinions that the words can be interpreted in many ways. Chapters 9–11 begin with a condemnation of Israel's Palestinian neighbors; then attention turns to the future of God's flock. Chapters 12–14 deal with the future of Jerusalem and the Jewish state. These six chapters were evidently quite familiar to the early Christians. For example, Jesus quotes 13:7 in Mark 14:27; verses 9:9 and 11:13 are cited in Matthew 21:5 and 27:9.

Zechariah, 'God remembers', is the most common name in the Bible; at least 30 different Zechariahs are mentioned. The author of this book comes from a priestly family and has much in common with Ezekiel. Both prophets emphasize purity and use a variety of thought-provoking symbols.

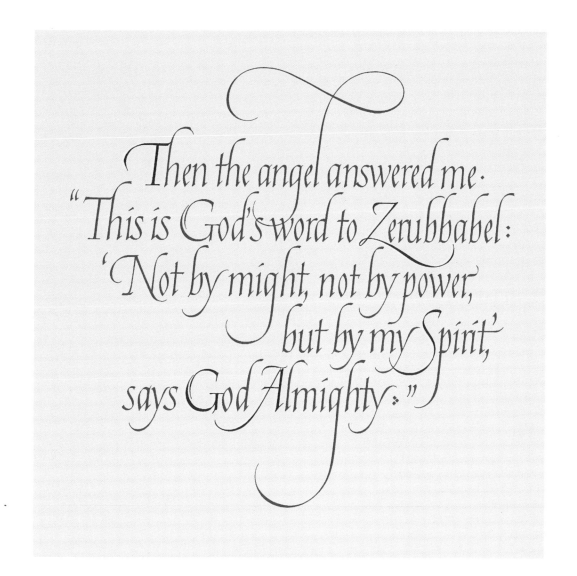

Then the angel answered me.
"This is God's word to Zerubbabel:
'Not by might, not by power,
but by my Spirit,'
says God Almighty.'"

Zechariah 4:6   Claude Mediavilla

THE SPIRIT OF GOD is mentioned frequently throughout the Bible, from Genesis 1:2 to Revelation 22:17. The children of Israel were instructed by God's Spirit during their sojourn in the wilderness (Nehemiah 9:20); the prophets of Israel received messages through God's Spirit (7:12 and Nehemiah 9:30); the artists and artisans of Israel were Spirit-filled (Exodus 31:3). Ezekiel 37:14 speaks of a time when Israel's dry bones will receive God's Spirit and come to life in their own land. Now the time for a genuine spiritual revival has arrived: Joshua the high priest, Zerubbabel the governor, and the returning exiles have indeed been inspired (Haggai 1:14) and told to be fearless because "My Spirit lives among you" (Haggai 2:5).

Verse 4:6 is part of Zechariah's fifth vision, in which he sees a golden lampstand with seven lamps (4:2; see Exodus 25:31 and 37), flanked by two olive trees (4:3). An angel has shown him all these things, and he asks the angel what they mean (4:4). The angel doesn't reply directly to the question until 4:10; therefore many people believe that the words from the middle of 4:6 to the middle of 4:10 have been misplaced from their original position, and many translators have moved this material to the end of Chapter 4 or to some other chapter. However, it is not necessary to reorder the verses, because the angel or the writer may well have preferred to address a more important issue before answering Zechariah's question about the vision.

ZECHARIAH 4:6

Then the angel answered me.
"This is God's word to Zerubbabel:
'Not by might, not by power,
but by my Spirit,' says God Almighty."

There's no foolproof way to tell the difference between an 'angel' and a 'messenger' in the Bible, because Hebrew and Greek each have a single word for both concepts. For example, Jacob meets 'angels' of God in Genesis 32:1, but immediately afterward in Genesis 32:3 he sends 'messengers' to his brother; the same Hebrew word is used in both cases. St. Paul likewise describes an 'angel of light' and a 'messenger of Satan' with the same Greek word, in 2 Corinthians 11:14 and 12:7. Bible translators generally use the term 'angel' when the context implies that a messenger is superhuman.

A similar ambiguity arises with other words as well. For example, Biblical Hebrew and Greek have no way to distinguish between 'spirit' and 'wind'; translators must make a choice. In verse 4:6 we have an angel and a spirit.

Zerubbabel receives here a dramatic message: A new era is dawning, in which Israel will achieve its ends spiritually, not by might or power. The

Hebrew word translated 'might' here can mean many things, from wealth (Genesis 34:29) to an army (Exodus 14:4); in general it signifies a force that's able to influence or control something else. The other word, translated 'power', stands for muscles, brute strength. These human resources are said to be nothing compared with God's Spirit. A similar sentiment appears in Psalm 20:7: "Some boast about their chariots, but we boast about Jehovah." (See also Isaiah 31:1 and Hosea 1:7.)

The task facing Zerubbabel seems almost hopeless by human calculations. His people are poor (8:10) and surrounded by hostile neighbors (Ezra 4:4). Yet the angel reassures him that God's Spirit will make it possible to reconstruct the holy Temple in a reasonable amount of time (4:7–9).

Verse 4:6 contains several layers of meaning. Zerubbabel is a descendant of David (1 Chronicles 3:19), and his name means 'sprout of Babylon'. Therefore he must be aware of the prophecies of Isaiah 11:1 and Jeremiah 23:5, which describe the promised Savior of Israel as a Branch from David's line. Moreover, Isaiah 11:2 specifically says that this Branch will be filled with the Spirit.

The message of 4:6 may appear at first to have no relation to Zechariah's vision, but closer inspection shows an intimate connection. The two olive trees represent Joshua and Zerubbabel (see 4:14), who are to be co-leaders of the people (6:12–13). This radical restructuring of the community government—a diarchy instead of a monarchy—must have involved considerable negotiation, and Zechariah gives it wholehearted support. A word is addressed to Joshua in 3:8, saying that although he is high priest, he should remember the Branch. Likewise, Zerubbabel is reminded in 4:6 about God's Spirit. Neither the church nor the state should dominate the other. Both are in God's service.

The lamps in Zechariah's vision represent the seven eyes of God (4:10), and the two olive trees represent two 'sons of oil' (4:14). Oil is the source of energy that makes the lamps give light; therefore several commentators have suggested that the oil may represent God's Spirit. Indeed, olive oil is often used to symbolize the Holy Spirit's presence within Christians today, when they are anointed in rituals of confirmation or in the last rites. (This symbolic interpretation is supported by a comparison of 1 John 2:27 with John 14:17, 26.)

Thousands of years have elapsed since Zechariah penned his prophecies, and time has demonstrated the great truth embodied in the words of this verse. Mighty military regimes come and go, but the fruits of God's Spirit survive. Zechariah 4:6 is a timeless message to heads of state in all generations.

THE BOOK OF MALACHI brings the Old Testament books of prophecy to a fitting conclusion. It addresses issues of vital concern to the people who lived in Jerusalem about fifty years after the prophecies of Haggai and Zechariah; and it still remains surprisingly relevant to God's people everywhere, some 2500 years later.

'Malachi' means 'my messenger' or 'my angel', and the earliest translations from Hebrew into other languages did not consider 'Malachi' to be a proper name. Therefore it is reasonable to believe that these prophecies were originally anonymous, like the two collections with similar titles (Zechariah 9:1 and 12:1) that come just before them in the Hebrew book of Twelve Prophets. However, it is convenient to identify the author of these verses by calling him Malachi. The 'angel of Jehovah' is frequently mentioned in the Bible (for example, in Genesis 16:7 and 1 Chronicles 21:16). Malachi 2:7 points out that every true priest is in fact an angel or messenger of God, and Haggai is given this title in Haggai 1:13.

Malachi has been called the Hebrew Socrates, because his prophecies are presented in an effective question-and-answer format. He buttonholes us and demands that we make decisions for ourselves. There are six major sections, each of which begins with a theological statement, followed by 'but you ask so-and-so'; here Malachi puts questions into our mouths that must have been asked by his contemporaries, since the same questions are still being asked today. Then he presents God's answer, which itself usually contains one or more questions.

The first section (1:2–5) is about God's love; the next (1:6–2:9) paints a vivid picture of religious leaders, both bad and good. A third section (2:10–16) addresses the abuse of divorce. God's justice is the subject of the fourth section (2:17–3:5); his covenant will be renewed when the priests and people have been purified. Proper gifts to God are discussed next (3:6–12). The final section (3:13–4:3) stresses the eternal value of piety. The main theme throughout is that God loves the children of Israel, even though they question the existence of this love. Their sins have unfortunately kept him from showering them with more blessings than they have received.

The end of this book prepares us for the New Testament (i.e., the New Covenant) by predicting that the great prophet Elijah will return, to help reconcile people before God's day of judgment (4:5). Jesus later identified this Elijah as John the Baptist (Matthew 11:10 and 17:13; Luke 1:17).

People who revere

have been conferring together,
and God has listened attentively.

A book has been written
in his presence,
Containing a permanent record
of those who revere him
and keep his name
in their thoughts.

Malachi 3:16

Darle Maveety

GOD'S ROLL BOOK is mentioned metaphorically in more than a dozen Bible passages. For example, God tells Moses in Exodus 32:33 that he will cross out the names of people who have sinned against him. (We can speculate that Malachi was especially familiar with Exodus 32:33, because the very next verse speaks of 'my angel'—'Malachi' in Hebrew—coming to guide the Israelites.) Jesus tells his disciples to rejoice that their names are "written in heaven" (Luke 10:20), and St. Paul speaks of the "Book of Life" (Philippians 4:3). Daniel 12:1 and Revelation 21:27 tell how everyone named in God's book will one day be saved; the other side of the coin is depicted in Revelation 20:15. Additional references can be found in Psalms 40:7, 69:28, and 139:16.

Malachi 3:16 contributes a new dimension to this symbolism by comparing God's book to a "scroll of remembrance," employing the same words that Esther 6:1 uses to describe a feature of Persian court life. *Herodotus* 8:85 tells us that Persian monarchs assiduously maintained lists of their benefactors, so

MALACHI 3:16

People who revere God have been conferring together, and God has listened attentively. A book has been written in his presence, containing a permanent record of those who revere him and keep his name in their thoughts.

that proper rewards could later be given to each of them.

Verse 17 speaks of the people in God's book as his most prized possession. This is God's reply to those who murmur in verses 14 and 15 that it's pointless to obey the law because evildoers seem to get away with their bad deeds. Malachi's dialog style of question-and-answer is well illustrated by these verses.

The questions raised in 3:14–15 are perennial problems for people who try to obey God. Does it make any difference if we behave honestly? Why do some perfidious people thrive? (See Psalm 73:13; Ecclesiastes 9:2; Isaiah 58:3; Jeremiah 12:1.) Many a college professor has encountered conscientious students who are convinced that they are the only ones who have not cheated on an exam.

Verse 16 can be interpreted in several ways, and commentators disagree about which meaning was originally intended. Many translations put the words into past tense: "Then people who revered God conferred together, and God listened attentively." This makes Malachi 3:16 the only verse of narrative style in the entire book, after 1:1, and some see this as a sign that it was added by another author. For example, Haggai 1:12 is a similar comment about people's response to prophecy. On the other hand, the ancient Greek and Syriac translations say, *"Thus* people who revered God conferred together," implying that devout people were conferring together by asking the questions of verses 14 and 15. Perhaps God did not like what he heard. The so-called Damascus Document, found among the Dead Sea Scrolls, supports the view that the original Hebrew was 'then', not 'thus'; yet verse 16 remains ambiguous.

The competing opinions basically boil down to this: Were there two groups of people, the murmurers of verses 14–15 and the faithful of verse 16? Or did the faithful people question God? The first interpretation makes it possible for us to imagine an idyllic picture of friends reinforcing each other's views by mutual exhortation. We are reminded of the steadfast fellowship of the first Christians (Acts 2:42). But the second interpretation is not really inconsistent with this, when we realize that it is natural for people to have doubts; our doubts must be aired before our faith can grow.

Verse 16 refers twice to people who 'revere' God; this word is sometimes translated 'fear'. God says in 2:5 that Levi "feared me, he stood in awe of my name"; similar expressions are in 3:5, in 4:2, and in many other parts of the Bible. The name of God, to a person of Malachi's day, is the same as God himself. When God is contemplated directly, he is indeed pretty scary—totally awesome, in the true meaning of that phrase.

The Hebrew verb *châshab* in verse 16, 'to keep in their thoughts', signifies creative thinking and invention (2 Chronicles 26:15; Amos 6:5), as well as placing a value on something (Isaiah 13:17). It corresponds to the Greek word *logízesthai* used in a similar context in Philippians 4:8. This is not merely reflection; it is deliberate, practical calculation that leads to action. Therefore it is reassuring to see the same verb used conversely in Psalm 40:17: God also keeps us in *his* thoughts.

Little children are taught that Santa Claus makes a list of who's naughty and who's nice; so they'd "better watch out." At a superficial level, God's roll book seems very similar to this. People with an immature understanding of religion do good deeds because of the promise of heaven, and avoid evil deeds because of the threat of hell. But Malachi's conception of a "scroll of remembrance" goes much deeper. With this image, the motive for good deeds is to do things that God will remember with pleasure; evil deeds are to be avoided because they make God 'weary' (2:17; Isaiah 43:24).

Let us therefore strive to live in such a way that all of our activities—even those things that are known only to God—are worth remembering.

THE GOSPEL OF MATTHEW is the first of four books that tell the *gōd spel*—the good news, the story of Jesus Christ. It tells how Jesus himself proclaimed the 'gospel of the kingdom' (4:23, 9:35) and how he predicted that this gospel would be preached throughout the world (24:14).

None of the four gospel writers identified themselves by name, but some ancient traditions state that the sayings of Jesus were written down in Hebrew or Aramaic by Matthew, one of the twelve disciples who accompanied Jesus throughout his ministry. Matthew was a tax collector for the Roman rulers of Palestine (9:9, 10:3), and as such he was despised by most of his fellow Jews (5:46, 9:11, 18:17, 21:31). But his experiences gathering taxes, together with the religious education he probably had received as a Levite (Mark 2:14; Luke 5:27), would have been useful for recording the gospel. The Greek text that has come down to us was probably prepared by a Christian teacher in Syria who belonged to the next generation of disciples; yet we can regard Matthew as the essential author, while realizing that the available evidence is inconclusive.

This book spans a rich variety of topics and ideas. The principal teachings of Jesus have been collected into six blocks of lessons, concerning morality (Chapters 5–7), missionary work (Chapter 10), parables of the kingdom (Chapter 13), relations between disciples (Chapter 18), hypocritical church leaders (Chapter 23), and the end of the world (Chapters 24–25). These discourses are skillfully interwoven with details about Jesus's life: his ancestry and birth (Chapters 1–2); his preparation for ministry (Chapters 3–4); his preaching, teaching, and healing in Galilee (Chapters 5–18); his journey to Jerusalem, where he is put to death (Chapters 19–27); his resurrection (Chapter 28).

Matthew writes especially for Jews, emphasizing that God's long-standing laws and promises have been not only fulfilled but perfected by Jesus. He quotes the Old Testament more than 100 times; thus his gospel is appropriately placed first, where it comes nearest to the Old Testament. He assumes that his readers are familiar with Jewish customs, in places where the other gospel writers have included explanations; for example, Matthew 15 does not mention the facts explained in Mark 7:3–4.

One of Matthew's trademarks is his phrase "the kingdom of heaven"—literally, 'the kingdom of the heavens'—which he uses more than 30 times (3:2, 4:17, 5:3, etc.). The other gospels consistently use a different expression, 'the kingdom of God' (for example, in Mark 1:15; Luke 6:20; John 3:3). Matthew's story ends with Jesus reigning in both heaven and earth (28:18).

AS SOON AS JESUS WAS BAPTIZED / HE CAME UP OUT OF THE WATER, AND AN AMAZING THING HAPPENED: THE HEAVENS OPENED, AND HE SAW THE SPIRIT OF GOD COMING DOWN LIKE A DOVE TO REST ON HIM·

MATTHEW 3:16

Matthew 3 : 16   Friedrich Neugebauer

JESUS PLUNGED IN to his life's work by being baptized in the Jordan river. This inaugural event was truly a new wave, destined to have a profound effect on human history. It is recorded in all four gospels (see Mark 1:9–11; Luke 3:21–22; John 1:32).

The Greek word *baptízō* signifies a ritualistic washing or purification, either of people (as here) or of objects (Mark 7:4). John the Baptist, a relative of Jesus (Luke 1:36), instituted an important religious revival in which people confessed their sins as he baptized them (Mark 1:5). When Jesus comes to the Jordan (verse 13), John protests that their roles should be reversed (verse 14). But Jesus insists that John should baptize him, in order to 'fulfill all righteousness' (verse 15), that is, to carry out God's wishes.

MATTHEW 3:16

As soon as Jesus was baptized, he came up out of the water, and an amazing thing happened: The heavens opened, and he saw the Spirit of God coming down like a dove, to rest on him.

Verse 16 says that Jesus came out of the water *immediately*, and this remark is probably significant because Matthew—unlike Mark—rarely stresses the speed of events. Jesus emerges with zest and energy, ready to embark on his public career as a teacher and savior. In sharp contrast to the proud religious leaders of his day (9:11), he identifies with ordinary people and encourages them by his example. People ever since have been able to feel closer to God because of their own baptism, linked to that of Jesus.

Pagan religions viewed seas and rivers as the abode of evil spirits (see Psalms 74:13 and 77:16). Early Christian baptismal rites therefore depicted Christ's baptism as a victory over the underworld, in which Jesus transformed the waters and made them holy.

An amazing thing happens next in verse 16. It's difficult to translate Matthew's exclamation into contemporary English, but older Bibles use the term 'lo' or 'behold'. In French we would say '*voilà!*'; the best English equivalent is probably 'look!' or 'hey!' or 'wow!'. Matthew is fond of this term, which comes from a common Hebrew idiom (see Genesis 8:11). He uses it again in verse 17, and more than 60 times altogether. For example, Jesus says "Lo, I am always with you" in the last verse of this Gospel (28:20).

Lo! The heavens opened! (See Acts 7:56 and Revelation 19:11.) Mark 1:10 says even more vividly that the heavens were 'torn apart', as in Isaiah 64:1. People of this time pictured the heavens as a huge dome over the earth.

160

Therefore they would describe a supernatural vision in which more than just the stars and planets were visible as a view of 'open heavens' (Ezekiel 1:1). Nowadays we might say instead that Jesus experienced a fourth dimension.

Malachi 3:10 speaks of 'windows of heaven' through which God can pour blessings. In this case Jesus receives a special gift: God's Spirit descends to him in the form of a dove. According to Luke 3:21, Jesus is praying when this happens. John the Baptist sees the dove, which remains with Jesus (John 1:32). Soon the Spirit will guide Jesus into the desert (4:1).

Why did the Spirit of God appear as a dove? Today's Christians are familiar with the dove as a symbol of the Spirit, because of the story of Christ's baptism; but when doves appear elsewhere in the Bible they signify something else. For example, doves are innocent (10:16); they are used in sacrificial offerings (21:12; Leviticus 1:14); they are mournful (Isaiah 38:14); they represent the children of Israel (Psalm 74:19; Isaiah 60:8; Hosea 11:11). But these analogies all make the dove more appropriately a symbol for Christ, not for the Spirit. What would a dove have meant to people at the scene?

Early church fathers saw a connection between the dove of verse 16 and the dove that once brought an olive branch to Noah (Genesis 8:11); Noah's dove symbolizes harmony between God and man after an encounter with water. Thomas Aquinas, in his *Summa Theologiæ* 3a:39.6, wrote that doves symbolize the seven gifts of the Spirit: wisdom, knowledge, counsel, understanding, piety, fortitude, reverence. But these comparisons seem rather forced.

A more plausible explanation can be found in the Song of Solomon, where doves symbolize love, as they did in all ancient cultures. Indeed, the Greek word for dove, *peristerá*, contains the name of the love-goddess Ishtar. The Holy Spirit was widely regarded by early Christians as the feminine aspect of God, personified as Wisdom in the Old Testament, the Mater Magna who is the divine source of creativity and nourishment. Thus the dove is the Spirit of Love. God is neither male nor female, but if we must choose a pronoun to refer to the Holy Spirit we can sensibly describe her as 'she'.

Verse 16 describes the moment Jesus's work officially begins. God underlines the importance of the occasion in verse 17 by proclaiming that Jesus is his beloved Son. (See Isaiah 42:1.) God is explicitly present here as a Trinity: The Father speaks, the Son ascends from the water, the Spirit descends as a dove. Jesus will ultimately ask his disciples to perpetuate this scene by baptizing all nations "in the name of the Father, Son, and Holy Spirit" (28:19).

THE GOSPEL OF MARK is a basic introduction to "the good news of Jesus Christ, the Son of God" (1:1). Early traditions state that this book contains the reminiscences of Peter, as told to a resident of Jerusalem named John Mark (see Acts 12:12; 1 Peter 5:13). The Coptic church in Egypt traces its founding to the missionary work of Mark in Alexandria, shortly after Peter had established a church in Rome.

All but about thirty of the verses in this book have parallels in the gospels of Matthew and/or Luke, yet Mark adds a lot of color and detail. The first three gospels are called synoptic, 'seeing together', since they share a common viewpoint and they can be fruitfully studied at the same time. Each gospel writer uses his own vocabulary and stresses particular aspects of the story, so that no verse in one gospel is exactly duplicated in another; yet there is considerable unity amid the diversity, especially when Jesus is being quoted. In one place all three gospels contain an identical sequence of 16 words, beginning with the final three words of Matthew 16:24, Mark 8:34, and Luke 9:23; this agreement would extend to 22 words if Mark had said 'whoever loses' instead of 'whoever will lose' in 8:35.

Most scholars believe that Mark's gospel was written first, because a careful comparison suggests that Matthew and Luke independently used Mark's work as a reference when composing their own gospels. Mark presents Jesus as an intensely human, emotional teacher who is called 'Rabbi' by his disciples. Mark's language is simple and direct, like spoken Greek. Matthew and Luke follow the order of incidents in Mark rather closely, but their style is more polished; they also call Jesus 'Lord' as Paul and other early Christians did. They soften some of Mark's frank realism in places where some readers might take offense. Thus, Mark's gospel is especially valuable for modern readers who seek the Jesus of history, portrayed with sensitivity but without sentimentality.

Peter's sermon in Acts 10:36–43 echoes the general outline of this book. Chapters 1–10 describe the ministry of Jesus as he proceeded from Galilee to Jerusalem; Chapters 11–16 describe the final week during which Jesus is put to death, then comes back to life.

Mark maintains a brisk pace. He loves the word 'immediately', and he pictures Jesus as continuously active. The verses unique to Mark include two parables (4:26–29 and 13:34–37), two accounts of healing (7:32–37 and 8:22–26), and several other remarks or incidents (1:1, 3:20–21, 5:4–5, 7:2–4, 9:49, 12:29, 14:51–52, 16:5).

JESVS CHOSE SIMON AND GAVE HIM A NEW NAME »ROCK«

Mark 3 : 16

Adolf Bernd

163

TWELVE DISCIPLES were selected by Jesus to accompany him, to preach, and to heal (verses 14 and 15). Their names are listed in verses 16–19, and similar lists appear in Matthew 10:2–4; Luke 6:14–16; Acts 1:13. Each of these lists mentions the disciples in a slightly different order; but in every case the first name is Peter, who was evidently the leader of the group.

'Peter'—in Greek *Pétros*—means 'Rock'. Verse 16 tells us that Peter's real name was Simon, and that Jesus literally 'laid a name' on him. Simon has already been mentioned in Chapter 1, verses 29, 30, and 36; Mark will henceforth refer to him as Peter (5:37, 8:29, etc.). On the other hand, Jesus will actually continue to address him by the original name Simon (14:37; Matthew 17:25; Luke 22:31; John 21:15), except in one case (Luke 22:34).

MARK 3:16
Jesus chose Simon, and gave him a new name: 'Rock'.

'Peter' is an extremely common name now, but at the time of Jesus it was not a name at all. No evidence has yet been discovered that any person outside the Christian community was ever given the Greek name *Pétros* until much later (278 A.D.). Simon's new name eventually became popular, but we can best understand the radical significance it originally had if we replace 'Peter' by 'Rock' throughout the New Testament.

Jesus and Simon spoke Aramaic, not Greek. The Aramaic word for rock, *kephâ'*, appears in another account of Peter's name-change: "'So you are Simon, son of John? You shall be known as Cephas,' which means Rock" (John 1:42). The letters of Paul, which were in circulation earlier than the gospels, consistently refer to 'Cephas' (1 Corinthians 1:12; 3:22; 9:5; 15:5; Galatians 1:18; 2:9, 11, 14), except in Galatians 2:7–8 where Paul says 'Peter'. This small anomaly may be due to later copyists who were trying to be helpful; several old manuscripts of Galatians have 'Peter' for 'Cephas' in other places.

It's possible that *Kephâ'* was in limited use as an Aramaic name in those days. But if so, it must have been rare; otherwise the Greek transcription *Kēphás* would never have been translated into the form *Pétros*. The only known instance of a man called *Kephâ'* occurs in a legal document dated 416 B.C., discovered in the remains of a Jewish colony near Aswan in Egypt. (In earlier times people did have names like 'Zur', which is Hebrew for 'Rock'; see Numbers 1:6, 3:35, 25:15, 31:8; 1 Chronicles 8:30.)

We can compare this situation with contemporary American practice. People didn't name their sons Rocky until very recently, after Rocky Marciano became a champion boxer. Marciano, incidentally, was christened Rocco, which is the Italian name of a 14th-century saint (St. Rock of Montpellier). A civil war general, George Henry Thomas, was known as the "Rock of Chickamauga."

Verses 17–19 include several other examples of nicknames either assigned by Jesus or adopted by the disciples: James and John were called *Boanergés* (from the Aramaic for 'Sons of Thunder'); another Simon was called *Kannaíos* (from the Aramaic for 'Zealot'). 'Thomas' was not then a Greek name; it came from the Aramaic *Te'ômâ'*, 'Twin' (Greek *Dídymos*, see John 11:16). Ancient tradition says that Thomas's real name was Judas. Another Judas, *Iskaríoth*, may have taken his name from the Aramaic word for 'Ruddy'. The most common name among Jewish men between 100 B.C. and 100 A.D. was Simon, also spelled Simeon (Acts 15:14), and Judas was next in popularity; hence nicknames were useful for identification.

The earliest extant manuscripts of Mark are not in agreement about the exact wording of verse 16, and this has caused a linguistic puzzle for translators. The word 'Simon' appears only in the dative case, while the names in verses 17–19 are accusative, and this makes no sense. Some ancient copyists apparently tried to rectify the text by repeating the phrase 'he appointed the twelve' from verse 14, but this doesn't really work out well. The best solution is probably found in a 3rd-century Sahidic (Coptic) translation, from which we can deduce that two Greek words were once dropped from verse 16 by mistake. Verse 16 can then be restored to read, literally, 'First Simon (and he laid a name onto Simon, Rock)'.

Why did Jesus choose to call Simon a Rock? Matthew 16:18 gives a reason: Peter, and/or his faith, will serve as a solid foundation stone on which Jesus's community will be built. This indeed becomes Peter's role later.

Peter must have thought a lot about his new name and worn it with pleasure. He used a variety of metaphors based on rocks of various kinds: In one of his early sermons (Acts 4:11), he quotes Psalm 118:22 concerning a rejected boulder that has become the chief cornerstone, and he compares this rock to Jesus (who had used the same quotation in 12:10). In 1 Peter 2:4–8 he repeats the same imagery and adds references to a stumbling-block (Isaiah 8:14) and to a precious granite foundation-stone (Isaiah 28:16). These allegories not only help us to understand the significance of Jesus, they also apply to us personally; for we ourselves are able to become living stones, from which a spiritual Temple can be constructed (see 1 Corinthians 3:16).

THE GOSPEL OF LUKE tells the story of Jesus from the standpoint of a Greek historian. Verses 1:1–4 explain that the author has done his best to prepare an orderly narrative, after gathering facts from eyewitnesses. Ancient church traditions ascribe this gospel to Luke, the "beloved physician" who accompanied Paul on some of his missionary journeys (Colossians 4:14). This book is especially popular because Luke's pleasant personality shines through his exposition.

About one third of Luke's gospel matches parallel verses in Mark, and about one third of the remainder has parallels in Matthew. Sometimes the agreement is very striking; for example, Luke 16:13 repeats all 27 words of Matthew 6:24 verbatim, inserting just one more word—'servant'. Many Bible scholars account for the similarities by supposing that there was once a document Q that recorded numerous sayings of Jesus. According to this theory, Luke wrote his gospel by referring to Q and to Mark, as well as to his own sources L (which may not have been written down before); similarly, Matthew is supposed to have been compiled independently from Q, Mark, and his own sources M. Luke and Mark both worked together with Paul in Rome (see Philemon 24). The Q hypothesis is still debated, but it nicely accounts for a dozen or so verses that Luke includes twice. For example, verses 8:16–18 probably come from Mark 4:21–25; when they occur again in 11:33, 12:2, 19:26, they have parallels in Matthew 5:15, 10:26, 25:29, which probably come from Q.

The general outline of this book is like that of Matthew and Mark: First we learn of the early life of John the Baptist and Jesus (Chapters 1–3), then there's a major section describing Jesus's ministry (4–19), leading up to the story of the week preceding Jesus's death (20–23), followed by his resurrection and ascension (24). A major turning point occurs when Jesus "sets his face toward Jerusalem" (9:51); the climax of the story will take place there. From 9:51 to Chapter 18, Luke includes many incidents that do not occur in the other gospels. We find many of Jesus's best known teachings here, including the parables of the Good Samaritan (10:29–37) and the Prodigal Son (15:11–32).

Unlike the other gospel writers, Luke was not a Jew (Colossians 4:11). He emphasizes the implications of his story for everybody (2:32, 24:47); one of his favorite words is *pás* ('all', 'every'). He champions the causes of downtrodden people, giving special prominence to Samaritans and to women. He often warns the rich and sympathizes with the poor. He balances tales of pain and sorrow with accounts of joy and praise.

JOHN TOLD EVERYBODY:

BUT
SOMEONE
MORE POWERFUL
IS COMING;
I am not
even fit
to untie his
shoes!

He will
baptize you
with a holy Spirit
and with fire.

Luke 3 : 16   Timothy R. Botts

167

JOHN THE BAPTIST was a great man. Jesus called him "a prophet, and more than a prophet" (7:26). He was filled with a holy Spirit from birth (1:15), and he became an outstanding religious reformer, judging from the samples of his preaching that we are given in verses 7–14. He persuaded people to be baptized and to renounce their sinful ways (Mark 1:5); he also taught his disciples to pray (5:33, 11:1). His influence must have been widespread, because Paul found people in Ephesus many years later who said they had been baptized "with John's baptism" (Acts 19:3). According to verse 15 and John 1:19, a delegation of priests was sent from Jerusalem to ask him whether he was the Savior who had been foretold by ancient prophets.

John replies in verse 16 with a magnificent declaration of humility: "I'm just a herald for someone else who is much mightier; in fact, I'm not even fit to stoop down and untie his shoes." (This statement is quoted also in Mark 1:7, John 1:27, and Acts 13:25; in Matthew 3:11 he says that he's unfit to *carry* the

LUKE 3:16

John told everybody, "I am baptizing you with water. But someone more powerful is coming; I am not even fit to untie his shoes! He will baptize you with a holy Spirit, and with fire."

shoes.) One of the duties of a slave in those days was to fetch a pair of shoes when his master was about to leave the house, and to untie them just after he came back. Biblical Greek distinguishes two different kinds of footgear: A high-quality shoe, *hypódēma* (here and in 15:22), outshines a simple *sandálion* (Acts 12:8). For example, humble disciples are not supposed to wear shoes (10:4), but sandals are no problem (Mark 6:9).

John deepens the contrast between himself and his successor by comparing his own water-based baptismal rites to something better that will follow. He says that his hearers will ultimately be baptized with *spirit* and *fire*.

Water. Spirit. Fire. These are powerful symbols, capable of many interpretations. For example, fire boils water, yet water quenches fire. What exactly did the words of verse 16 originally mean to John the Baptist and his hearers? What did they mean to Luke and his original readers? We can get some insights by looking at other Bible passages where the same images occur.

John might be referring to a holy Wind and fire, since there's no difference in Greek or Aramaic between the words 'spirit' and 'wind'. Verse 17 may therefore help to clarify verse 16: It speaks of a fork-like 'winnowing shovel', which tosses grain into the air so that wind can carry the worthless chaff away

(22:31; Psalm 1:4). The chaff is then burnt; it shares the fate of unfruitful trees (verse 9).

A holy Wind can indeed sweep clean (Isaiah 4:4), but the significance of verse 16 probably goes well beyond the analogy of verse 17. Just as a master chess player makes moves that accomplish several goals simultaneously, a master theologian like John makes statements that carry many levels of meaning at once. John's hearers know that a holy Spirit has religious significance (Isaiah 32:15), and they know that fire refines as well as destroys (Malachi 3:3). Indeed, our word 'purify' has a curious similarity to the Greek word *pýr*, 'fire'. Jewish rites of purification traditionally use fire as well as water (Numbers 31:23). The so-called Manual of Discipline found among the Dead Sea Scrolls describes a community roughly contemporary with John that expected God to come soon and cleanse them with a holy Spirit, and with water, while destroying evil spirits with fire. (See Isaiah 33:14, 44:3.)

Nowadays a "baptism of fire" denotes a person's inauguration into the thick of difficult fighting. Did John have that meaning in mind when he first uttered the phrase? (See Psalm 66:12; Isaiah 43:2; 1 Corinthians 3:15.)

Luke often uses a definite article to refer to *the* Holy Spirit, for example in 2:26 and 3:22. But 3:16 and many other passages omit the word 'the'; they say 'with holy Spirit'. This extra nuance is often lost in translation.

Jesus will echo the last part of verse 16 by saying, enigmatically, "I've come to throw fire upon the earth...; there's a baptism I must still receive" (12:49–50). He will also refer to the first part of the verse, telling his disciples that they will soon be baptized with a holy Spirit (Acts 1:5, 11:16). He speaks of birth by water and Spirit in John 3:5; his disciples baptize with water (John 3:22, 4:1–2).

John Calvin interpreted verse 16 by comparing John the Baptist to anyone who now performs Christian baptism. A human being, acting as a servant of God, can apply the water; but God himself, the master, bestows spiritual blessings and makes changes in a person's soul.

On the day of Pentecost, the disciples became filled with a holy Spirit, after hearing a mighty wind and after flames seemed to touch them (Acts 2:2–4). This fire was understood to be an illuminating, kindling force. The book of Acts explains in detail how God's Spirit continued to guide them and to inflame others as they spread the teachings of Jesus throughout the world. "We have all been baptized into a single body with one Spirit" (1 Corinthians 12:13).

THE GOSPEL OF JOHN is for many people the most precious book in the Bible. It has been compared to a symphony, in which exquisite themes are stated separately then knit together until they build to a triumphant climax. The 3rd-century scholar Clement of Alexandria characterized it aptly as a "spiritual gospel"; John's story of Jesus is expressed in poetic, transcendental language that emphasizes eternal truths as well as historic facts. It is the product of a lifelong quest for a deep understanding of divine mysteries.

The author is identified only indirectly, as the "disciple whom Jesus loved" (13:23, 19:26, 20:2, 21:20, 21:24); but we can easily deduce that this must be the disciple John who is prominent in the other gospels and in the early church (Galatians 2:9). Further study of ancient material suggests that the fourth gospel was a joint work, which may have been written down in its present form by John the Elder, a noted associate of the disciple John.

John's gospel is quite different from the other three, although there are many parallels—just as we would expect to find in independent accounts of any complicated sequence of events. The most striking differences are in the sayings attributed to Jesus. Instead of down-to-earth parables and short, pithy maxims, we find a series of rather argumentative dialogs, interleaved with methodical discourses about abstract ideas. Parables are not absent from John (e.g., 4:35–38, 10:1–6, 12:24–26), and John-like discourses appear elsewhere (Matthew 11:27; Luke 10:22); but the balance is clearly different here.

One of John's strong themes is embodied in Jesus's declaration, "Before Abraham was, I am" (8:58; Exodus 3:14). This "I am" is combined with many other symbols to describe Jesus's mission: "I am the bread (6:35); the light (8:12); the gate (10:7); the shepherd (10:11); the resurrection (11:25); the vine (15:1); the way, the truth, and the life (14:6)." Believers find enlightenment in these phrases, but are sometimes troubled by such assertiveness; the statements seem to be intolerably arrogant—unless they are true! Since the other gospels describe a more approachable Savior, we suspect that John may have colored his account with aspects of his own personality (Mark 9:38; Luke 9:54). On the other hand, John also emphasizes the humanity of Jesus, who became tired (4:6) and thirsty (19:28); Jesus wept (11:35) and died (19:33).

Recent archaeological discoveries have led Bible scholars to reconsider previous doubts about this book's authenticity. Many contemporary critics find this gospel largely free of Hellenistic influences, assign it a relatively early date of composition, and take its historical data seriously.

Yes, God *JOHN 3:16*
loved the world
so much that he
GAVE HIS
ONLY CHILD,
SO THAT ALL
PEOPLE WITH FAITH IN HIM CAN
ESCAPE DESTRUCTION,
AND LIVE FOREVER·

John 3:16   Hermann Zapf

MARTIN LUTHER called John 3:16 "the Gospel in miniature," and this verse may well be the most popular sentence in the entire Bible. Football fans are often seen on television waving banners that say simply 'John 3:16'. The 1985 edition of *Sacred Choral Music in Print* lists thirty-nine different composers who have set this great verse to music: Palestrina, Prætorius, Scheidt, Schütz, Bach, Telemann, Bruckner, Stainer, and many more. The words have become so familiar that their meaning is often forgotten; I have purposely paraphrased them so that we might understand this verse in a fresh way.

What is the context? Jesus is speaking to Nicodemus, one of the seventy members of the official Jewish court. Nicodemus later will insist on a fair trial for Jesus (7:50) and will help to bury him (19:39). He doesn't appear elsewhere in the Bible, although there is an apocryphal Gospel of Nicodemus. On this occasion he comes to Jesus by night (3:2), seeking to be taught. Jesus immediately tells him to start his life over. Jesus uses a significant phrase that means both 'to be born anew' and 'to be born from above' (3:3). He implicitly tells Nicodemus to be baptized and to have a spiritual rebirth (3:5). He notes that the Spirit, like the night wind, blows freely; it moves us even though we don't know its source or destination (3:8–12). The gulf between the physical and spiritual worlds can be bridged by someone who comes from above (3:13–15).

JOHN 3:16

Yes, God loved the world so much
that he gave his only child,
so that all people with faith in him
can escape destruction, and live forever.

The other gospels frequently speak of entering the 'kingdom of heaven' or 'kingdom of God', but this key phrase occurs in John's gospel only in Jesus's opening words to Nicodemus (3:3, 5). John prefers to use the term 'eternal life' (Matthew 25:46; Mark 10:30; Luke 10:25), which he introduces in verse 15; it appears sixteen more times in his gospel, and six times in 1 John.

Since Nicodemus isn't mentioned after verse 9, it isn't clear just when he leaves the scene. Commentators differ widely in their opinions about where the words of Jesus that begin in 3:11 come to an end. Quotation marks hadn't been invented when this gospel was written, and John doesn't distinguish conversations from soliloquies. Some translators close the quote after verse 12, others after verses 13, 15, 17, or 21. Is verse 16 a statement by Jesus, or a summary by John? In either case the meaning is the same; a decision needs to be made only by printers who prepare "red-letter editions" of the Bible.

172

The discourse begins to speak of God explicitly in verse 16. God is said to be motivated by an active love (*agápe*) for the world of human beings (*kósmos*); *agápe* and *kósmos* are important words throughout John's book. We learn here that God's love is directed to the whole world—not just to one nation or race, not just to virtuous people, but to all.

God loved the world in the following remarkable way: He gave all he could, his only child. Instead of sending an angel or a prophet, he sent his unique, precious Son (Romans 8:32; 1 John 4:9). This is the nearest human analogy to what God did for us; it recalls the powerful story of Abraham and Isaac in Genesis 22. Rereading that story, we notice that Isaac carried the wood for the fire on which he was to be sacrificed (Genesis 22:6), just as Jesus later carried the cross for his crucifixion (John 19:17).

All human analogies are imperfect when applied to God, but we can gain some understanding if we try to imagine ourselves in God's place—loving the world, yet knowing the faults of its inhabitants. How could God help such a world? As a computer programmer, I can glimpse what the situation might have been like, because I can effectively create new worlds inside a computing machine. The ultimate act of love would be to become part of those worlds myself, if I could. John tells us that God's decision was to send his only child. Significantly, God chose to do this in the days before videotape and mass communication would allow his acts to be recorded unambiguously for posterity. I think this was infinitely wise. Religion would soon be disregarded if there were ironclad proofs of God's existence. No personal commitment would be needed.

Now we come to the punch line: Everyone who has faith—a personal trust that Jesus is God's Son—has eternal life, lives forever. Faith or belief (*pístis*) is another key word in this gospel; indeed, John tells us in 20:31 that his whole purpose in writing it is to inspire faith. Eternal life does not come from obeying laws, as Nicodemus thought; it comes from faith.

The Greek words 'in him' don't specify whether faith in Jesus or faith in God is meant here. But there is no real difference, according to 12:44. Believing in Jesus entails believing that God is what Jesus declared him to be.

The opposite of eternal life is destruction. John's Greek word, *apóllymi*, means to perish, to be lost (Matthew 8:25; Luke 19:10). Verses 17 and 18 tell us that this is not a punishment inflicted by God upon unbelievers; such people have chosen by themselves to be separate from God. John points out that we must make a choice. There is no middle ground. He urges us to choose life.

THE ACTS OF THE APOSTLES is a sequel to the Gospel of Luke, written by the same author. An *apóstolos* is someone 'sent forth'; this word originally referred to the disciples of Jesus (1:2; Luke 6:13), and it was used later to designate early missionaries (14:14; Romans 1:1).

The book of Acts is a history of early Christianity. Its theme is stated in 1:8, where Jesus says, "You will be my witnesses in Jerusalem, in Palestine, and throughout the earth." It covers a period of about 30 years, during which the word of God spreads rapidly and the faith of Christ's followers continues to grow (6:7, 9:31, 12:24, 16:5, 19:20); finally, the gospel is being preached without hindrance in Rome (28:31).

This is surely one of the most fascinating books of the Bible. It is filled with stories about men and women in challenging situations, told with a great variety of interesting details about lifestyles in the ancient world. It tells, among other things, how the apostles struggle with the problems of incorporating Gentiles into a movement that has purely Jewish roots. It is a story of spiritual energy and revolution, as God's Spirit continually guides the activities of the young church's pioneer leaders.

Chapters 1–5 describe the original community in Jerusalem, and Chapters 6–12 tell of early mission work reaching to the north. The dominant personality in this part of the book is Peter, who had been Jesus's most prominent disciple. Another strong individual, Saul, enters the story in 7:58 as a persecutor of the early Christians. Saul is dramatically converted to Christianity in Chapter 9, and from Chapter 13 on he plays a leading role, using his Roman name Paul (13:9). Therefore this book has sometimes been called The Acts of Peter and Paul. Chapters 13–20 tell about Paul's three major missionary journeys to Asia Minor, Macedonia, and Greece; this part of the book also summarizes the events of an important church council meeting (Chapter 15). In Chapters 21–26, Paul is arrested and he defends himself before various Jewish and Roman tribunals in Jerusalem and Cæsarea. Paul is ultimately sent to Rome, where he awaits a final trial (Chapters 27–28).

Ancient traditions tell us that Luke was a native of Antioch in Syria, the city where people "were first called Christians" (11:26). Luke is a master of Greek style, except where he is evidently quoting from other documents, and he faithfully reflects the standards of historical scholarship in the first century A.D. He begins in 16:10 to say "*We* did so-and-so," indicating that this portion of his book is the travel diary of an eyewitness.

174

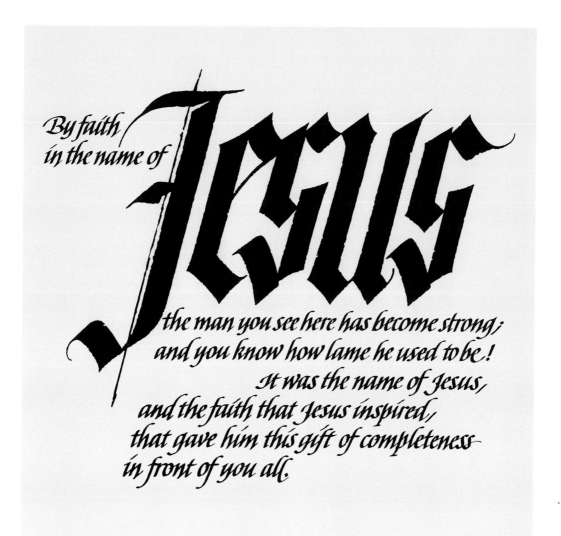

By faith in the name of **Jesus** the man you see here has become strong; and you know how lame he used to be! It was the name of Jesus, and the faith that Jesus inspired, that gave him this gift of completeness in front of you all.

Acts 3 : 16

Lothar Hoffmann

"IN THE NAME of Jesus Christ of Nazareth: Walk!" So speaks Peter in verse 6, to a poor beggar who has been lame all his life. And suddenly this man is cured! He enters the Temple, walking and leaping and praising God (verse 8). This attracts a crowd, and it gives Peter a chance to preach an impromptu sermon that aptly summarizes the gospel message (verses 12–26).

The name of a person was essentially inseparable from that person, in all ancient cultures. For example, the Temple was built "for the name of Jehovah" (1 Chronicles 22:19). The Psalms speak repeatedly about praising the name of God; this means praising God. "O God, save me by thy name" (Psalm 54:1); "How excellent is thy name throughout the earth" (Psalm 8:1). Jesus taught his followers to pray, "Hallowed be thy name" (Matthew 6:9). He also said that God will give "whatever you ask in my name" (John 15:16). John wrote his gospel so that we might have life "in Jesus's name" (John 20:31). Paul said that God gave Jesus "the name above every name" (Philippians 2:9–11).

ACTS 3:16

By faith in the name of Jesus,
the man you see here has become strong;
and you know how lame he used to be!
It was the name of Jesus, and the faith that
Jesus inspired, that gave him this gift of
completeness in front of you all.

Nowadays we do not take names so seriously, but many vestiges of older thought patterns remain. People are still anxious to preserve their family names through their children, and still pleased to have their names displayed prominently on buildings. Christians still wince when other people casually misuse epithets like 'God' or 'Jesus' or 'Christ', even when the offenders clearly intend no offense. I have found names to be amazingly significant in my own work as a computer programmer; for example, when I write a program I frequently find myself blurring the distinction between a reference to an object and the object itself. I've often noticed that new computer software systems seem to jell and to take on a life of their own once they have been given a name, but not before.

To do something in another person's name means to act in that person's place, with delegated authority. For example, prophets speak in the name of God (Deuteronomy 18:22). Peter says, in another story, "Jesus Christ heals you" (9:34); Jesus himself in similar situations said simply "Arise and walk" (Luke 5:24, 7:14). The Jewish authorities who put Jesus to death a few weeks earlier will soon arrest Peter and John and warn them never again to make statements in his name (4:18).

The name of Jesus is, of course, not merely a formula of incantation by which healing occurs magically. Peter emphasizes in verse 16 that faith is the essential ingredient. Jesus often said, "Your faith has healed you" (Mark 5:34, 10:52); Paul, likewise, will observe that a cripple has the faith to be made well (14:9). The lame man healed by Peter most likely knew the beggar whose blindness had been cured by Jesus (John 9:8). On the other hand, he may also have heard that the name of Jesus was affixed to the cross where a condemned criminal had recently been executed (John 19:19). If he had been skeptical about the power inherent in Jesus's name, he surely wouldn't have made a serious effort to obey Peter's command; he would have regarded Peter's words in verse 6 as absurd and insulting.

Some commentators think that verse 16 refers to Peter's faith rather than to the faith of the cripple. Peter undoubtedly has strong faith, but he is probably not claiming any credit for himself here. The thrust of his message is to ascribe glory to Jesus. "By him you have faith in God" (1 Peter 1:21).

The Greek text of verse 16 uses a pronoun that doesn't clarify whether Peter ascribes this faith to Jesus or to Jesus's name. However, both interpretations mean the same thing to Peter's audience. He proclaims that Jesus Christ has caused the faith that made this healing possible. Jesus is "the author and perfecter of faith" (Hebrews 12:2); thus, he is "the author of life" (verse 15).

In Peter's previous sermon, on the day of Pentecost, he had encouraged his audience to "be baptized in the name of Jesus Christ, for the forgiveness of sins" (2:38). After submitting to the rite of baptism and being instructed and touched by the apostles, early converts to Christianity received a holy Spirit (8:16–17, 19:5–6; see Luke 3:16).

It's interesting to compare Chapter 3 with the story in 19:13–16, which indicates that attempts to heal in Jesus's name do *not* work when faith is lacking. Jesus doesn't mind when people appoint themselves to act in his name (Luke 9:49–50), but he has no sympathy with such people when they fall out of harmony with God's wishes (Matthew 7:22–23).

Peter points out to his hearers that they can now see the results of faith for themselves. Most of them know the lame man personally. They know that he has been a fixture at the Temple for a long time. In fact, he's more than forty years old (4:22). And now he obviously can walk!

The moral of this story is clear: The name of Jesus, and the faith that Jesus inspires, can work wonders in us too.

THE LETTER TO THE ROMANS is the first and greatest of the "epistles" in the Bible, the letters that were written to early churches and preserved for posterity. It is the Apostle Paul's masterwork, a magnificent synthesis of his beliefs, composed at the height of his career. Unlike his other letters, it is almost a self-contained theological treatise, a systematic exposition of the central elements that he taught during his pioneering missionary journeys.

Rome was the leading city of the world. Paul had not been there (1:13), but a Christian community was already thriving (1:8). Paul's readers probably included prominent people who traveled frequently. Paul was inspired to write them about the core of religion, about the relationship between the transcendent God and the sinful human race. He addressed many of the subtle questions that he knew his readers were asking themselves.

Chapter 1 begins with greetings and states the major theme: The gospel reveals the gift of divine justice, a harmony between people and God, which is entirely a result of faith (1:17). The next verses (1:18–3:20) emphasize the utter depravity of humankind and our inability to justify ourselves; however, Paul explains that believers in Jesus Christ need not feel guilty (3:21–31). Chapter 4 presents the example of faithful Abraham, and Chapters 5–8 develop in detail the principles of justification by faith. The relationship between Judaism and Christianity, the Old Testament and the New, is discussed in Chapters 9–11. Chapters 12–15 apply these abstract ideas to daily life. The letter closes with several postscripts in Chapter 16.

Paul probably wrote this letter from Corinth about 56 A.D., when he had a few months of leisure before making a fateful trip to Jerusalem (15:24–28; Acts 19:21, 20:3, 24:17; 1 Corinthians 16:6).

Many of the world's greatest theologians have been profoundly influenced by serious study of this book. Martin Luther wrote that it is "the Gospel in its purest expression. Christians will find it well worthwhile not only to know it word for word by heart, but also to meditate on it day by day. ... The more you probe into it, the more precious it becomes, the better its flavor." John Wesley had his momentous Aldersgate experience in 1738 while listening to Luther's preface to this epistle: "While he was describing the change which God works in the heart through faith in Christ, I felt my heart strangely warmed." Karl Barth said in 1918 that his commentary on Romans was "written with the joy of discovery. Paul's powerful voice was new to me; ... clearly much remains that I haven't yet heard."

THEY LEAVE A TRAIL OF WRECKAGE AND MISERY.

ROMANS 3:16

Romans 3:16   Alfred Linz

179

PAUL QUOTES THE OLD TESTAMENT frequently in his letters, and especially in his letter to the Romans, which contains more than sixty citations drawn from thirteen different books. He expects his readers to be familiar with the Bible, because he uses these quotations to support the points he is making.

The sequence of quotations in verses 10–18 is an especially interesting example of his technique. Paul has begun his theological argument in 1:18 by discussing the universal prevalence of sin. The entire world is disobedient to God. Paul has demonstrated this from personal experience, in Chapters 1 and 2. Now he shows that the Scriptures confirm the indictment.

Verses 10–12 are quoted from Psalm 14:1–3, or from the nearly identical words of Psalm 53:1–3, coupled with a hint of Ecclesiastes 7:20. Verse 13 cites Psalm 5:9 and then Psalm 140:3; verse 14 comes from Psalm 10:7. Verses 15–17 are extracted

ROMANS 3:16
They leave a trail of wreckage and misery.

from Isaiah 59:7–8, and verse 18 is the beginning of Psalm 36. Although many different texts have been cut apart and pasted together here, the result is a pleasing, poetic unity that does not do violence to the original contexts.

Rabbinical scholars were fond of assembling Biblical texts in this way. They called the method *chârats*, from the Hebrew word for strings of beads. A "chain of testimonies" such as verses 10–18 was often used at the beginning of a sermon in the synagogues of Paul's day.

Paul's poetic chain begins by stating its main thesis: "No one does right, not a single one" (verses 10 and 12). Then it enumerates various parts of the human body—throat, tongue, lips, feet, eyes—to emphasize how thoroughly we are tainted. Sinfulness progresses dramatically from a lack of seeking after God (verse 11) to lies (verse 13), then to anger (verse 14) and even murder (verse 15). Sinners are ultimately surrounded by a wasteland (verse 16); they know neither peace (verse 17) nor reverence (verse 18).

The seven Greek words of verse 16 agree precisely with the words of Isaiah 59:7 as they appear in the Septuagint, a Greek translation of the Old Testament that was widely used by Hellenistic Jews. Verses 12, 13, 17, and 18 also show verbatim agreement with the Septuagint, except that the final word of verse 18 has been changed from 'his' to 'their' so that the plural sense of verses 13–17 is retained. Verses 10, 11, and 15 are close to their Septuagint counterparts, but verse 14 is a paraphrase. In general, when Paul quotes the Bible his words tend to match the Septuagint perfectly about half the time,

180

and they agree very closely in almost all the remaining cases. Therefore it's reasonable to suppose that he is quoting from memory, a memory that is filled with phrases from several different languages.

Several surviving manuscripts of the Septuagint exhibit an interesting phenomenon: The entire text of Romans 3:12–18 has been substituted for the text of Psalm 14:3! Apparently some Christian copyist—trying to be helpful—decided that Paul's construction was more complete than the original. This is the only place where the New Testament is known to have become part of the Old, instead of vice versa. The error found its way into the Latin Vulgate, then into Coverdale's English Bible of 1535, and it eventually became part of the Psalter in the Episcopal Book of Common Prayer. Thus it happened that the official Prayer Book version of Psalm 14 contained several spurious (though Biblical) verses, until the new Prayer Book was issued in 1976.

Verse 16 paints an eloquent picture of godless human nature in one of its aspects: People go charging off to indulge their whims, leaving nothing but wreckage in their wake. Ruins and rubble can be seen everywhere in the Mediterranean today, and it must have been the same when Paul wrote.

Indeed, we are still surrounded by the detritus of civilization wherever we look. Verse 16 reminds us of the industrial waste material that pollutes our environment, the scribbles of graffiti that deface things of beauty, the litter that characterizes human carelessness.

The trail of sin is marked by misery and distress as well as by debris. The more we indulge our "natural instincts," the more unhappy we seem to be. The more power a person has, the more pain he seems to inflict. The entire passage of Isaiah 59:2–15, which Paul has excerpted, discusses human wretchedness.

Paul concludes in verses 19 and 20 that the function of the Law (the Old Testament) is to clarify the nature of sin. Nobody can be justified in God's sight by keeping the Law. (This is quoted from Psalm 143:2.) From the standpoint of divine justice, Jews have no more merit than Gentiles; Christians have no more merit than unbelievers. God sees the rottenness, deceit, and hypocrisy in every one of us, and if we were in his position we might well decide to wipe out the human race and start over.

But there is good news, beginning in verse 21. Because of Jesus's life and death, God has a way of putting people in harmony with himself. This happens by faith, not by doing what the Law specifies (verse 28). Thus, according to 11:26, Jesus can be identified as the Rescuer promised by God in Isaiah 59:20.

THE FIRST LETTER TO THE CORINTHIANS is filled with practical advice about church-related problems. We know more about the early Christians in Corinth than about any other first-century congregation, because of the vivid details in this letter and in its sequel.

Corinth was a great seaport, one of the Roman empire's leading cities, ranking with Ephesus and Alexandria. The Mediterranean topography helps to explain why: The southern half of mainland Greece is connected near Corinth to the northern half by a narrow neck of land less than 4 miles wide. Ships and goods traveling between Asia and Rome could easily portage here, avoiding some 200 miles of dangerous seas. Thus Corinth was a busy hub of commerce, a gateway not only between north and south but also between east and west. It was also a center for the manufacture of fine pottery and bronze.

Corinth's unique history made its population unusually diverse. After being devastated by war in 146 B.C., it became a Roman colony in 44 B.C., with settlers recruited primarily from liberated slaves having a wide variety of cultural and ethnic backgrounds. By the time Paul arrived, about 50 A.D., Corinth was a fast-growing metropolis that probably surpassed Athens in size. Archaeologists have unearthed more than a dozen Greek, Roman, and Egyptian temples at this site, along with evidence of at least one Jewish synagogue.

Corinth was also notorious as a wide-open center of immorality. All of these factors made it an ideal place for Paul to gain insights about the human condition and to gain converts for Christianity. He stayed eighteen months after establishing an active church here (Acts 18:11), and he kept in close touch as the congregation continued to grow.

Paul tries in the first part of this letter to resolve disputes that have been reported to him (1:11): Chapters 1–4 warn against factionalism; Chapters 5–6 deal with matters of community discipline, lawsuits, and sexual morality. Then he answers a series of questions that the Corinthians had specifically asked (7:1): Chapter 7 discusses marriage; Chapters 8–10 are about proper food; Chapter 11 concerns worship; Chapters 12–14 discuss spiritual gifts and emphasize the supremacy of love (Chapter 13); Chapter 15 is about the resurrection of Christ and of believers. The letter closes in Chapter 16 with Paul's immediate plans and his final exhortations.

Throughout this letter Paul is able to surmount petty crises by leading the discussion to general theological principles. He converts controversies into supremely positive statements that have inspired church members everywhere.

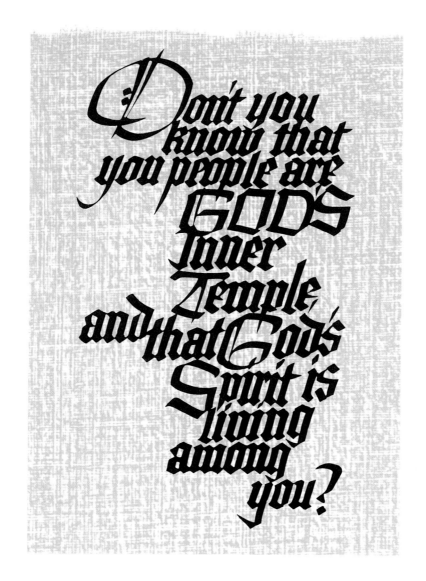

Don't you know that you people are GODS Inner Temple, and that Gods Spirit is living among you?

1 Corinthians 3 : 16

Villu Toots

INSIDE EVERY ANCIENT TEMPLE was an inner sanctuary where a god was thought to live. Indeed, the Greek word for temple, *naós*, comes from the verb *naíō*, 'to dwell'.

Travelers to the excavations at ancient Corinth can visit an oracular shrine with a concealed doorway, near which is a 2500-year-old sign warning people not to enter these sacred precincts. The Mediterranean traveler Pausanias wrote in 175 A.D. that "whoever swears falsely here, be he Corinthian or stranger, can by no means escape from his oath." (See Matthew 23:21.)

The innermost sanctuary of the Jewish Temple was called the Holy of Holies (Hebrews 9:3). This is where the Ark of the Covenant had been placed to symbolize God's presence, although God was understood to be all-encompassing, not limited to this one place (2 Chronicles 6:11, 18).

1 CORINTHIANS 3:16

Don't you know that you people are
God's Inner Temple,
and that God's Spirit is living among you?

Thus Paul's readers, both Gentile and Jew, knew exactly what he meant when he said that they themselves are God's Inner Temple. The Spirit of God was dwelling within them in such a way that they could actually feel God's presence (12:7).

Verse 16 begins with the phrase "Don't you know," which Paul will use nine more times in this letter (5:6; 6:2, 3, 9, 15, 16, 19; 9:13, 24); he also uses it in Romans 6:16 and 11:2. He does this in order to emphasize important things that everybody ought to know. Some of his readers may have found this phrase a bit intimidating; but Jesus and James also used the same expression (Mark 4:13; James 4:4), so it was evidently a common teaching device.

Paul realizes that human beings have lots of faults. Indeed, we cannot help noticing a sharp contrast between this passage and Romans 3:16, which comments on universal depravity. Paul is well aware of "sin living in me" (Romans 7:20); yet he knows that God's Spirit lives there too (Romans 8:9). Somehow we have been purified, and God is actually part of us: "God lives in us as we share his Spirit" (1 John 4:13). "The Spirit of truth is in you; my Father and I will make our home with whoever loves me" (John 14:17, 23). "Jesus Christ is in you" (2 Corinthians 13:5). "When two or three meet in my name, I'm right in their midst" (Matthew 18:20).

The image of Christians as God's Inner Temple is one of Paul's favorites. For example, he uses it in 6:19 as a powerful argument against contaminating our bodies by illicit sexual practices. One of the principal ideas in his letter to

184

the Ephesians is the notion of church members fitting together harmoniously to make a suitable residence for God (Ephesians 2:21–22). Peter uses a similar metaphor when he speaks of a "spiritual house built from living stones" (1 Peter 2:5).

Hebrew scrolls found at Qumran, the site of an ancient monastery near the Dead Sea, show that the men of this community regarded themselves as God's new Inner Temple, a Holy of Holies to replace the one in Jerusalem (Qumran Manual of Discipline 8:5, 9:6). The close connection between their beliefs and 2 Corinthians 6:14–7:1 suggests that some of the Corinthian Christians may have had theological roots in Qumran.

Verse 16 is part of Paul's general discussion in Chapters 1–4 about unity in the church. Several factions had apparently developed in Corinth, threatening to split the congregation. Some of the people claimed loyalty to Paul, some to Peter, and some to another leader named Apollos (1:12). Paul says it is wrong to pay too much attention to human leaders like himself. He addresses his letter to "the church of God in Corinth" (1:2), not to his own adherents. "I planted and Apollos watered, but God made you grow" (verse 6). Nobody in the church should put men in God's place (verse 23); Paul sees no need for any hierarchical arrangement.

The Temple metaphor begins in verse 9 when Paul says, "You are all God's building." God has laid the foundation (verse 10), which is Jesus Christ (verse 11), and others have helped and will help with the construction (verses 12–15). But the important point is that everybody in the church collectively constitutes God's Inner Temple (verse 16).

This verse should be required reading at church meetings, when human weaknesses often become all too prevalent. A community that understands itself as God's Inner Temple will know how to give each member proper respect. Once we perceive that God is truly present in a faithful church, we realize our sacred duty to provide God with a worthy home; we realize what a tragedy it would be to spoil the Inner Temple in any way (verse 17). Squabbles will melt away when people become aware of the Spirit that unifies them. Then men and women will be able to walk humbly and to keep their egos under control (verses 18–20).

Pagan temples were made of stone and inhabited by idols. God's Inner Temple is made of believers and inhabited by his Spirit. This is the sort of temple that lasts! Let us aspire to be its pillars (Revelation 3:12).

THE SECOND LETTER TO THE CORINTHIANS contains urgent communications to a church that is in turmoil. Paul, who has recently escaped death after severe persecution in Asia (1:8–10, 11:23–26), speaks frankly and forthrightly about how he views his ministry. His main theme is the role of a Christian leader as a servant of God and of God's people. Like Jeremiah, he gives intimate details about the agonies he must sometimes suffer.

Chapters 1–9 are generally joyful and confident, while Chapters 10–13 have a very different tone. For example, 7:16 is almost the exact opposite of 12:20. Therefore it is difficult to understand how these sentences could both be part of the same letter, and most Bible scholars now believe that the present text of 2 Corinthians is a compilation of separate epistles. Early church records imply that copies of 1 Corinthians were being circulated long before people were reading 2 Corinthians; hence this material might well have remained in Corinth for many years before anyone decided to make it widely available. Parts of the originals may have been lost by that time. Examples from Greek and Latin literature show that letters from this era were often combined and edited before they were published.

Paul wrote 1 Corinthians after learning about specific problems, but the trouble-makers in Corinth did not immediately mend their ways; a new crisis seems to have arisen. Paul was in Ephesus, about 250 nautical miles distant (1 Corinthians 16:8); he evidently decided to go back and straighten things out (2:1, 13:2). But his second visit must have been painful, because afterward he wrote them a letter "with many tears" (2:4). If someone had deliberately insulted him during his visit and questioned the authenticity of his teaching, it makes sense to regard Chapters 10–13 as a major part of the letter written with tears, since these chapters explain why he believes his credentials are as good as anybody's (10:7, 11:5, 12:12).

After writing the tearful letter, Paul changed his plans to stop in Corinth on the way to Macedonia (1:17, 23). Instead, he sent Titus, from whom he was anxious to hear the latest developments (2:13). Fortunately he soon learned that all was well (7:7–9). The letter in Chapters 1–7 celebrates the successful healing of the church's wounds, and it offers forgiveness and encouragement to the chief offender (2:7). Chapters 8 and 9 are a renewed appeal for funds to help needy Christians in Jerusalem. The stage is set for Paul to have another pleasant stay in Corinth, during which time he will write his magnificent letter to Rome.

186

But when a person
turns
to the LORD,
the heavy veil is
removed.

2. CORINTHIANS 3:16

Edit Zigány

MOSES REGULARLY VEILED HIS FACE, which had begun to shine after he spoke with God (Exodus 34:29–35). As Paul recalls this ancient story, he sees that it has special significance for his Christian readers.

Christians who gathered for worship in Corinth probably began their meetings by reading from Scripture, just as their Jewish contemporaries did. Therefore Paul can assume that his readers know the Bible, which in Paul's day consisted of what we now call the Old Testament. (He refers in verse 14 to the 'old covenant', which means 'old testament'; this may have suggested the name that was eventually adopted.) Today's Christians, too, need to know the Old Testament in order to understand Paul's comments.

Exodus 34:29 says that the skin of Moses's face was shining. The Hebrew word *qâran* used there, 'to shine', can also mean 'to sprout horns' (Psalm 69:31); this alternative meaning led to a mistranslation

2 CORINTHIANS 3:16
But when a person turns to the Lord,
the heavy veil is removed.

in the Latin Bible (the Vulgate), after which Michelangelo and many other artists decided to depict Moses with horns. A similar ambiguity occurs in Habakkuk 3:4, where some Bibles say 'horns' instead of 'rays of light'. A fresco by Botticelli in the Sistine Chapel shows beams of light radiating from Moses's forehead; this is the real meaning of Exodus 34:29. In the Greek Bible that Paul knew (the Septuagint), Moses's face was said to be 'glorified'.

This radiance was too much for the Israelites, who were afraid to come near Moses; but he summoned them anyway (Exodus 34:30–31). Then he made a cover for his face, and wore it regularly except when he was talking to God or reporting to the people (Exodus 34:33–35). The Hebrew word for this head covering, *maçveh*, doesn't appear elsewhere in the Bible, and nobody knows what it looked like; it may have been a mask of some sort. The Septuagint calls it *kálymma*, 'veil', using a word related to *apokálypsis*, 'revelation'. Such a veil seems to have been quite opaque, not flimsy.

Verse 16 is Paul's paraphrase of Exodus 34:34: "But when Moses went before God ... the heavy veil was removed." Paul changes the verbs to the present tense and substitutes another common Biblical idiom, obtaining this: "But when he turns to Lord, the heavy veil is removed." The Greek words 'turn to Lord'—not 'to the Lord', just 'to Lord'—appear five times in the Septuagint (Deuteronomy 4:30; 2 Chronicles 24:19, 30:9; Psalm 22:27; Isaiah 19:22), where they translate the Hebrew phrase 'turn to Jehovah'.

188

When Paul speaks of 'Lord' he nearly always means Jesus Christ (1:2, 1:14, 4:5, etc.), except when he is quoting Scripture (6:17–18). Therefore it's not clear whether he means to say 'turns to Jesus' or 'turns to God' in verse 16. Perhaps he means both, since he associates turning to God with having faith in Jesus (verse 14).

Paul's Greek words in verse 16 are ambiguous also in another sense: They do not specify exactly who is turning to the Lord. Commentators have suggested four different ways to interpret this aspect of the verse. The subject of 'turns' may be the noun at the end of verse 15 (the heart of the Israelites), or it may be Moses as a representative of Israel; in these cases verse 16 refers specifically to conversion from Judaism to Christianity. A third possibility, adopted in most modern translations, assumes that Paul is extending Exodus 34:34 to all people, because he does this explicitly in verse 18. Still another possibility was suggested by John Calvin, who noted that verse 15 refers to 'reading Moses', reading the Law. Therefore verse 16 might refer to the Law, the Torah itself, turning to Christ, who was the 'end' or 'successful fulfillment' of the Law (Romans 10:4). A subtle interpretation like this might very well have been in Paul's mind.

Paul has spoken in verses 3 and 6 of a new covenant in which the letters of the Law, carved in tablets of stone, are replaced by the Spirit, written in human hearts. "The letter kills but the Spirit gives life." Now in verse 17 he says that turning to the Lord is turning to the Spirit.

The heavy veil represents an obstacle to spiritual vision. The ancient Israelites couldn't look steadily at Moses because of the blinding light of the Old Testament Law (verse 7). The New Testament Gospel shines even brighter (verse 9). But now, because of Jesus Christ, Paul says we can all be like Moses and turn to God. Then the veil is immediately removed (verse 16), and we have a new understanding, a new freedom (verse 17). "The veil that is spread over all nations will be destroyed" (Isaiah 25:7). Paul may have been thinking of his own conversion, after which scales fell from his eyes (Acts 9:18).

Jesus lifted a veil and opened people's minds by explaining the significance of the Old Testament (Luke 24:32, 45). The Bible becomes unveiled as a new book when a person changes course and sincerely turns to the Lord. (Nowadays we might say 'turns on' instead of 'turns'.) Paul has succeeded here in capturing some of the radiant feeling that fills Christians when they approach God "with faces unveiled" (verse 18).

THE LETTER TO THE GALATIANS is often called the Magna Charta of Christianity, because it was the first document to state that obedience to rules and regulations is not the way to please God. Paul argues that Christ has fulfilled the Old Testament laws, and that ordinary humans cannot do so. "Christ has set us free" (5:1). Yet God is not an angry tyrant who needs to be placated. Our own deeds earn no heavenly rewards (2:16); the good things we do flow from God's Spirit inside us (5:22), and we have God's Spirit because of our faith (3:5).

This letter can be regarded as a prototype of Paul's letter to the Romans, which develops everything in much greater detail. Paul's emotions are more intense here, because an urgent problem has arisen: "I'm shocked that you are turning so quickly from the gospel I taught" (1:6). People have been trying to coerce the Galatian Gentiles into adopting the Jewish rite of circumcision (6:12). Paul is convinced that circumcision is no longer important (6:15).

Who were the Galatians? Nobody knows for sure, because place names were then in a state of flux. Gallic tribes had conquered part of Asia Minor and settled near present-day Ankara; this area is called 'the Galatian region' in Acts 16:6 and 18:23. But the Roman province of Galatia was larger; it included two districts further south, called Lycaonia and Pisidia in Acts 14:6 and 24. Paul generally refers to places by their official Roman names (e.g., Cilicia, Syria, Judea in 1:21–22; Achaia, Asia, Macedonia in 2 Corinthians 1:1, 8, 16).

Paul and Barnabas had founded churches in the southern part of Roman Galatia during their first missionary journey (Acts 14:23). Paul may well be writing to these churches now, because 2:13 assumes that his readers know Barnabas. When he says "You foolish Galatians" in 3:1, he might mean "You Lycaonians are acting like slaves," since many Gallic people were slaves.

Some scholars think this letter was written from Antioch in Syria, at the time of the controversy reported in Acts 15:1. If so, this would be the earliest of Paul's letters to have survived. Others think that the similarity to Romans makes it likely that both letters were written at the same time, some five or six years later. Such arguments are inconclusive, because Paul had been teaching the same concepts ever since he had been in Galatia (1:8; Acts 13:39).

Chapters 1 and 2 contain interesting autobiographical material and introduce Paul's strong feelings about being "right with God." Chapters 3 and 4 develop the doctrine of justification by faith. Chapters 5 and 6 apply these principles to daily life, explaining that Christian liberty is not license.

Notice
(The passage does not say
that the promises
'and to offsprings' in the plural;
were addressed to Abraham
it uses the singular,
and to his offspring,
'and to your offspring'
meaning Christ.)

Galatians 3 : 16

Lubomír Krátky

191

PAUL WAS EDUCATED at the world's leading center of Jewish studies. "I surpassed many fellow students with boundless enthusiasm for the traditions of my ancestors" (1:14). His teacher was none other than Rabbi Gamaliel the Elder (Acts 5:34 and 22:3), the president of the Sanhedrin council, a grandson of the great Rabbi Hillel. Several of Gamaliel's other students became prominent Jewish leaders. Some teachings of Gamaliel are preserved in the Jewish Mishnah, a legal code based on the law of Moses.

Paul's rabbinical training is evident in much of his writing; and Bible commentators generally rank Galatians 3:16 as the most rabbinical verse he ever wrote. Here he analyzes Genesis 13:15 and Genesis 17:8, observing that God made promises 'to Abraham and to his offspring'. The Hebrew and Greek words that correspond to 'offspring' in Genesis are collective nouns, just as 'offspring' is collective in English; thus, the same word can stand for one offspring and for many offspring. Paul boldly interprets this word as a reference to Jesus Christ.

GALATIANS 3:16

Notice that the promises were addressed to Abraham and to his offspring. (The passage does not say 'and to offsprings' in the plural; it uses the singular, 'and to your offspring'—meaning Christ.)

Such hairsplitting seems far-fetched to a 20th-century mind, but we can understand Paul's point if we look more closely at the methods of interpretation he had learned. Rabbi Tanḥuma in the fourth century saw a reference to the Messiah in the phrase 'other offspring' of Genesis 4:25. The Mishnah argues in *Sanhedrin* 4:5 that a man who is responsible for another man's wrongful death is also responsible for that man's unborn 'offsprings' (plural, meaning generations of descendants), because Genesis 4:10 says that the 'bloods' (plural) of Abel cried out. Another Mishnaic passage says that it is permissible to plant different kinds of seeds in a small garden, because Isaiah 61:11 says that God will make righteousness spring up just as a garden makes its seeds grow. "It is not written 'seed' but 'seeds'" (*Shabbath* 9:2). This passage has an interesting connection with verse 16 because the Hebrew word for 'seed' is very similar to the word for 'offspring'.

The plural of 'offspring' occurs only once in the Hebrew Bible, where it means 'crops' (1 Samuel 8:15). And in Greek Bibles, it appears only in an ancient translation of Daniel 11:31, where 'offsprings' incorrectly translates 'armies' (a Hebrew word with the same consonants). Thus, linguistic studies show that 'offsprings' rarely means 'people', but 'offspring' often does.

192

Surely Paul knew that 'offspring' was being used in a collective sense by the author of Genesis; the word 'offsprings' was not a serious alternative. For example, Genesis 13:16 says "I will make your offspring as numerous as specks of dust." Paul himself says in verse 29 that all Christians are, in essence, offspring of Abraham; he doesn't say 'offsprings' there.

But Paul saw a special significance in the way Genesis is worded, because he knew that the promises were not made to all of Abraham's offspring. For example, Abraham's son Isaac received them, but Ishmael did not (4:28); Isaac's son Jacob received them, but Esau did not (Romans 9:12). The promises passed eventually through David (1 Kings 11:13) and ultimately to the Messiah (Micah 5:2), the Christ. Therefore Paul can say that all of Abraham's offspring can essentially be summed up in one. And with hindsight he finds it interesting that Genesis hints of this.

Of course Paul does not rest his case on such wordplay; his faith does not stand or fall on the fact that Genesis 17:8 doesn't say 'offsprings'! The insight in verse 16 merely enriches his general argument and makes it more appealing to those who already understand. His equating of Abraham's offspring with Christ sharpens the point of verse 8, because God promised Abraham that "all nations of the world will bless themselves by your offspring" (Genesis 22:18). He also returns to the idea in verse 19, where he states that the law of Moses was a temporary measure pending the arrival of the promised Offspring.

The main thrust of verses 15–17 is that God gave these promises to Abraham long before he gave the law to Moses. The law could not have annulled the promises; for if human beings do not abrogate their agreements, God himself will surely abide by his. (This reasoning, incidentally, illustrates another principle of rabbinic scholarship, an argument from lesser to greater.) The promises were made because of Abraham's faith (verse 6; Genesis 15:6). Therefore faith was, and still is, the basis for being in harmony with God.

Many of Paul's readers in Galatia were Gentiles (4:8), so we might suspect that they were barely able to follow his rabbinic argumentation. But this style may have been just right for the occasion; Paul's opponents, who were trying to enforce the practices of Judaism, were probably using similar methods.

The Christians in Galatia had heard Paul discuss these things in person, but we are not so fortunate. Chapter 3 is difficult to understand in isolation. We can, however, turn to the book of Romans for clarification; Romans 4:13–16 aptly summarizes the lessons that Paul wishes to teach here.

THE LETTER TO THE EPHESIANS has been called the Queen of the Epistles; St. John Chrysostom commented that it "overflows with lofty thoughts and doctrines." Like the Gospel of John, it is filled with devotional material intended to enrich and deepen the faith of people who have already become Christians. Paul wrote these words from prison (3:1, 4:1, 6:20), probably when he was in Rome (Acts 28:16); it represents a summing up of his most profound and mature thoughts about religion.

This letter has traditionally been associated with Ephesus, an important city that was the Roman capital of Asia Minor. But the oldest surviving Greek manuscripts make no mention of Ephesus in 1:1. Paul had spent more time in Ephesus than anywhere else during his travels (see Acts 19:10 and 20:31); yet this letter includes no personal greetings. Therefore he probably did not write it specifically for the Christians of any one city. He probably wanted Tychicus to carry it to many different churches (6:21). Christians in America can therefore regard it as Paul's Letter to the Americans; indeed, this letter is highly relevant for all churches in all places at all times.

The style and content of this letter are rather different from Paul's other writings. For example, the ratio of verbs to nouns is 231/158, compared to 139/202 in Galatians. Therefore some Bible scholars believe that the writer was a disciple of Paul, not Paul himself. But such arguments are far from conclusive. Paul often dictated his letters to another person who wrote them down (see Romans 16:22; 1 Corinthians 16:21; Galatians 6:11). Paul could certainly have decided to write a letter in a liturgical, hymnodic style; his other letters include several similar passages where he is moved to adopt an exalted language of adoration and prayer (for example, in Romans 8:38–39 and 11:33–36).

Chapters 1–3 summarize God's grand plan, running throughout history, under which Christ and Christians help to bring all creation together (1:10). "You have been saved by faith, a gift of God" (2:8). Chapters 4–6 deal with the moral issues of how we should live with each other in our churches and homes. Paul writes primarily to Gentiles (2:11, 3:1), who are urged to live in harmony and equality with Jews (2:14). He compares the church to a body whose head is Christ (1:23, 5:30); he also compares it to a building, whose cornerstone is Christ (2:20); and he compares it to a wife, whose husband is Christ (5:25). He asks everyone to "pray as the Spirit leads you, on all occasions" (6:18).

May GOD,
who is
SO RICH IN GLORY,
grant you
additional strength
through HIS SPIRIT,
so that
your inner selves
will be
powerful.

Ephesians 3 : 16

Kerstin Anckers

195

PAUL'S PRAYER for his readers (verses 16–19), which is his prayer for us, has been called the high point of his letter to the Ephesians. In the original Greek it is all part of one sustained, sonorous sentence beginning at verse 14. English translations usually break it into parts so that modern readers can more easily appreciate his beautiful words and thoughts, savoring them one by one.

He prays to God the Father (verse 14), who he also calls "our Father" (1:2), "the Father of glory" (1:17). In 1:7 and 2:7 he has said that God is rich in grace; in 2:4 he has said that God is rich in mercy. Now in verse 16 (as also in Romans 9:23 and Philippians 4:19) he says that God is rich in glory. He emphasizes God's bountiful treasures because he is thinking of God as a giver of gifts; Paul sees no limit to the resources with which God will supply all of our needs.

EPHESIANS 3:16

May God, who is so rich in glory, grant you additional strength through his Spirit, so that your inner selves will be powerful.

But what exactly is 'glory'? The word *dóxa* means 'reputation' or 'prestige' in secular Greek literature, and it occasionally retains this meaning in the Bible (1 Thessalonians 2:6). We often consider glory and honor to be synonymous concepts. But when the Greek Bible refers to the *dóxa* of God, the word takes on special theological significance; it stands for divine splendor and majesty, the very essence of God's perfection. When we contemplate the vastness of the starry skies, we quickly realize that "the heavens declare the *dóxa* of God" (Psalm 19:1). Such glory is often associated with bright light; for example, God's *dóxa* shone on the shepherds when Jesus was born (Luke 2:9). Paul asks in verse 16 that God impart some of his radiant energy to us.

God's holy Spirit is the medium by which we are strengthened; the Spirit is a source of revelation (1 Corinthians 2:10). Paul emphasizes in this letter that God's Spirit is also a source of unity among Christians (2:18, 4:3). His readers already have spiritual gifts (1:13); but Paul asks for additional strengthening from God, just as John the Baptist and Jesus Christ were said to have grown strong in the Spirit (Luke 1:80, 2:40).

We never advance so far that we can't grow a little more. John Calvin aptly commented on this passage that believers are "not only born again but growing daily." Calvin also noted that Paul doesn't pray for us to become strong by our own power; spiritual strength is a gift from God, it is nothing for us to boast about (2:9).

This additional strength is to be directed to our 'inner selves', and we come now to the most important part of verse 16. Paul has referred to an 'inner self' also in Romans 7:22 and in 2 Corinthians 4:16; a similar phrase appears in the writings of Greek philosophers (Plato's *Republic* 9:589; Plotinus's *Ennead* 5:1.10). The inner self is the real essence of our being. It is our conscience, our consciousness. Deep down inside myself lies the real me; a recent book calls it the "mind's I". Peter speaks of "the hidden person of the heart" (1 Peter 3:4); Paul may have a similar idea in mind when he prays that God may enlighten "the eyes of your hearts" (1:18).

Philosophers have been exploring the concept of self for centuries without being able to clarify it. The advent of computers in recent years has stimulated considerable research into artificial intelligence, but so far this work has been unable to shed much new light on the subject—except to reveal how little anybody actually understands about consciousness.

Although we don't know what our inner self really is, we can sense that it is more important than our outer, external self. The inner self is the aspect of our personality that we are least able to control; hence we have a special need to pray that it be directed by God's Spirit. If people are asked what they want most, chances are they will choose health, honor, riches, beauty, or some other external gratification. Paul's prayer, by contrast, is for our inner selves, indeed for my inner self; the inner self is what really counts.

Verse 16 calls for an infusion of power to be sent into my innermost being. The Greek word used here for power, *dýnamis*, means the ability to do things, and the following verses explain why inner fortification is so important: In some mysterious way, Jesus Christ will take up residence inside of me by means of faith (verse 17); I will then have the strength to understand four dimensions—breadth, length, height, depth—that is, everything in the universe (verse 18); and I will know the love of Christ, which surpasses all knowledge (verse 19). "Knowledge puffs up, but love builds up" (1 Corinthians 8:1). Rooted in love (verse 17), I will finally be "filled with God's utter fullness" (verse 19). It is easy to see from these verses why Ephesians is reckoned as one of the high points of the Bible.

Paul closes his prayer with a *doxology* in verses 20 and 21: "To the One who can give us infinitely more than we could ever think of requesting, to Him be *dóxa*—in the church and in Christ Jesus, throughout all generations to come—forever and ever! Amen." Amen!

THE LETTER TO THE PHILIPPIANS is a friendly, personal letter from Paul to his favorite group of Christians, his "joy and crown" (4:1). The church at Philippi was the first he had founded in Europe (Acts 16), and it seems to have been as close to an ideal congregation as any he had known.

Philippi was a small but prosperous Roman colony, strategically located on the chief road from Asia to the West. Paul usually earned his own living during his missionary journeys (Acts 18:3; 1 Thessalonians 2:9), but the Philippians had helped him generously on several occasions (4:16; 2 Corinthians 11:9). Now he was in prison (1:13), and they had sent Epaphroditus to look after his needs (2:25, 4:18). Unfortunately Epaphroditus had become seriously ill; Paul writes this letter in part to commend this faithful co-worker, who now has recovered and is returning home (2:26–30).

Paul knows well that he might soon die a martyr's death (1:21, 2:17). Yet the outstanding characteristic of this letter is his evident joy—a deeply felt, serene happiness that cannot be taken from him. "I pray with joy" (1:4); "I am happy and will continue to be happy" (1:18). "Rejoice in the Lord always! I say it again: Rejoice!" (4:4).

We don't know exactly when Paul wrote this letter. He might have been imprisoned at Ephesus during his third missionary journey (see 2 Corinthians 1:9), or he may have been writing from captivity in Rome (Acts 28:16).

Like all spontaneous, informal letters, this one moves gradually through a number of important topics. Chapter 1 is a hearty greeting followed by a report on Paul's current situation. He tells his friends not to worry about him, as he is not worried about the people in Philippi. Chapter 2 begins with a call for increased unity and a magnificent description of Christ's life of service; then Paul discusses his future plans. Chapter 3 is an ardent warning against false propaganda that might tempt the Philippians to other religions. This chapter also contains a brief but eloquent summary of what it means to be a Christian. Chapter 4 contains final exhortations, personal greetings, and warm thanks for all of the help he has received.

I once visited Riverside Church in New York City, keenly anticipating an outstanding sermon by its well known pastor, Rev. William Sloane Coffin, Jr. But on that particular Sunday, he decided to do something different: Instead of delivering a newly prepared sermon, he simply read to us the book of Philippians, from beginning to end. And it was, in fact, one of the best sermons I've ever heard.

let us keep
in step

Meanwhile

with the
pace
we have set.

Philippians 3:16

Guillermo Rodríguez-Benítez

RUNNERS like to run every day so that they can build up their strength to go farther and faster. Paul often compares the life of a Christian to a foot race (2:16; Galatians 2:2, 5:7). In verse 13, as in 1 Corinthians 9:24–26, he recommends straining forward and going flat out toward the finish line, like a champion racer. "Christ took hold of me so that I could take hold of the prize" (verse 12). But Paul hasn't reached his goal yet; he keeps running (verse 14).

English translations of verse 16 tend to be quite different from each other, because Paul's original Greek words are difficult to render in our language. A literal translation goes something like this: "Hey, to what we've reached, by this to march!" The first word, *plén*, is especially hard to translate adequately; it means 'yet', 'moreover', 'indeed', 'besides', 'nevertheless', 'here is another important point'. Paul tends to use sentences beginning with *plén* at the close of a discussion, when he wants to stress a particularly significant idea (1:18, 4:14; 1 Corinthians 11:11; Ephesians 5:33).

PHILIPPIANS 3:16

Meanwhile, let us keep in step with the pace we have set.

The middle Greek word of verse 16 means 'we have reached or arrived at'. Romans 9:31 says that "Israel pursued a law of justification but didn't reach it." Paul was a Jew of the tribe of Benjamin, and he had been a devout Pharisee (verse 5); this meant that he strove to please God by living a spotless life, obeying many laws (verse 6). But when he became a Christian, he realized that attempts to achieve perfection by his own efforts were inadequate, and he turned to a perfection based on faith, a perfection that originates with God (verse 9).

The final Greek word of verse 16 means 'to march in step'. Paul's construction here is interesting to students of Greek grammar, because this word is infinitive in form but imperative in meaning. English speakers might say, similarly, "To work!" Imperative infinitives are found mostly in ancient Greek literature, but another instance occurs in Romans 12:15: "To rejoice with those who rejoice; to mourn with those who mourn."

Putting all these words together, we can see what verse 16 means: "Let's keep progressing from the point we've reached." It is analogous to Galatians 5:25, "Let's march in step with the Spirit."

Some old manuscripts of the New Testament have four additional Greek words in the text of verse 16; the extra words make it say, "Let us all be of one mind and march according to the same rule." But these words do not appear in the oldest and best manuscripts, so they apparently were inserted by a later scribe who was trying to help interpret a somewhat obscure phrase. The addition is not incompatible with what Paul says elsewhere (in 2:2 and Galatians 6:16); but the extra words actually miss the main point that Paul is trying to make in verse 16, and in Chapter 3 as a whole.

Paul's main point is that the Christian life is a process of continual striving for greater faith, for greater knowledge of God. We never reach perfection; we continue to depend on God for growth. As Luther put it, "The essence of Christianity is not what we have become, but what we are becoming."

This is a confusing concept for many people. Surely it would be much easier to say that a person either has faith or doesn't. Everything would be so simple if there were definite answers to all questions. But God does not want things to be so pat. Paul knows that he himself has not achieved a perfect faith, so he continues to run toward the goal (verses 12–14).

Scientists are quite familiar with this state of affairs. Experiments never produce complete knowledge about nature; they only help to narrow down the possibilities. Even in mathematics, where it is possible to prove conclusively that certain things are true, we find that the more we know, the more we realize is unknown. Every answer suggests more questions; we never reach the end, but we always try to keep moving forward.

If there are degrees of faith, and degrees of understanding, it must be true that some people are less advanced than others. But this is not a reason for anyone to be proud, since faith comes from God (verse 9). The fact that different people are at different stages of development is, instead, a reason for tolerance of those who disagree with us; they may be ahead or behind, we don't always know. God will continue to reveal himself to them and to us by his Spirit (verse 15; 1 Corinthians 2:10). We keep running, precisely because our knowledge is incomplete.

Thank goodness we aren't engaged in a rat race. As we progress on our spiritual journey, God sustains us and whets our appetite for more. As we turn into the home stretch, verse 16 encourages us not to rest on our laurels but rather to maintain the momentum we already have. We don't need to get ahead of the competition, yet we're motivated to make our best effort.

Furthermore, we shouldn't go running off in all directions. Once we've gotten off to a good start, we should all march together toward the same goal, from wherever we are.

THE LETTER TO THE COLOSSIANS presents Jesus Christ in a cosmic context. It can be regarded as a first draft of the letter to the Ephesians, just as Galatians is thought to be a preliminary version of Romans. Paul wrote this letter in order to counteract the influences of occultism and other beliefs that were threatening to undermine the gospel message in this early Christian community.

Colossæ was a small city about 110 miles east of Ephesus, on the main road between Ephesus and the eastern Roman empire. There was nothing particularly colossal about it; in fact, it has been called the least important town to which Paul ever wrote. Colossæ was known for fine woolen goods that were dyed in a certain way; but the twin cities of Laodicea and Hierapolis (4:13), a dozen miles to the west, were much more prominent. Paul himself may never have visited this region (2:1), but several of his friends came from there. One of these was Epaphras, founder of the church in that district (1:7, 4:12); another was Onesimus (4:9), a runaway slave on whose behalf Paul wrote a short, touching letter to Philemon. Paul also knew Philemon, in whose house the church at Colossæ seems to have met (Philemon 2). Like the letters to Ephesians and Philemon, this one was written from prison (4:3) and delivered by Tychicus (4:7). Therefore all three letters were apparently sent at the same time, probably from Rome, about five years after Christianity had reached Colossæ.

Chapter 1 begins with prayer, then describes the supremacy of Christ, in whom "the fullness of God lives" (1:19). Chapter 2 warns against "deceptive philosophy" (2:8) by which people are trying to mix harmful additives with the pure Christian gospel. These dangerous embellishments include angel worship (2:18), abstinence from certain foods (2:16, 21), and extreme forms of self-discipline (2:23). Chapter 3 contrasts such practices with a Christ-filled life; verses 5–9 summarize bad things that are to be avoided, and the following verses (3:10–4:6) summarize good things that are to be enjoyed. Chapter 4 closes with personal greetings and Paul's signature. Both Mark (4:10) and Luke (4:14) are among those who send their regards.

Paul knows that the issues addressed here are of general importance, for he wants this letter to be read also in Laodicea (4:16). He may have foreseen that letters like this would be copied and preserved. But he surely never dreamed how valuable his letters would become during the next twenty centuries, as the heretical tendencies he warned about continued to spring up regularly.

Let Christ's Word live
exuberantly among you.
Teach and guide each other
in all wisdom.
Sing psalms and hymns and
spiritual songs;
Praise God with all your hearts!

Colossians 3:16   Neenie Billawala

THE JOY OF WORSHIP is central to Paul's description in Chapter 3 of the Christian life. Verse 16 is a beautiful summary of the ideal way for members of a congregation to act together. It's part of a three-fold discussion of the "peace of Christ" (verse 15), the "word of Christ" (verse 16), and the "name of the Lord Jesus" (verse 17), supporting Paul's emphasis in this letter on the supremacy of Jesus Christ.

Christós is a Greek word meaning 'Anointed'; it is a translation of the Hebrew *Mâshîyach*, Messiah. Israel's kings and priests were anointed with olive oil (Exodus 29:7; 1 Kings 1:39); prophets later spoke of a future savior-king (Isaiah 11:1; Jeremiah 23:5; Ezekiel 34:23; Micah 5:2), who came to be known as the Messiah, a title that was given to Jesus (John 4:25, 29).

COLOSSIANS 3:16

Let Christ's word live exuberantly among you.
Teach and guide each other in all wisdom.
Sing psalms and hymns and spiritual songs;
praise God with all your hearts!

Verse 16 refers to 'the word of Christ', the *lógos* of Christ, and this term can be understood in several ways. It may refer to Christ's sayings (Matthew 28:20; Acts 20:35); but in such a case Paul would probably have said 'words', not 'word'. Another possibility is that *lógos* refers to Jesus himself, the Word or Essence of God in human form (John 1:14). But the best clues to Paul's meaning here are found in 1:5, 1:25, and 4:3, where Paul uses 'the word' to stand for the gospel message; this is what he calls 'the word of the Lord' in 1 Thessalonians 1:8 and 2 Thessalonians 3:1. Nowadays we might legitimately substitute 'the New Testament' for 'Christ's word' in verse 16, because the gospel message has now been written down.

Christ's word should live among us, just as God's Spirit does (1 Corinthians 3:16); the word stays with us, is at home with us (1 John 2:14). In fact, it should be abundantly, exuberantly present in every Christian gathering. Verse 16 suggests holding a worship service in a magnificent theological library.

The remaining parts of verse 16 explain how Christ's word can be lavishly present when Christians meet: We teach each other, guide each other, and sing to each other. An emphasis on 'each other' is carried over from verse 13: Paul has said in 1:28 that he is guiding and teaching, but now he points out that such responsibilities belong to all. Everybody can be a teacher, counselor, and/or vocalist (Romans 12:6–8). Mutual edification is best.

Teaching means educating (Acts 5:42); it also implies studying and learning (2 Timothy 3:15–16). Guiding or admonishing helps to correct behavior, just as parents train children (Acts 20:31; 1 Corinthians 4:14; Ephesians 6:4; 2 Thessalonians 3:15). Paul is suggesting the formation of Christian support groups here. His phrase 'all wisdom', used also in 1:9 and 1:28, refers to the spiritual understanding that goes with Christ's word. The goal of teaching and guiding is to be able to "walk in wisdom" (4:5); this is contrasted to the mere "appearance of wisdom" (2:23).

Christians have inherited a great musical tradition, typified by Psalm 66:1: "Let all the earth make a joyful noise to God." Jesus sang a hymn with his disciples the night before he died (Mark 14:26). Paul and Silas sang in prison (Acts 16:25). James 5:13 says, "If you're happy, sing a psalm."

Verse 16 speaks of psalms, hymns, and spiritual songs. A *psalmós* in Greek usually has instrumental accompaniment; a *hýmnos* is a song of praise; and the third word, *ōdé*, denotes a song in general, especially a folk song. A 'spiritual ode' may therefore be like the popular spirituals and gospel music of our day. But we need not look for precise differences among these three ways to sing; Paul's point is that there are many ways to do it, and they're all highly recommended.

About one fifth of Paul's letter to the Colossians has close parallels with his letter to the Ephesians, and this verse is a case in point. Ephesians 5:19 reads, "Speak to each other with psalms and hymns and spiritual songs; sing and play to the Lord with all your heart!"

The Greek text at the end of verse 16 is difficult to translate. Literally, it says 'in the grace singing to God with your hearts', and the phrase about grace can be interpreted in several ways. The word *cháris*, 'grace', comes from *chará*, 'joy', and it means anything that delights. Thus it means both a favor bestowed by a gracious giver and a thank-you returned by a grateful receiver. Paul refers frequently to God's grace in the first sense (1:6, 4:18); thus, 'in the grace' could designate the state of the singers. But *cháris* can also be directed to God in the second sense (1 Corinthians 15:57; 2 Corinthians 2:14); then verse 16 illustrates a way to be thankful (see verse 15). A third meaning is also possible: The singing might be 'graceful', a treat for the hearers (4:6; Ephesians 4:29; Luke 4:22). Musicians prefer this interpretation.

A true song comes from the heart, not just from our lips (Isaiah 29:13). Similarly, good workers do their jobs with all their hearts (verse 23), where the peace of Christ rules (verse 15). Singing heartily means that our minds as well as our emotions are entirely caught up in song (1 Corinthians 14:15).

THE FIRST LETTER TO THE THESSALONIANS is generally regarded as the earliest of Paul's letters that has been preserved; the only other potential candidate for this honor is his letter to the Galatians. The letters appear in our Bible in order of decreasing size, and this sometimes obscures the fact that Paul didn't write some of the longer ones until many years after he wrote the shorter ones.

Thessalonica was and still is a teeming metropolis, founded in 316 B.C. by one of Alexander the Great's generals and named after one of his sisters. It was the capital of the Roman province of Macedonia; today Thessaloníki is the second largest city of modern Greece.

Paul came to Thessalonica in 50 A.D., immediately after being forced to leave Philippi, 100 miles to the east. He established a Christian community consisting of a few Jewish converts and a large number of Greeks (Acts 17:4), who "turned from idols to serve a living God" (1:9). Other Jews forced him to leave, but he was able to strengthen and encourage the Thessalonian Christians by sending Timothy to them from Athens (3:2). Timothy rejoined Paul in Corinth shortly before this letter was written (3:6; Acts 18:5,11). Thus we have a unique opportunity in this letter to experience Paul's missionary work as it is taking place. He is writing to people who have just recently learned of the gospel, some twenty years after Christ's ascension.

He begins Chapter 1 with warm thanks for the example they are setting, saying that their faith is "known everywhere" (1:8), even though they are persecuted (1:6). In Chapter 2, he summarizes his mission work among them, and in Chapter 3 he says, "Don't worry about me; keep up the good work."

Chapters 4 and 5 provide additional guidance for this fledgling congregation. Paul encourages everyone to live a chaste life and to grow even stronger in brotherly love. He answers a question about the fate of dead people at the time of Jesus's second coming, and he points out that nobody knows exactly when this will happen. Meanwhile, he says, "rejoice always" (5:16) and "pray continually" (5:17); these are two of the shortest but best verses in the Bible.

Paul doesn't dwell on fine points of doctrine in this brief letter. But he masterfully covers all the highlights of Christianity, stressing faith, love, and hope (1:3, 5:8). His readers are still unfamiliar with the Old Testament, so he doesn't quote directly from it, but he does paraphrase it in subtle ways (compare 2:16 with Genesis 15:16; 3:13 with Zechariah 14:5; 4:5 with Psalm 79:6; 5:8 with Isaiah 59:17).

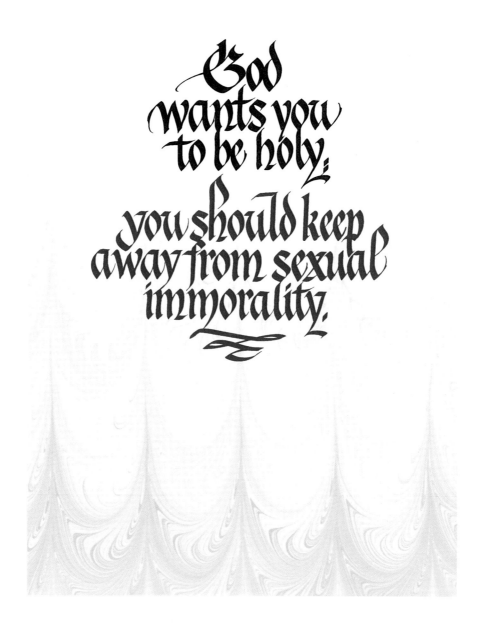

God
wants you
to be holy;
you should keep
away from sexual
immorality.

1 Thessalonians 4 : 3

Margo Snape

CHASTITY was a rarity in the Greco-Roman world. Extramarital sex was considered normal, as long as it wasn't carried to excess. For example, Cicero once asked (in 56 B.C., *Pro Cælio* 20:48), "When was it not common practice for youths to have affairs with courtesans? When was it blamed?" Cicero had, incidentally, been living in Thessalonica a year before saying this.

Jewish people adhered to a much stricter code than their neighbors. Therefore Paul and the other early Christian missionaries who had grown up under Judaism had to decide how many of the laws of Moses should be binding on converts to Christianity. A church council meeting in Jerusalem concluded that the number of special restrictions should be reduced to four: Christians should not eat food sacrificed to idols, nor blood, nor an animal that had been strangled, nor should they engage in illicit sex (Acts 15:29). The last of these prohibitions is echoed by Paul in verse 4:3; he did not think

1 THESSALONIANS 4:3
God wants you to be holy; you should keep away from sexual immorality.

that the others were very important unless they caused offense to other people (Colossians 2:16; 1 Corinthians 10:32).

Several of Paul's letters contain lists of vices, which he contrasts with the fruits of God's Spirit. In each case, sexual immorality is the first item on Paul's vice list (Galatians 5:19; Ephesians 5:3; Colossians 3:5). Jesus also condemned adultery in a similar list, headed by "evil thoughts" (Matthew 15:19).

Paul is writing from Corinth, which (like Thessalonica) is a large seaport notorious for its licentiousness. Therefore it is easy to understand why he begins the exhortations in his letter with a lesson about sexual mores. The word he uses, *porneía*, comes from the Greek word for prostitute; prostitution was the most common type of sexual offense, but *porneía* had also acquired a more general meaning including incestuous marriages (1 Corinthians 5:1). Jesus said that a man who remarries after divorcing his wife commits adultery (*moicheía*) unless the grounds for divorce were his ex-wife's *porneía* (Matthew 5:32, 19:9).

Verse 4:3 begins literally with the words 'Indeed, this is the will of God'. This phrase, which appears also in 5:18, expresses the fundamental governing principle of a Christian life: We wish to please God (4:1). Conversely, we try not to sin because that is against God's will (4:8). "Teach me to do your will, for you are my God" (Psalm 143:10). When we pray "Thy will be done" (Matthew 6:10), we want our actions to be consistent with God's intentions.

208

And what does God want? He wants us to be holy (Leviticus 11:45). That means we should be sacred, consecrated, sanctified, like a saint; like God. Holiness is the opposite of uncleanness and impurity (4:7; 2 Thessalonians 2:13). Christians are called to be saints (Romans 1:7; 1 Corinthians 1:2).

And why is holiness associated with sexual morality? Paul only hints at the reasons in this letter when he says in 4:6 that sexual license exploits another person. He will discuss the problem in more detail several years later when he writes to the Corinthians, pointing out that a Christian's body is part of God's Temple (1 Corinthians 3:16, 6:19). "Your body is part of Christ's body; therefore it's out of the question to join it with the body of a prostitute" (1 Corinthians 6:15).

Of course, the human sex drive is a powerful force, part of our God-given makeup. "It is not good for a man to be alone" (Genesis 2:18). Paul admires the man or woman who can suppress this urge (1 Corinthians 7:1,8); but he knows that abstinence is impossible for most people. So he advocates monogamous marriage (1 Corinthians 7:2), saying "It's better to marry than to burn with passion" (1 Corinthians 7:9).

Verse 4:4 presents the positive side of the coin, by commenting on what is desirable as an alternative to what is forbidden in 4:3. But unfortunately the exact meaning of 4:4 is unclear, because it uses an unusual Greek expression whose interpretation has been the subject of endless debate. Literally, 4:4 says that everyone should know enough 'to acquire or possess one's own *skeúos*', where *skeúos* normally means 'vessel' or 'container'. Some translations render this 'to take a wife', because 1 Peter 3:7 tells husbands to respect their wives although a wife is a 'weaker vessel'. Then 4:4 is saying that marriage is the proper outlet for sexual passion, that a man should honor his wife. Other translations say 'to control your body', because *skeúos* sometimes means 'reproductive organ' in secular Greek. A third possibility, 'to have marital intercourse', is based on rabbinic discourses from Paul's time in which 'using as a vessel' is a euphemism for sexual relations. All three of these interpretations are consistent with Paul's more complete discussion in 1 Corinthians 7.

The important part of verse 4:4 is its punch line: Acquiring a vessel (whatever that means) can and should be done in a holy and honorable manner, not in a lustful way. Here again we see an emphasis on holiness, which returns us to the thought of 4:3. Every part of our life—especially our sex life, in which many temptations arise—should be holy. For that is what God wants.

THE SECOND LETTER TO THE THESSALONIANS is a sequel to the first, probably written only a month or two later. Paul's purpose is to clarify some things that the Thessalonians have misunderstood, and to help them resolve a conflict that is troubling them.

The central issues discussed here revolve around the second coming of Christ, an anxiously anticipated event that was also a significant theme in Paul's first letter. He had described the Thessalonians as "waiting for God's Son from heaven" (1 Thessalonians 1:10) and encouraged them to be "blameless at the coming of our Lord" (1 Thessalonians 3:13, 5:23). Now he emphasizes that relief from the present struggles will come when Jesus appears (1:7).

Like all predictions of the future, the forecasts of Christ's return are paradoxical and difficult to understand. Paul had told the Thessalonians, repeating Jesus's words (Matthew 24:43), that the event will be a surprise when it happens: It will come "like a thief in the night" (1 Thessalonians 5:2). Yet he had also told them (2:5) that the event will have historical portents (2:3), so they shouldn't be surprised that it hasn't already happened. Jesus had said the same thing (Matthew 24:6). Paul tries in Chapters 1 and 2 to give the Thessalonians a balanced understanding of the mystery, using numerous paraphrases of Old Testament prophecies.

In Chapter 3 he explains how Christians are to wait: We should work and pray. Some of the Thessalonians had evidently been so convinced that Jesus was coming immediately, they had simply decided to sit idle and let the rest of the community take care of them. Some hints of this can be found in 1 Thessalonians 4:11 and 5:14; now Paul is more explicit in condemning such laziness. "Anybody who refuses to work shouldn't eat" (3:10). But he gives advice about how to apply discipline in a loving manner (3:14–15).

Paul's affection for this fervent young community is evident throughout both of these letters. He addresses the Thessalonians frequently as his 'brothers', 24 times in all. (Jesus recommends this term in Matthew 23:8.) Nowadays Paul would call them his 'brothers and sisters' (see Mark 3:35 and Luke 8:21).

The Thessalonian church evidently continued to thrive after these letters were received. A Jewish convert from Thessalonica named Aristarchus would later become one of Paul's principal companions (Acts 19:29, 20:4, 27:2; Colossians 4:10; Philemon 24). But 2 Timothy 4:10 reminds us that problems also persisted: "Demas, in love with the present world, has deserted me and gone to Thessalonica."

May the Lord of peace himself give you PEACE at all times and in all ways. The Lord be with you all·

2. THESSALONIANS 3:16

2 Thessalonians 3 : 16   Gudrun Zapf von Hesse

THE PEACE OF THE LORD! Christians in thousands of churches around the world regularly "share the peace" with each other as part of their Sunday worship, saying "The peace of the Lord be with you." This phrase becomes more and more meaningful the more we read the Bible and grow in faith. Christianity is the "good news of peace through Jesus Christ" (Acts 10:36).

Paul is coming to the end of his second letter to the Thessalonians, and he is moved to say a prayer for them. Verse 16 is one of four short prayers in these letters that begin with the same two Greek words, literally 'Himself now'; the other three prayers are found in 2:16 and in 1 Thessalonians 3:11, 5:23. Indeed, 1 Thessalonians 5:23 begins with almost the same thought as 2 Thessalonians 3:16, but it says "May the God of peace himself make you completely holy." Romans 15:33 is another very similar verse: "May the God of peace be with you all."

2 THESSALONIANS 3:16
May the Lord of peace himself give you peace, at all times and in all ways. The Lord be with you all.

Paul usually means Jesus Christ when he speaks of 'the Lord'; but sometimes he uses 'Lord' as a term for God the Father, especially when quoting from the Old Testament (see 1 Corinthians 10:9). Verse 2:13, which speaks of 'brothers loved by the Lord', has a parallel in 1 Thessalonians 1:4, 'brothers loved by God'. Although verses 6 and 12 speak of the Lord Jesus Christ, we cannot be absolutely certain that Paul's references to 'Lord' in verse 16 point specifically to Jesus. Peace comes from both Father and Son (1:2).

The Greek word for peace, *eirēnē*, means the absence of hostility. Paul has this notion of peace in mind when he says that Christ is the basis for peace between Jews and Gentiles (Ephesians 2:14). He also explains that faith in Jesus Christ leads to peace with God (Romans 3:22, 5:1). Such peace is a wonderful state of harmony.

But the Hebrew word *shâlôm* has an even richer meaning, including health and prosperity. When Jesus says "Peace I leave with you" (John 14:27) and "Peace be with you" (John 20:19, 21, 26), he is speaking in a Hebrew dialect and thereby implying much more than abatement of conflicts. He clearly deserves the title Prince of Peace (Isaiah 9:6).

Paul's prayer in verse 16 includes three uses of the word 'all', each of which is significant in itself and reinforces the others. First, Paul asks for peace *at all times*. This means that the peace should be continual, continuous; "peace like a river" (Isaiah 48:18).

212

Secondly, Paul asks for peace *in all ways*. Several ancient manuscripts of the New Testament have a different word here (Greek *tópō* instead of *trópō*), which would make it 'in all places' instead; but the oldest and best surviving copies of Paul's letter say 'in all ways', and this phrase has a much more profound meaning. Paul is not asking for a superficial peace, a Pax Romana that is enforced by military might. Nor is he asking for just one kind of peace. He is asking for peace in its broadest possible sense.

Earlier in the letter he has referred to persecution that the Thessalonians are suffering (1:4–5), and in the third chapter he has just discussed an internal conflict about lazy people in the church who interfere with everybody else (verses 6–15). Now Paul asks God for peace of all kinds, including an end to these struggles, and including the concept of *shâlôm*.

Finally, Paul asks for the Lord's presence as well as his peace. To have God as our companion, as part of ourselves, is his fervent wish; this will be a permanent source and guarantee of peace. And—most significantly—Paul wishes it for *all*, including the idlers he has just been castigating. Nobody is left out of this prayer; true peace involves everyone.

The same words 'with you all' occur at the very end of this letter (verse 18), where Paul includes an additional prayer for the Lord's grace (that is, for God's generous gifts). Grace and peace traditionally go together (see 1:2 and Numbers 6:24–26).

Different translations of the Bible almost always exhibit different choices of words. But the last part of verse 16 is an exception to this general rule; twelve of the fifteen most prominent English translations, from the King James Version to the New Jerusalem Bible, say exactly the same thing at this point: "The Lord be with you all." Here, it seems, is a case where Paul was almost writing in English.

Once I was camping in a desert region; I had time to forget everyday concerns and to think about my life as a whole. And I remember especially being struck by a realization that, deep down, in some way I can't define, I am at peace with God and with the world. This means a lot to me; in fact, I think it's the basis of my whole life. And I think this is what is meant by the peace of the Lord, the peace that transcends all understanding (Philippians 4:7). It must be the greatest of God's gifts. "Great peace have they who love God's law" (Psalm 119:165). No wonder we often end our own letters, as Paul did, by saying "Peace."

THE FIRST LETTER TO TIMOTHY is the first of three epistles called the Pastoral Letters, addressed to pastors instead of to churches. In these letters Paul discusses church affairs with his co-workers Timothy and Titus, who have become leaders of the congregations at Ephesus and Crete. He teaches them how to be good 'shepherds' (Latin *pastori*, see Ephesians 4:11).

Chapter 1 gives introductory background information and a warning against false teachers. Chapter 2 is about public worship; Chapter 3 emphasizes the character and qualifications of church leaders and helpers. The remaining chapters, 4–6, are concerned with administering the life of the congregation. The letter to Titus has a similar structure and seems to have been written at about the same time.

The Pastoral Letters have a distinctive style and vocabulary that differs from Paul's other writings, and many influential scholars have therefore questioned whether these letters were really by Paul himself or by a disciple writing in Paul's name. But many other scholars believe that the differences are no more than we would expect, considering that (a) letters to friends are generally quite different from letters intended for large groups of people; (b) our own style changes noticeably as we get older; (c) Paul did not write his own letters but had the help of secretaries (Romans 16:22; 2 Thessalonians 3:17). Furthermore, these letters are full of personal details that have the ring of authenticity: "Take a little wine for your health" (5:23); "Please bring the cloak I left at Troas" (2 Timothy 4:13). A disciple would hardly make Paul say "I am the worst sinner" (1:15).

Modern readers of this letter often have a hard time accepting Paul's comments about the subordination of women to men (2:9–15). Similar remarks appear in 1 Peter 3:3–6. Why should women be considered inferior because they were created last (2:13)? By the same reasoning, men would then be inferior to animals! In such matters Paul did not wish to "disgrace the message of God" by deviating radically from the social norms of his day (Titus 2:5). We can well imagine the increased persecution that would have resulted otherwise. But now that times have changed, the rules that he laid down more than 1900 years ago are no more normative than his rules for obedience of slaves to their masters; those rules had precisely the same motivation (6:1).

The remaining advice in this letter is still timely. For example, "Corrupt people suppose that religion is a way to make a profit. Religion does enrich us, but only if we are content with what we already have" (6:5–6).

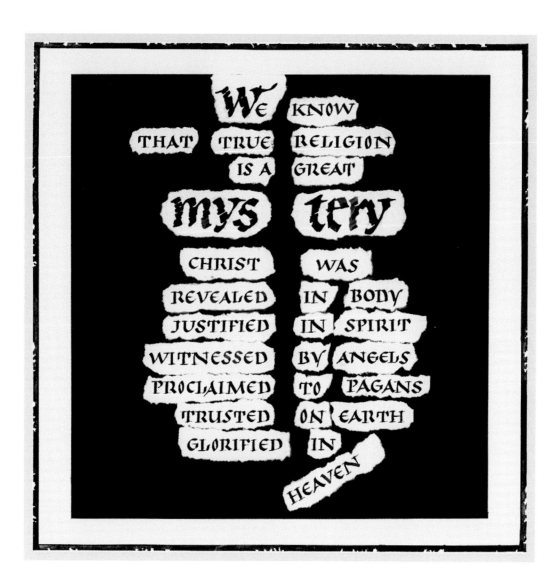

1 Timothy 3 : 16

Leonid Pronenko

AN ANCIENT HYMN, the earliest known example of Christian poetry, is quoted here by Paul as he contemplates the great principles of his faith. Colossians 3:16 tells us that Christians in his congregations like to sing; here we are treated to one of their sonorous texts. Fragments of early hymns probably survive also in 1:17 and 6:15–16, and in other letters (2 Timothy 2:11–13; Ephesians 5:14; Philippians 2:6–11; Colossians 1:15–20); but the words of verse 16 are most clearly constructed to have rhythm and assonance. Indeed, this verse has been called the finest written part of the New Testament.

The hymn at the end of verse 16 has six short lines, each of which consists of words like *ephanerōthē én sarkí*, fitting the pattern '___*thē én* ___'. (But '*én*' in the third line is replaced by the first syllable of *angélois*, which sounds the

1 TIMOTHY 3:16

We know that true religion
is a great mystery: Christ was
   revealed in body,
      justified in spirit,
  witnessed by angels,
     proclaimed to pagans,
 trusted on earth,
    glorified in heaven.

same.) Each line represents a different aspect of Christ's life. The English translation given here attempts to capture the flavor of the original by rendering all six lines as terse phrases having a similar parallelism. The lines divide naturally into three groups of two, emphasizing contrasts of body/spirit, angels/pagans, earth/heaven, each pair combining a natural and a supernatural aspect. Christ was

   ◆ revealed in body: The Greek verb in the first line of the hymn, often translated as 'manifested', means 'lit up'; it implies that Christ existed before he assumed a human form. "The Word became flesh" (John 1:14).

   ◆ justified in spirit: Paul often used this verb 'justified' in a special theological sense (Romans 3:28), but here the ordinary sense of 'vindicated', 'proved right' is relevant (Romans 3:4; Luke 7:35). Christ was condemned and executed as a common criminal, but his spirit—his inner self (Mark 2:8)—was justified because he had done no wrong (2 Corinthians 5:21). "In the body put to death, in the spirit raised to life" (1 Peter 3:18).

   ◆ witnessed by angels: We are told that "angels long to glimpse these things" (1 Peter 1:12; Ephesians 3:10); that "every knee bows to Christ, in heaven and on earth and under the earth" (Philippians 2:10). The sense of the Greek words here is not only that angels watched Christ and helped him (Luke 2:13; Mark 1:13), but that Christ actively showed himself to them.

216

♦ **proclaimed to pagans:** The news of Christ's sacrifice for the sins of all is preached to people everywhere, not just to a special group and not just to angels. "On earth as in heaven" (Matthew 6:10).

♦ **trusted on earth:** And people all over the world believe in him; Christ's prayer in John 17:21 has been answered.

♦ **glorified in heaven:** The closing Greek words mean literally 'ascended in glory'; the grand climax is Christ's elevation to a position of supreme splendor.

Some commentators see in this hymn a six-stage chronological progression: incarnation → resurrection → ascension → preaching → response → second coming. Others arrange the lines as two groups of three instead of three groups of two: Christ became man, was proved spiritually spotless, and rose to join the heavenly hosts; his victory was proclaimed, and believed, his reign is glorious. Such a multitude of appealing interpretations reflects the beauty of these words, which have inspired several other hymns.

Paul and Timothy presumably know this hymn well. So Paul naturally recites it when he is contemplating the mystery of faith (verse 9), the truths upheld by the church (verse 15). True religion, he declares, is a great mystery— great not in the sense of obscure or puzzling but great in the sense of profound, wonder-full, tremendous (Ephesians 5:32). How great it is! The Greek word translated here as 'true religion' is a term that connotes deep reverence for God; Paul uses that word frequently in this letter (2:2; 4:7, 8; 6:3, 5, 6, 11).

But what does he mean by a mystery? Jesus referred to the "mystery of God's kingdom" (Mark 4:11). Paul said, "The mystery is that Christ is in you" (Colossians 1:27). The Greek *mystérion* means a secret, something that is hidden, yet a source of wonder and awe. Plato spoke of mysteries as forms of knowledge that could be understood emotionally, by means of allegories and symbols, but not comprehended rationally by human reasoning. Mystery cults sprung up whose initiates were sworn to silence about the secrets they knew. By contrast, the mysteries of Christianity were proclaimed openly.

Oriental philosophy sees mysteries as a tension between opposites, yin and yang. From this standpoint it is entirely natural for the hymn of verse 16 to express the mystery of Christ in terms of sharp contrasts.

A rational mind like mine generally wants to nail everything down, to understand concepts fully. Yet I am glad that true religion is a great mystery, something I can feel but not describe, something I can ponder and learn about, something that will always remain tantalizingly beyond my grasp.

THE SECOND LETTER TO TIMOTHY is sometimes called Paul's last will and testament, because he wrote it when he sensed that his life would soon be over. During his first captivity in Rome, he was able to write with optimism about his impending release (Philippians 2:24; Philemon 22); but now he says "the hour of my departure is at hand" (4:6).

The year is perhaps 67 A.D.; Paul is again imprisoned in Rome (1:8,17); the emperor Nero's persecutions of the Christians have increased. Paul's general message to Timothy is, "Carry on, and keep up your faithful work in spite of suffering and opposition."

From remarks in this letter and the other Pastoral Letters, we learn something about Paul's activities after the close of the book of Acts. At that time Paul lived under house arrest for two years in Rome (Acts 28:16,30). Regaining the freedom to travel, he left Timothy in Ephesus while enroute to Macedonia (1 Timothy 1:3), after which he planned to spend the winter in Nicopolis, northwest of Greece (Titus 3:12). Paul visited Troas, Corinth, and Miletus before returning to Rome (4:13,20). We don't know whether he was able to complete his planned journey to Spain (Romans 15:24,28), but it is clear from the data in these letters that he continued his missionary journeys on behalf of the church as long as he could.

Timothy hailed from the southern part of Galatia. His father was Greek, but his mother and grandmother were Jews who converted to Christianity after Paul's first missionary journey (1:5; Acts 16:1). For more than ten years, Timothy traveled extensively with Paul (Acts 17:15, 18:5, 19:22, 20:4) and seems to have been his chief assistant. Indeed, six of Paul's letters (1 & 2 Thessalonians, 2 Corinthians, Philippians, Colossians, Philemon) are entitled "from Paul and Timothy," so Timothy may have been the secretary who wrote them down. Paul refers to him as "my beloved son" (2:1; 1 Corinthians 4:17; Philippians 2:22).

Chapter 1 opens with some of Paul's reminiscences, then Chapter 2 encourages Timothy to be a faithful servant of Christ. Chapter 3 paints a contrast between impostors and true Christians.

Finally, Chapter 4 is Paul's farewell. "Proclaim the Word, both in season and out of season" (4:2). "I have fought the good fight, I have completed the race, I have kept the faith. Now the garland of victory, of being in harmony with God, is in store for me, and for all who have waited with love for Christ's appearance" (4:7–8).

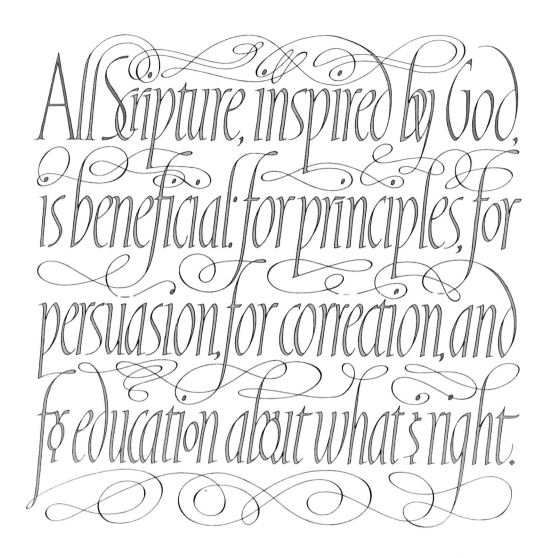

All Scripture, inspired by God, is beneficial: for principles, for persuasion, for correction, and for education about what's right.

2 Timothy 3 : 16

David Kindersley

219

BIBLE STUDY is valuable—so says the Bible; and the more we study it, the more we appreciate that fact. Martin Luther inscribed this famous verse on a copy of the German Bible that he gave to his friend Johann Wilhelm Reiffenstein in 1545. J. B. Phillips featured this verse on the book jacket of his New Testament translation in 1958.

Paul has been discussing impostors who maintain the outward appearance of religion while denying its inner power (verse 5). Timothy knows better; he has been familiar with the Bible since his childhood (verse 15).

Verse 16 opens by relating the Bible to God in words that can be interpreted two ways: (1) "All Scripture is inspired by God, and beneficial"; (2) "Every Scripture inspired by God is also beneficial." Interpretation 2 was adopted in translations by Jerome, Wycliffe, Tyndale, Luther, and more recently in the New English Bible; Interpretation 1 was adopted in the King James and Revised Standard versions, and also in recent translations such as the Jerusalem Bible and the New International Version. The Greek words make grammatical sense either way, so my own translation attempts to capture this ambiguity in contemporary English.

All Scripture, inspired by God, is beneficial: for principles, for persuasion, for correction, and for education about what is right.

The phrase 'inspired by God' corresponds to the eloquent Greek adjective *theópneustos*, 'God-breathed'. What does this mean? In Psalms 33:6 and 147:18, the breath of God is equated to God's commands; thus, God-breathed might signify 'exhaled by God', in the sense that he speaks directly (Exodus 24:12). On the other hand, God breathed life into man in Genesis 2:7; this act corresponds to our word 'inspiration' (Ezekiel 2:2; 2 Peter 1:21).

In any case, verse 16 implies that the holy writings mentioned in verse 15 are in some supernatural way a gift from God. Of course we don't believe that a book is inspired by God just because it explicitly claims to be; self-testimony means nothing unless it is supported by additional evidence (John 5:31). As I write this book I often feel that God is putting words and ideas into my head; but I may be deluding myself. The value of what I write will depend on how much its readers get from it. For similar reasons, I don't think Paul is implicitly including his own letter to Timothy among the Scriptures he is discussing here; in verse 15 he uses the contemporary name for the Old Testament (1 Maccabees 12:9). However, 1 Timothy 5:18 does refer to a saying of Jesus as part of Scripture (see Deuteronomy 25:4 and Luke 10:7); see also 1 Corinthians 15:3–4. Paul puts no limits on what might be God-breathed.

Many theories have been proposed to explain exactly how God's inspiration takes place. Indeed, this issue has become a major dividing line between "conservative" and "liberal" Christians. Some people believe in a dictation theory, according to which each word was miraculously communicated; others think that God's Spirit enhanced the abilities of the Bible's many authors, who wrote in their own words; some admit only that the Bible is inspired because it is inspiring. The debate is between "inspired words" versus "inspired people."

Verse 16 doesn't answer the question, because it is not concerned with the mechanism of inspiration but rather with the result. Indeed, Paul is exhorting Timothy (and us) to *use* the God-breathed Scripture; his main point is that the Bible is basic equipment for a person of God. He states this even though he no longer submits to all the Old Testament laws (Galatians 3:23–25).

Timothy's contemporaries were probably claiming that the Old Testament was no longer worthy of study. But Paul insists otherwise (Romans 15:4). The Bereans studied Scripture daily when Paul preached to them (Acts 17:11). Jesus once said, "Surely you know this scripture" (Mark 12:10).

Paul observes that Bible study is beneficial in four ways: (1) for principles—ideas and ideals to be upheld; (2) for persuasion—aids to reasoning by which we can reinforce our beliefs and discover our errors; (3) for correction—literally 'straightening out' our lives; and (4) for education and training. The Greek concept of education included discipline; Pontius Pilate said, "I will teach him (Jesus) a lesson (with a whip) and let him go" (Luke 23:16).

The final word in verse 16 is the noun *dikaiosýnē*: 'what is right'. This word, a favorite of Paul's, means holy living, living in conformity to God's will. It can be associated with all four of the scriptural benefits cited earlier.

Incidentally, Paul does *not* say that the Bible is easy to understand, or that it is infallible or historically accurate or free of paradox. Indeed, the Bible states that God sometimes misleads people deliberately (Ezekiel 20:25). Paul emphasizes the importance of Bible study for guidance and nourishment, but he does not encourage us to idolize the words themselves. If we have superior knowledge and faith but lack love, we are nothing (1 Corinthians 13:2).

I have written this book because I'm convinced that God wants people to study the Bible regularly. Bible study truly helps to make God's people complete (verse 17).

THE LETTER TO THE HEBREWS was prepared for early Jewish Christians whose faith needed to be strengthened in the face of peer pressure and persecution. It summarizes the doctrine that the New Testament gospel is the perfection and completion of the Old Testament.

We don't know who the author was; but we do know that he or she was a master of the Greek language. This book has been called "the Isaiah of the New Testament" because of its rhythmic cadences, its artistic wordplay, its stately prose. The opening verse, in which five of the first twelve words begin with the letter p, is one of many key sentences that have proved to be especially memorable to people fluent in Greek.

If we assume that the anonymous author is mentioned elsewhere in the New Testament, the person most likely to have written such a text is Apollos of Alexandria (Acts 18:24; 1 Corinthians 1:12; Titus 3:13), because the writer of Hebrews is evidently a Jewish-Christian scholar with a Greek background and a gift of rhetoric. If Apollos didn't write this book, the writer must have been somebody very much like him—perhaps one of his teachers, Aquila or Priscilla (Acts 18:2, 26; Romans 16:3–4; 1 Corinthians 16:19).

The original addressees of this letter aren't identified explicitly; they must have been Christian converts from Judaism who were intimately familiar with the Greek version of the Old Testament. Such people lived throughout the Mediterranean region. We can learn much from their perspective, which is rather different from that of a typical 20th-century Christian. I once found that I could understand the book of Hebrews much better after living a few days with some orthodox Jewish friends.

This book has the literary form of a Hebrew *midrash* or commentary on Scripture, in which exposition alternates with exhortation. It also contains remarks addressed to the readers (for example, in 5:11–12 and 6:9–12). Thus it can justly be called both a theological treatise and a personal letter.

The contents have been arranged systematically and with great care. Jesus Christ is presented first as Son of God, superior to angels in the celestial sphere (Chapters 1–2); he is also superior to Moses as a leader on earth (3–4). Moreover, Jesus is superior in the role of high priest (5–10), having made a sacrifice sufficient to replace the cultic sacrifices previously offered in the Temple. Chapter 11 is a celebration and review of the great faith demonstrated by stalwart heroes of the Old Testament era. Finally, Chapters 12 and 13 give specific details about how to live a life that pleases God.

✝

CONSIDER THE PEOPLE WHO LISTENED AND REBELLED · ALMOST EVERYBODY WHO LEFT EGYPT WITH MOSES DID *Hebrews 3:16* THIS.

Hebrews 3 : 16   John Stevens

MOSES LED a massive exodus of Israelites from Egypt, in accordance with God's instructions, back toward the territory of Canaan where their ancestors had lived. But just as the people were about to march into this promised land, they got cold feet and said that they would rather not have come. We are told in Numbers 13–14 and Deuteronomy 1:19–45 that God was angered by their rebellion; God resolved that they should spend forty years wandering in the desert until a new generation was ready to take their place. God decreed that none of the original emigrants of military age would experience the eventual victory march into Canaan, not even Moses himself (Numbers 20:12)—nobody, that is, except Caleb and Joshua, who had been the only leaders urging an invasion according to God's original orders (Numbers 14:30, 26:65). A few of the priests were also exempt from the punishment (see Numbers 16:37 and Joshua 24:33).

HEBREWS 3:16
Consider the people who listened and rebelled. Almost everybody who left Egypt with Moses did this.

This famous story is recounted at the end of Psalm 95, a beloved psalm whose opening words "Come let us sing unto the Lord" are the *Venite* often chanted at Matins. The author of Hebrews quotes the less familiar final verses of that psalm, because those lines contain an instructive lesson for his readers (verses 7–11): "Listen to God today! 'Don't close your minds, as your ancestors did when they rebelled.... Their hearts went astray, and they failed to respect my ways; so I vowed in anger that they should not enter my place of rest.'"

Verse 16 can be read in two ways, depending on whether its first word is taken to be *tinès*, 'some', or *tínes*, 'who?'. Both alternatives look the same in a Greek manuscript, because accents were not written down in those days. The first interpretation was adopted by early translators such as Jerome, Luther, and the preparers of the King James Bible; it means "Some of those who listened also rebelled, but not all did so." The second interpretation has been adopted in almost all modern translations; it means "Who were those who listened and rebelled? Didn't everybody do so?" For example, the Jerusalem Bible of 1966 followed the first interpretation, but the New Jerusalem Bible of 1985 uses the second. In the second case, the implied answer to the second rhetorical question is "Yes"; but in the first case, the reader is supposed to be more familiar with the original Bible story and to know that Caleb and Joshua were exceptions to the general rule.

The second interpretation has much to commend it, because verses 17 and 18 contain rhetorical questions of a similar kind, in classical midrashic diatribe style. But those verses aren't strictly parallel to verse 16, and the first interpretation has certain advantages because it makes the author's point even stronger. The early Christian readers of Hebrews were, like Caleb and Joshua, a small minority surrounded by a vast majority who did not believe the good news they had recently learned from God (4:2). Thus, like Caleb and Joshua, they would ultimately be able to enter the promised land (4:3), if they didn't take the easy way out by going along with the majority opinion. Paul, similarly, uses this some-but-not-all interpretation when he discusses the same episode of Jewish history in 1 Corinthians 10:5–10.

The psalm (verse 11) calls the promised land God's 'place of rest'. This concept has always been a key idea for the descendants of Abraham. For thousands of years they have been striving to reach such a place. The author of Hebrews points out in 4:4–9 that there is an important sense in which the Israelites did not reach God's place of rest even after Joshua had led them into Canaan—namely that there is a spiritual, heavenly resting place, much more significant than an earthly home. Just as God rested after creating the world (Genesis 2:2), those who enter God's place of rest will also rest from their own labors. This is the true promised land, the heavenly Jerusalem (12:22), a lasting city of the future (13:14). (Incidentally, the Hellenistic Jewish philosopher Philo of Alexandria had expressed similar sentiments in *De Cherubim* 26.) Therefore the writer of Hebrews sees the Israelites of his day as marching to their true place of heavenly rest guided by Jesus Christ, who is infinitely superior to the former leaders Moses (verse 3) and Joshua (4:8). His illustration is enhanced by the fact that Jesus and Joshua both have exactly the same name, *Iēsoús*, in Greek.

The Israelites rebelled against God's orders because they didn't believe God's pledge to them (Numbers 14:11). It was this lack of faith that prevented them from reaching the promised land in Moses's day (verses 17–19). Indeed, the author of Psalm 95 and the author of Hebrews both emphasize that this lesson from the past is an urgent lesson for all time: "Listen today! Don't close your minds to God." The stakes are as high as ever. We can only come to a true place of rest, a state of sabbatical peace and harmony with God, if we listen attentively and overcome our tendency to rebel—even when almost everybody else we know is part of the rebellion.

THE LETTER OF JAMES is the first of seven "catholic" or "general" epistles intended for Christians in a variety of communities instead of being addressed to one particular church or individual. This letter is from James "to the twelve tribes of the dispersion" (1:1); in other words, like the letter to Hebrews, it was written for Jewish Christians who lived in many different places. (The original twelve tribes of Israel were descendants of Jacob, and the Hebrew name Jacob is identical to James when translated into Greek.)

Many people were named Jacob/James in New Testament times, but the James of this letter was almost surely James the Just, a brother of Jesus (Mark 3:32, 6:3; Acts 1:14; 1 Corinthians 15:7; Galatians 1:19). James was the leader of the first Christian congregation in Jerusalem (Acts 12:17, 15:13, 21:18). Indeed, Paul refers to James, Peter, and John as "pillars of the church" (Galatians 2:9); these three pillars became authors of the first six catholic epistles, and James's brother Jude wrote the seventh.

The pattern of this book has been compared to a musical rondo: Chapter 1 states the main themes briefly, then Chapters 2–4 develop them and elaborate on them, and Chapter 5 gives a final recapitulation. The major themes are poverty, piety, and prayer. James praises the poor, warns the rich, and encourages generosity; he explains how to control our tongues and have good relations with our neighbors; he emphasizes the power of prayer; he stresses that true Christians will not be content with an abstract religious faith that produces nothing concrete.

One of the main sections (2:14–26) explains that a living faith leads naturally to positive actions. James may have known people who misunderstood Paul's discussion of faith as the mainspring of Christian life (Romans 3:22–31; Galatians 2:16; Philippians 3:9). Paul's sentiments were not really at odds with those of James (Romans 8:9, 12:8–13; Galatians 5:6).

If verse 1:1 is removed, the remaining 107 verses of this book become a written sermon instead of a letter. James writes earnestly and passionately, using imperative verbs often (49 times). For this reason he has been called "the Amos of the New Testament." His sermon has the same flavor as the sermons of Jesus recorded in Matthew, Mark, and Luke; for example, 5:12 is very similar to Matthew 5:37. James uses lively metaphors from nature—flowers, grass, trees, birds, waves, sun, and fire—to illustrate his points. He deals with basic issues that aren't specific to any particular time or place, so this book remains as fresh and relevant today as ever.

James 3:16

Wherever
there is
jealousy or greed,
there will be
turmoil &
all kinds of
foul play.

EARTHLY WISDOM is contrasted sharply with heavenly wisdom in this instructive passage. James, as an experienced mediator of heated disputes in the early church (Acts 15 and 21), knows that human nature includes animal instincts that can have diabolical effects (verse 15).

In verse 16 James highlights the dangers of two vices, *zélos* and *eritheía*, which can be freely translated into English as 'jealousy' and 'greed'. Both of these vices have already been mentioned in verse 14. If we wish to understand more precisely what James is saying, we need to understand the significance of the Greek words he uses.

The first word, *zélos*, corresponds to 'zeal' in English, and it comes from the Greek word for heat. Zeal can be both good and bad. The good kind of zeal occurs in 2 Corinthians 9:2, where Greek people enthusiastically come to the aid of impoverished Christians in Palestine. The bad kind occurs in Philippians 3:6, where Paul recalls how he once persecuted the church (Acts 8:3). Ardor and passion are tremendous attributes; God himself is zealous (Exodus 20:5 and 34:14), and Paul speaks of being 'zealous with a Godly zeal' (2 Corinthians 11:2). But a misplaced zeal becomes blind fanaticism. Zeal can also connote jealousy concerning a spouse, or envy of somebody else's possessions, or rivalry about status, as in 1 Corinthians 3:3. James specifies the bad type of zeal by inserting an adjective when he introduces the concept in verse 14; that verse speaks of 'bitter' or 'harsh' zeal.

The other word, *eritheía*, is more difficult to characterize. It stems from a verb that means 'to work for hire'. Aristotle uses it in his *Politics* 1302 b4 to denote party spirit or factionalism, presumably because political demonstrators could be rented like day-laborers. The term occurs in Romans 2:8 and Philippians 1:17, 2:3, where it seems to stand for selfish ambition or pride—the attitude of a social climber, or of a poor man who wants to get rich.

Both *zélos* and *eritheía* are listed as vices of human nature in Galatians 5:20, where we also find the similar word *éris*, 'strife'. Some translators have mistakenly assumed a linguistic connection between *eritheía* and *éris*, but the similarity is just coincidental. Still, James observes in verse 16 that *zélos* and *eritheía* lead directly to *akatastasía*, 'turmoil', and to evils of all sorts. We can paraphrase verse 16 by saying that misplaced zeal and selfishness are the roots of all evil. All three of these dangers, *zélos*, *eritheía*, and *akatastasía*—

JAMES 3:16

Wherever there is jealousy or greed, there will be turmoil and all kinds of foul play.

228

jealousy, greed, and turmoil—are listed in 2 Corinthians 12:20 among Paul's greatest worries.

But verse 17 tells us about an alternative, the wisdom "from above," a wisdom that is the antidote for *zḗlos* and *eritheía*. Heavenly wisdom is pure, peaceable, patient, open-minded, compassionate, fruitful, unbiased, sincere. (This list of wonderful qualities is especially euphonious when recited in the Greek language.) "God is not a God of turmoil but of peace" (1 Corinthians 14:33). Moreover, James says in verse 18 that peacemakers reap a harvest of justice, which they can sow again for more peace. "Blessed are the peacemakers; they will be called God's children" (Matthew 5:9).

A nationalistic political party called the Zealots was gaining prominence during James's day. One of the twelve disciples of Jesus was, in fact, called Simon the Zealot (Luke 6:15; Acts 1:13). This party wanted to overthrow the Roman governors of Israel and restore Jewish sovereignty; eventually it became a revolutionary, anarchical movement. The anti-Gentile mob that plotted to kill Paul in Acts 23:12 may have consisted of people from the Zealot party. Therefore some interpreters think that James was referring specifically to this political situation when he wrote verse 16; according to their view, James was telling Christian Jews to respect their present government and not to join the Zealots. Similarly, Jesus, Paul, and Peter counseled submission to the emperor (Mark 12:17; Romans 13:1–7; 1 Peter 2:13–17). However, the context makes it clear that James is giving advice about general principles, not restricting himself to current political problems.

Some commentators think James is talking only about minor squabbles between members of his congregation. James, however, is warning about turmoil 'of all kinds', including murder and war. "You want something that you can't have, so you kill for it" (4:2). He sees tragic misery on all sides resulting from people's earthly wisdom, from their human natures. He sees that if we refuse to learn wisdom that is peaceable, open-minded, compassionate, and sincere, we are doomed. Indeed, if James were alive today he would surely fear that we will destroy ourselves with the bombs our earthly cleverness has devised.

The cure is to be "quick to listen, slow to speak, slow to become angry" (1:19); to love our neighbors as we love ourselves (2:8); in fact to love everyone, including our enemies (Matthew 5:44). If we cannot change our human natures, let us ask God to help us find some harmless outlet into which we can channel the destructive urges of our *zḗlos* and *eritheía*.

THE FIRST LETTER OF PETER is one of the best-liked books of the Bible, perhaps because it was written by the most popular disciple of Jesus. Peter was a natural leader, a frequent spokesman for the other disciples (Mark 10:28; John 6:68), known for his impetuosity and sincerity (Matthew 14:28–30; Mark 14:29). He is writing to churches in Asia Minor (1:1), especially to Gentile Christians there (1:14, 18); he had been the first to baptize Gentiles (Acts 10:48). The Bible says little of his later life except that he traveled with his wife on missionary journeys and possibly visited Corinth (1 Corinthians 1:12, 9:5). According to other ancient records, Peter became head of the church at Rome, where he died a martyr's death during the reign of Nero, about 65 A.D.

Peter had no formal education (Acts 4:13), so it's unlikely that he could have composed the excellent Greek of this letter by himself. He probably enlisted the help of Silvanus (5:12), who was co-author of two of Paul's epistles (1 & 2 Thessalonians 1:1; see Acts 15:22, 32, 40).

Many strands have been woven together in this letter, which has been called "a microcosm of the Christian faith." Peter writes with a vigorous confidence, combining theology and ethics, sending both encouragement and testimony to his readers (5:12). His style is devotional and practical, never argumentative. His main themes are faith and fortitude, based on the exemplary life and teachings of Jesus Christ.

The first part of this letter deals generally with the idea of Christian identity, leading up to the statement that "You once were not a people, but now you are the people of God" (2:10). The next part, from 2:11 to 3:12, deals generally with a Christian's responsibilities in society. The traditional relationships of Peter's day—between slaves and their masters, between people and their rulers, between wives and their husbands—are to be upheld in a spirit of loving kindness (3:8). "If you want to enjoy life, ... turn away from evil" (3:10–12, quoted from Psalm 34:12–16).

The final portion of this letter, from 3:13 to 5:11, is the major section in which Peter discusses Christian suffering. The Christians of his day are an oppressed minority group; he writes to give them comfort and hope. "Leave your worries with God, because he cares for you" (5:7).

Nowadays Peter's message speaks louder and louder, as Christians are once again becoming a minority group in many parts of our culture. Today's Christians probably understand Peter better than their parents could.

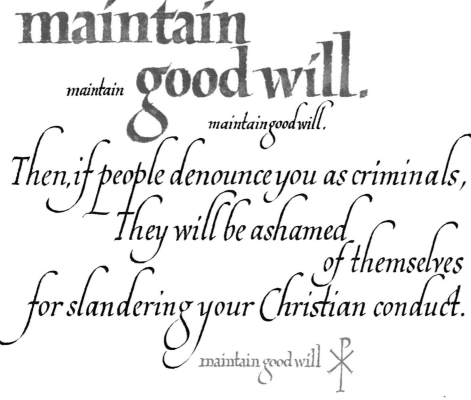

1 PETER 3:16

maintain

maintain good will.

maintain good will.

Then, if people denounce you as criminals,
They will be ashamed
of themselves
for slandering your Christian conduct.

maintain good will ☧

1 Peter 3 : 16   José Mendoza y Almeida

231

INTIMIDATION comes in many forms. Peter was once afraid to admit that he knew Jesus (Mark 14:66–72); a few weeks later, on Pentecost day, he had become bolder, but then people taunted him and said he was drunk (Acts 2:13). Soon afterward he was thrown in prison and ordered not to speak about Christ (Acts 4:3, 18). Paul and other missionaries were often brutally attacked and/or expelled from cities (Acts 13:50; 14:6, 19; 16:23–24). Jesus himself had been condemned to death by a mob (Mark 15:14).

Today's newspapers are filled with stories of intimidation from all over the world. Even in our own relatively sheltered lives we are tempted every day to choose expedience over conscience. For example, as a university professor surrounded by people who are mostly atheistic or agnostic, I was reluctant for a long time to tell anybody that I was working on a book about the Bible. Thus our own personal experiences give us insight into the much more severe conditions faced by the people to whom Peter is writing this

1 PETER 3:16

Maintain good will.
Then, if people denounce you as criminals,
  they will be ashamed of themselves
for slandering your Christian conduct.

letter. Peter's readers are small groups of people with an unconventional lifestyle, and they've been accused of crimes they didn't commit (2:12); they are abused for not carousing with the crowds (4:4); they are insulted for proclaiming the name of Christ (4:14). Christians throughout the world are suffering (5:9). Many of them will in fact die as martyrs because of their faith (Revelation 2:13, 17:6).

Peter's advice is to follow the example of Jesus (2:23), who repaid bad will with good (verse 9). Peter had once pulled out a sword and begun to fight, but Jesus stopped him (John 18:11). Instead of retaliating, Jesus counsels us to bless those who curse us, to pray for those who vilify us (Luke 6:28). In verse 15 Peter says we should answer our persecutors with gentleness and respect. This thought continues in verse 16, where we are advised to maintain good will.

Many translators of verse 16 begin with the words "Maintain a good conscience," or something similar, because the Greek word *syneídēsis* can mean 'conscience' as well as 'consciousness'. The concept of a person's conscience is difficult to characterize: Conscience is the consciousness we have of our own morality. In Bible passages like 1 Timothy 1:5, *syneídēsis* does seem to mean conscience, but in 1 Peter 2:19 it means consciousness. Passages like Acts 23:1

232

or Hebrews 13:18 can be read either way, with 'good *syneídēsis*' meaning either a favorable attitude toward one's self or toward others. If verse 16 refers to our conscience, it means that we have our own house in order; hence we aren't inwardly denouncing ourselves. This gives us the confidence necessary to continue doing good in the face of accusations, and our accusers will be pricked by their own consciences. However, it is simpler and more in keeping with verse 15 to assume that *syneídēsis* here means a cooperative attitude of good will toward others, because Peter's point is that Christians should not be self-righteous or arrogant when they are unjustly maligned. Similarly, 'good *syneídēsis*' in verse 21 denotes good will toward God.

Modern translations of verse 16 often omit the words that are translated 'as criminals' here. These extra words appear in the Textus Receptus, the traditional version of the Greek Bible that was edited by Erasmus in the 16th century and used to prepare the King James Bible in the 17th; but they are not present in today's Greek Bibles. Recent discoveries of ancient manuscripts show that the extra words were not always present, and scholars now believe that the original Greek text of verse 16 involved an unusual grammatical construction. According to this theory, some ancient scribe copied a few words from 2:12 into verse 16 so that the Greek would read more smoothly.

The closing words of verse 16, 'your Christian conduct', have a deeper significance in Greek; they read, literally, 'your conduct in Christ'. This phrase, 'in Christ', appears also in 5:10 and 5:14. It is a favorite expression of the apostle Paul, who uses it 164 times in his letters (see, for example, Romans 3:24, 6:11, 8:2, 12:5). To be 'in Christ' means more than just to be a member of a Christian church; there also is a mystical significance, in which Christ somehow forms the spiritual atmosphere breathed by a believer's soul. This concept is central to John's gospel: "Remain in me and I will remain in you" (John 6:56, 15:4–7).

Verse 16 says that if our adversaries have nothing against us except that we are followers of Jesus Christ, they will sooner or later understand their mistake. Moral strength wins over physical strength. Verse 2:12 goes further and says that good behavior will not only silence our accusers, it may also convince them to praise God. Our job is to "let our light shine" (Matthew 5:16; Colossians 4:5–6). However, we may still have to suffer unjustly; this may in fact be part of God's plan (verse 17). Sometimes it is a privilege to endure abuse for a righteous cause (verse 14).

THE SECOND LETTER OF PETER may have been the last book of the Bible to be written. Most Bible scholars believe that it was composed by a devoted disciple of Peter who wrote many years after his master's death, a person who attempted to imagine as closely as possible what Peter would have wished his final words to be.

Such compositions were quite common in the literature of that time. For example, many works were written in the name of Solomon, or in the names of other revered figures like Adam, Enoch, or Moses. The Testaments of the Twelve Patriarchs formulated advice in the names of Israel's ancestors; one of those patriarchs was Simeon, Peter's original Hebrew name (1:1; Mark 3:16; Acts 15:14). Several early Christian books use Peter's adopted Greek name, notably the Apocalypse of Peter, the Preaching of Peter, the Gospel of Peter, and the Acts of Peter. Early Christian writers who mention 2 Peter all express admiration for its content but uncertainty about its real author. The available evidence suggests that this letter was probably written during the first half of the second century A.D.; some branches of Christianity hesitated to include it in their Bibles until the sixth century. Their reservations were overcome when they recognized its religious value and its inspired nature.

The language of 2 Peter is majestic and churchly, quite different from that of 1 Peter and from all other New Testament books. In fact, 2 Peter repeats almost all of the short letter of Jude, but with a more elegant vocabulary. A comparison of 2 Peter 2:1–18 with Jude 4–13 reveals startling parallels of text and imagery. For example, the last six words of 2:17 come from the end of Jude 13; a rare Greek word for darkness appears in those verses, and also in 2:4 and Jude 6, but nowhere else in the Bible. Moreover, there are close correspondences between 1:12 and Jude 5, between 3:2–3 and Jude 17–18, and between portions of other verses.

This letter gives instruction and guidance to Christian communities that are beginning to take root in many parts of the world as Christianity enters a more stable phase. Chapter 1 is a call to virtue and a reminder of the majesty of Jesus Christ, as it was revealed to Peter at the transfiguration (1:16–18; Mark 9:2–8). Chapter 2 warns against false teachers who will try to pervert orthodox doctrine. Chapter 3 speaks about Christ's long-awaited second coming, pointing out that a thousand years are like one day in God's eyes (3:8; Psalm 90:4). "God is not slow about fulfilling his promise; he is patiently waiting for more people to turn away from their sins" (3:9).

PAUL
SAYS THIS IN ALL
OF HIS LETTERS,
WHENEVER HE REFERS TO
THESE THINGS. SOME OF
HIS WRITING IS
HARD TO UNDERSTAND;
IGNORANT AND INSECURE
PEOPLE DISTORT HIS WORDS,
JUST AS THEY TWIST THE
REST OF THE SCRIPTURES,
AND THEY DESTROY
THEMSELVES IN
THE PROCESS.

2 Peter 3:16   Jean Evans

235

"PAUL'S WRITING is sometimes hard to understand." After making a careful study of Romans 3:16, 1 & 2 Corinthians 3:16, Galatians 3:16, Ephesians 3:16, Philippians 3:16, Colossians 3:16, 1 & 2 Thessalonians 3:16, and 1 & 2 Timothy 3:16, we can certainly testify to that! It is SO TRUE. If we find we're having trouble comprehending some of the things Paul says in his letters, 2 Peter 3:16 tells us we're in good company.

Paul had the courage to try explaining the unexplainable, "God's hidden wisdom" (1 Corinthians 2:7). He was, of course, not being obscure on purpose; God gave him insights into abstract questions that people have been grappling with for years, and his theological discussions have provided endless food for thought. Furthermore, the subtle ideas he expresses are not inscrutable; they can in fact be understood, if we take the time to do it. In 2 Corinthians 1:13 Paul says "We write only about what you can read and also understand."

2 PETER 3:16
Paul says this in all of his letters,
whenever he refers to these things.
Some of his writing is hard to understand;
ignorant and insecure people distort his words,
just as they twist the rest of the Scriptures,
and they destroy themselves in the process.

Thus the complexity of Paul's letters is not a defect. It is rather a sign of the rich layers of meaning to be found there. How tiresome it would be if the Bible were filled only with trivial truisms! How rewarding it is when we are able to get fresh insights every time we re-read! God's word is "a lamp for our feet, a light for our path" (Psalm 119:105), yet we don't see everything at first glance. Illumination comes gradually as we get used to the light (see Luke 8:10).

The first part of verse 16 refers back to verses 9 and 15, which speak of the patience of Jesus in delaying his second coming so that more people can be saved from their sins. Paul does not state precisely this idea in his letters, but he does come close in Romans 2:4, Romans 11:23, and 1 Timothy 1:16; see also 1 Thessalonians 5:2, which has an echo in verse 10. Paul often urges Christians to be morally prepared for Christ's return (Romans 13:11–14; 1 Corinthians 7:29–31; Philippians 2:14–16).

Notice that Paul's writing is compared here to "the rest of the Scriptures." At the time of Christ, 'the Scriptures' meant the Old Testament; but by the time 2 Peter was written, at least some of Paul's letters were already considered to hold equal rank as Scripture. They had already been widely copied and presumably were being read in churches. From a historical standpoint, verse 16

236

is significant as the first indication that the Old and New Testaments were destined to become united in one Bible.

Verse 16 also brings up a serious problem: Ignorant and insecure people are distorting Paul's words. People who are ignorant (uneducated) have no stable foundation on which to build an understanding. Without clear principles learned from experience and study, we can easily be misled into making completely wrong interpretations of Paul's writing. Paul himself once mentioned that he was being misunderstood and slandered (Romans 3:8).

The Greek word that is translated 'insecure' means 'unsteady', 'vacillating', 'not firmly established'; it appears also in 2:14 ("false teachers seduce insecure souls") and nowhere else in the Bible. The opposite word, 'stability', appears in verse 17 (and nowhere else).

Insecure people distort and twist the words of Scripture. This word 'twist' is another example of 2 Peter's unique Greek vocabulary. It originally meant to tighten a cable by turning a crank; then it acquired another meaning, to torture on the rack. Thus, Scripture's words are being stretched out of shape until they seem to mean something else. Then "corrupt doctrine spreads like gangrene" (2 Timothy 2:17).

Such distortion and perversion of meaning has terrible consequences: It leads to destruction (2:1, 3) on the day of judgment (verse 7). As a result, the opportunity to enter a new heaven and earth will be lost (verse 13).

What shall we do with the Bible then? If it is so difficult to understand, and if misunderstanding is so deadly dangerous, we should perhaps keep it locked up so that billions of people aren't exposed to such risks. Maybe ordinary folks should stop trying to understand such a difficult book; when so much is at stake, it seems that we should withdraw, and trust the experts to interpret the Bible for us.

No, by no means! Verses 17 and 18 make it clear that verse 16 is not intended to scare us away from the Bible, but rather to give us fair warning that misrepresentations and distortions are to be expected, even from well-meaning people within the church. We should be fully aware that heretics will try to corrupt the truth; and we should be prepared to make our own decisions.

We know that the Bible is challenging. So our job is to remain balanced and stable, growing in grace and knowledge. Indeed, this idea of continued spiritual growth through continued study is perhaps the main lesson I have learned from the Bible's 3:16s.

THE FIRST LETTER OF JOHN is the first of three letters that share distinctive characteristics of style and terminology with the Gospel of John. This letter, like the fourth Gospel, is anonymous; in fact, it begins without a salutation and ends without a valediction, so it doesn't really fit the pattern of a normal letter. But it is clearly a personal communication, because of phrases like "I am writing to you" (1:4; 2:1, 12; 5:13). And it is so closely related to John's Gospel that, if we select one of its phrases at random, expert Bible scholars have difficulty recalling whether the words come from 1 John or from John.

The other two letters, 2 John and 3 John, are the shortest books in the Bible. They do have the format of personal letters, from a man who calls himself simply 'the Elder'. Ancient documents imply that two people, John the Apostle and John the Elder, both lived and died in Ephesus at about the same time. So these letters were probably written either by Jesus's disciple John when he was elderly, or by John's disciple who wrote the words "we know that his testimony is true" (John 21:24).

1 John is a beautiful letter, filled with memorable expressions of religious ideas and ideals. It is a devotional commentary on the Gospel of John and an excellent companion to that book. It assumes that the readers are familiar with basic Christian principles; it affirms the testimony of John without arguing about why the doctrines are correct. The language is simple but the thoughts are profound.

The author writes earnestly, with an undertone of anxiety, because his readers face disruption from "antichrists" who do not believe that God came to earth in human form (2:18, 4:3; 2 John 7). He denounces such heretics as malicious liars (2:22; 3 John 10). Yet the overall tone of this letter is positive, even joyful (1:4).

This book blends together a number of variations on the related themes of light, piety, truth, love, faith, and the essence of God. The first half revolves to some extent about the key phrase "God is light" (1:5); the second half, similarly, features the words "God is love" (4:8 and 16). Scholars who have tried to find an orderly arrangement of ideas have compared 1 John to the river Meander, which takes a winding course through Asia Minor; each verse flows smoothly into the next, but progress does not occur along a straight line. This technique of exposition may not be considered efficient by modern standards, but it certainly has proved to be effective.

We have
learned the
meaning of *Love,*
because
the Holy One
laid down his *Life.*

Just as he did this for us,
we too should lay down our lives
for each other.

1 John 3 : 16

Jeanyee Wong

239

TRUE LOVE is the Bible's most radical concept, a notion so unusual that the writers of the New Testament could explain it best by giving a new meaning to the Greek word *agápē*. The Greek language had always had the verb *agapán*, with its comparatively neutral meaning 'to like' or 'to respect'; but the corresponding noun *agápē* was rare until the Bible came along. The New Testament writers use both *agapán* and *agápē* to denote a special, selfless kind of love. These words occur a total of 257 times, including 52 appearances in John's letters and 43 in John's gospel.

Love is central to John's message, so he wants to define exactly what *agápē* means. That is the purpose of verse 16, which is an echo of John 3:16 and of John 15:12–13: "Love each other as I have loved you; the greatest love is to lay down one's life."

The Greek text of verse 16 begins literally with the words 'In this we have known the love'. John likes to begin a thought with the word 'this' pointing forward, instead of pointing back to the preceding context. (See 1:5; 2:3; 3:10,11; 4:9,10,13; 5:2; John 4:37; 9:30; 13:35; 15:8; 2 John 6; 3 John 4.) He points here not simply to 'love' but to 'the love', the thing called *agápē*. In verse 12 he has already explained the opposite of love, by the example of Cain, who murdered his brother (Genesis 4:8).

A literal translation of verse 16 continues 'because that One, for us, laid down his own life; and we too should, for the brothers, lay down our lives'. John's readers don't need to be told who 'that One' is (2:6; 3:3,5,7; 4:17; John 1:18). They also know what it means to 'lay down one's life', although this unusual idiom is found only in John's gospel: "A good shepherd lays down his life for the sheep" (John 10:11–18). John uses the same verb, 'to lay down', when Jesus lays down his outer clothing (John 13:4).

Now that we understand the individual words of verse 16, we're ready to comprehend their overall meaning. And the meaning is devastating, to most people who think that they are capable of genuine love: True love implies a willingness to give up our own lives for the sake of others, to make the supreme sacrifice. For example, St. Paul mentions that Aquila and Priscilla once risked their lives for him (Romans 16:4).

How many people, if any, do I love that much? Do I love God that much?

240

The idea of giving up my life makes me imagine that I might some day be on a sinking ship that doesn't have enough lifeboats to save everybody; staying aboard that ship will mean certain death for me, but it will allow others to live. I also think of a burning house, from which I might be able to rescue someone before an explosion occurs. I might enter such a house if my chances of dying are only 10 percent, say, but not if they are 20 percent or worse; does that mean I love the person inside the house only 10 percent?

Love is self-denial but not self-torture. We give our lives to help somebody else, not simply to "prove our love." Thus verse 16 emphasizes that Jesus laid down his life for a purpose, for our benefit; indeed, verse 2:2 says that he died on behalf of the entire world. "He died for all, so that we would no longer live for ourselves" (2 Corinthians 5:15; see also Mark 10:45; Romans 5:8; Ephesians 5:2). From Christ's example we should therefore be ready to lay down our lives for anyone, not just for our family and friends.

Of course there's a paradox here: We can't be *forced* to love anybody, not in the true sense of *agápē*. The word 'should' in verse 16 gives us a way to test our capacity for love, but it doesn't tell us that we must love each other because it's the law. "We ought to love because God loved us so much" (4:11), yet this love comes not by decree but as a natural response to God's love (4:19). We do things for others without making conscious decisions.

Many issues about love are unclear. Consider, for example, a young woman whose twin brother needs a kidney transplant; is she guilty of insufficient love if she decides not to donate one of her own kidneys?

Verse 4:20 says that we do not love God if we do not love our brother. Does each person either love or hate, or is there a middle ground?

These are difficult questions. But they are purely theoretical for most of us, because we are rarely called on to do anything heroic. We can always say, "Yes, in such an emergency I would lay down my life," just as Peter did (John 13:38). But inside, we are counting on the fact that such dramatic opportunities will probably never arise. Therefore verse 17 moves from theory to practice, telling us that love makes us act frequently, whenever we see a person we can help. Verse 17 may seem at first to be very mild compared to verse 16, but in fact it is even stronger, because it applies all the time.

Love isn't just genuine sympathy, it's constant generosity. "Dear children, our love should not be just words or mere talk, it should be real and active" (verse 18).

THE BOOK OF REVELATION stands at the end of the Bible and points to the future. 'Revelation', or *apokálypsis* in Greek, means 'uncovering'; yet this book remains tantalizingly enigmatic and obscure. It is the New Testament's book of prophecy (1:3; 10:11; 22:7, 10, 18), having a basic structure somewhat like the book of Ezekiel in the Old Testament. The author experiences a series of visions that he is directed to write down and send to seven churches in Asia Minor (1:10–11); he discusses present conditions (Chapters 2–3) and describes God's heavenly court (Chapters 4–5), then points out woes that will overtake sinners (Chapters 6–11). In these visions a cataclysmic struggle between the forces of good and evil (Chapters 12–20) finally results in God's decisive victory (Chapters 21–22).

The author's name is John (1:9, 22:8), and he is sometimes identified with the John of the gospels. However, John was a common name in Palestine, so the prophet of Revelation may well have been someone completely different. He writes with authority and uses a distinctively Hebraic Greek grammar that is quite unlike anything else in the Bible. He is intimately familiar with the Old Testament, to which he makes hundreds of allusions.

Revelation has been called a book of songs, a kaleidoscope of pictures. Everything in this book is expressed in terms of symbols; for example, horns represent power, eyes represent knowledge. The symbols involve sights, sounds, smells, colors, textures, and strange creatures. Numbers receive special significance: For example, 4 represents the world, 7 represents completeness, 1000 represents an extremely large quantity. Sometimes the symbolism is explained (1:20; 5:6, 8); sometimes we are challenged to discover a hidden meaning (13:18; 17:9). Many of these symbols appear also in Daniel 7–12 and in other "apocalyptic" literature that was popular at the time of Christ.

The great mathematicians John Napier and Isaac Newton published scholarly treatises giving keys to the interpretation of this book. Dozens of theologians have also discovered what they believe is the true meaning of all the symbols. But every solution has been different. Adam Clarke said, "I have read elaborate works on the subject, and each seemed right until another was examined." Perhaps Revelation is not supposed to be understood in detail, but rather in its essence, in its total impression of inexhaustible mystery and majesty. As Jesus said, some things are "hidden from learned men but revealed to little children" (Matthew 11:25). These powerful images stir our imagination; do we also need to understand them?

Since you
are merely lukewarm—
neither cold nor hot—
I'm going to spit you out
of my mouth!

Revelation 3 : 16

Rick Cusick

APATHY can be much worse than staunch support of the wrong cause; lack of spirit can be much worse than open wickedness. That is the astonishing message of this famous verse addressed to the young Christian church at Laodicea.

Chapters 2 and 3 contain letters to seven churches in the vicinity of Ephesus, summarizing the strengths and weaknesses of each congregation from Jesus's point of view. The seventh letter (verses 14–22) is addressed to Laodicea, which is the only church for which Jesus has no words of commendation. He doesn't single out any grave errors of doctrine; he simply accuses the Laodiceans of being lukewarm. And lukewarmness is the gravest error of all.

Verse 15 says, "I wish you were either cold or hot." It's easy to understand why God wants our religious fervor to be hot. Deuteronomy 6:5 tells us to love God with our whole heart, our whole soul, our whole strength. Romans 12:11 tells us to serve God with a 'boiling spirit'. And Matthew 24:12 warns of a day when many people's love will grow cold. Why then would God prefer coldness to an alternative that is at least partly warm?

REVELATION 3:16

Since you are merely lukewarm—
neither cold nor hot—
I'm going to spit you out of my mouth!

The main reason is that complacency makes people oblivious to their faults. By contrast, people who frankly reject God are under no illusions about their relationship, and they may perhaps be converted later. But the rich Laodiceans, pleased with themselves (verse 17), are utterly unaware of their spiritual poverty (verse 18). They don't even realize that they have effectively shut Christ out of their lives—that he now stands outside, knocking at the door, hoping that they will hear him and invite him back in (verse 20).

The Laodiceans' indifference is a kind of hypocrisy, an outward show of religion with no divine glow inside. Jesus repeatedly denounces hypocrites, pointing out that tax collectors and prostitutes enter God's kingdom more readily than insincere religious leaders do (Matthew 21:31).

Sometimes things have to get worse before they can get better. Paul says in 1 Corinthians 3:18 that people who think they're smart need to become fools before they can gain true wisdom. One of my most devout friends once told me that he actually spent an evening throwing stones at church buildings, shortly before deciding to become a church member.

The American educator Robert Morss Lovett records in his autobiography that he started a so-called Laodicean Society with George Santayana and a few

244

other Harvard friends in 1892. Lukewarm tea was served, and the members were not allowed to be enthusiastic about anything. "It was the rule that if at any meeting a quorum should be present the club should *ipso facto* cease to exist. As a result, the second meeting was the last." Lovett also notes that this very act of promoting indifference and rebelling against traditional religion coincided with a resurgence of religious feeling in his own life.

Thus, extremes of emotion, positive or negative, prove to be better than a lethargic zero. Verse 16 makes this point with an apt analogy to water: Cold water can be refreshing and hot water is good for healing, but tepid water just makes people throw up! The Laodiceans understood this easily because of the famous hot springs in the city of Hierapolis, just six miles to the north (Colossians 4:13); some of that sulphurous hot water bubbled over a nearby cliff, at which point it was lukewarm and nauseating. Their drinking supply, piped in via Roman aqueducts to the south, may also have been less than satisfactory.

It's easy to fall into the trap of letting our religious convictions go stagnant. We like to be warm and comfortable, shielded from difficult questions; we might even congratulate ourselves on our moderation. But there is no room for neutrality in religion. Elijah said, "If Jehovah is God, worship him; if Baal is God, worship him" (1 Kings 18:21). God wants us to worship one or the other, not to keep our spirits earth-bound. He prefers hostility to detachment.

Dante's *Inferno* 3:34–42 mentions a large band of miserable folk who had lived bland lives "without disgrace and without praise." These people were condemned to run in circles forever; neither Heaven nor Hell wanted them.

But verse 16 isn't quite as harsh as it seems. The Greek words can also be translated 'I'm ready to spit', not 'I'm going to spit'. God is sick of lukewarm people, and he holds out hope for the cold ones, but he hasn't permanently rejected anybody.

The Laodiceans did, in fact, gain strength in later years. Their church had several notable bishops, and they hosted an important council called the Synod of Laodicea late in the fourth century. (But that Synod decided not to include Revelation in its list of approved New Testament books.)

Revelation 3:16 is the final 3:16 of the Bible. I hope that my detailed studies of these verses have not simply been amusing intellectual exercises that leave me and my readers with vaguely warm feelings. I pray, rather, that the messages of these verses may come through and kindle an intense, God-pleasing heat.

AFTERWORD

OUR JOURNEY through the 3:16s of the Bible is now complete, and we are led to an inescapable conclusion: Either God contrived to put unusually excellent material into verse 16 of nearly every Chapter 3, or else the entire Bible is extraordinarily rich in its contents. Although we selected Bible verses almost at random, we have found that nearly all of them would make good sermon texts. Who could have predicted that 1 John 3:16 would be nearly as memorable as John 3:16? Or that 2 Timothy 3:16 and 2 Peter 3:16 would be commentaries on Bible study itself?

After I finished leading a Bible class on this subject, my overwhelming feeling was that the verses we had studied were much more profound and interesting than I had expected. When I began to teach the course, I was confident that we would learn a lot; but I was bowled over by the number of hitherto-unfamiliar verses that turned out to be really inspirational and enlightening. A glance at the index to this book makes it plain that the 3:16s touch on a great number of significant topics; it's hard to think of any important issues that are left out.

In fact, I worried a little that the experiment might have worked almost too well. After reaching Revelation 3:16, I felt that I knew a great deal about every book in the Bible—except for the gospel of John, where the selected verse was not randomly chosen. I had to remind myself that I had looked closely at only one verse in each book, and that there were more than 500 times as many verses that I still knew very little about.

Of course, the 3:16s aren't the only verses we have looked at. In order to understand those verses fully, we have studied their contexts and examined many other verses that use the same words or speak of the same ideas. The index to Bible passages at the end of this book shows that we have in fact encountered quite a lot of the Bible. But we've looked at the other verses only briefly, while we have studied the 3:16s in almost excruciating detail. We have learned "everything about something and something about everything."

As I prepared this book, I learned much more than I did when I first taught the Bible class, mostly because of my decision to translate each of the 3:16s personally. That idea was scary at first, but in retrospect it proved to be one of the best decisions of my life. There is no better way to study a verse of the Bible than to try making a new translation; I now recommend the practice to everyone. Of course I often felt inadequate to the task of capturing the meaning of the original text in the best way; I'm sure that I can do much better if I keep learning and keep trying. But the exercise of choosing the best English renderings from among the many alternatives already published was an ideal way to penetrate into the meaning of the verses and to illuminate unsuspected gaps in my knowledge.

Bible translation by diligent laypeople isn't as difficult as it might seem, because Bible scholars have done an excellent job of making their knowledge accessible to nonspecialists. More and more wonderful resource books are being published every year. I have found Interlinear Bibles to be especially helpful; these are Bibles in which Hebrew or Greek lines of text alternate with English, so that it's easy to see word-for-word what the original says. This means that I don't have to be lost when I'm reading scholarly works that involve Hebrew or Greek, even though I'm almost totally unfamiliar with those languages myself. I'm not competent to take part in theological debates, but I can at least match words easily enough to understand controversial points that the experts bring up in their publications. Besides Interlinear Bibles, I regularly consult theological dictionaries and concordances, which make it possible to locate other instances of each word; the related texts are often significant. I'm glad to see that such aids are now becoming computerized so that many more people will find it easy to discover the rewards of do-it-yourself translation.

While preparing my own versions of the 3:16 verses, I was surprised at first to find a great disparity between existing translations. Different groups of translators have identified several of the 3:16s as "obscure" in the original languages, because the only extant manuscripts incorporate errors that have crept in during centuries of copying; but rarely do the translators agree on which verses belong in this category. The troublesome verses for some people seem to be no problem for others. If you look at a dozen different translations, you'll find that most of the 3:16s have been translated in twelve different ways; moreover, the various translations often differ in meaning as well as in their choices of words. I knew, of course, that each translation would be distinctive; but I had no idea that there would be such a lack of consensus. After I had gained more experience, I was able to understand why this is so, because I began to look at detailed textual comparisons of ancient Biblical manuscripts and learned that variant readings are extremely common; the task of interpretation and reconstruction is much more complex than I had imagined because an enormous number of decisions have to be made. In the verses that I sampled, I found unusually felicitous phrases in each of the major translations; but no one translation proved to be consistently superior to the others.

My experience with the 3:16s has demonstrated that a sampling method can indeed provide considerable insight into the Bible, but I was pleased to discover that the method works even more effectively with respect to the auxiliary literature. A person can read the Bible in its entirety without difficulty; but nobody could possibly digest all the thousands of additional books that have been published about the subject. I found that it was easy to look up the 3:16 verses in dozens of commentaries and translations, thereby getting a very good feeling for the spirit of each of those study helps. I doubt if there's any other way to evaluate so many of those books so quickly and so accurately. In this way I was able to read significant sections of many great books from many centuries, getting a new appreciation of the works of people like Luther and Calvin that I would never have obtained otherwise. I discovered a series of books called the *Pulpit Commentary*, published about 1900, that regularly provided stimulating ideas I had not found in other works. I encountered some commentaries that left me cold, because the authors seemed to be too interested in academic gamesmanship or other human concerns; but I found many others, especially from recent times, that left me decidedly encouraged about the future of Bible scholarship. I was particularly impressed by a number of books about the Old Testament issued by the Jewish Publication Society.

As a mathematician, I have a peculiar liking for numerical data, so I was interested to see how well the sampling method would work with respect to quantitative considerations as well as to the more important qualitative ones. Numerical facts about the Bible are generally classified as "trivia," but I couldn't resist the opportunity to gather some statistics about questions that have precise answers. For example, let's suppose that we want to estimate how many verses are present in the whole Bible, by using stratified sampling. Exactly 60 books of the Bible have a Chapter 3, and by tabulating the number of verses in those 60 chapters it's easy to discover that the average Chapter 3 has about 22.9 verses, with a standard deviation of 10.1. Multiplying by the total number of chapters, which is easily found to be 1189, we can estimate that the Bible contains $27{,}200 \pm 1550$ verses. (Here $1550 = 1189 \times 10.1 \, / \sqrt{60}$.) The true number, in the King James Version, is known to be 31,101; other translations are slightly different. (I was surprised to see that stratified sampling gave such a low estimate. The Bible's longer chapters tend to be in the Bible's longer books; therefore any method that chooses just one chapter from each book is likely to underestimate the total number of verses.) Another experiment worked better: I used stratified sampling to predict the number of words per Bible verse. In the King James Version, the 59 verses selected by our 3:16 rule have 1567 words altogether, so we predict an average of $1567/59 = 26.6$; this is very close to the true value $788767/31101 = 25.4$.

Incidentally, on the basis of the 3:16s, I can state with some confidence that the Revised Standard Version contains approximately 95% as many words as the King James Version; the New English Bible is a little bit shorter yet. The second edition of the Revised Standard New Testament seems to have been a rather substantial revision, because 4 of the 22 verses I studied were altered in some way between 1946 and 1971. Curiously, I noticed that the Good News Bible (Today's English Version) has significantly fewer words than the King James, roughly 85%, in its translations of the Old Testament 3:16s; but it has significantly *more* words per verse, roughly 110%, in the New Testament. The same is true of the Living Bible paraphrase. Could these statistics account for the fact that I find these two translations especially readable and clear?

Sixteen of the 59 verses we have studied turn out to contain Hebrew or Greek poetry; that's a ratio of slightly more than 1 in 4. I don't know the true figures, but I doubt that 25% of the Bible actually has a poetic structure. On the other hand, the true percentage is probably not much lower than 20%.

The ancient Hebrew name of God, the sacred Tetragrammaton 'YHWH', appears 19 times among the 3:16s. If we multiply 19 by a factor of $23144/37$, to account for the fact that we looked at just 37 of the 23144 verses in the Old Testament, we get 11,885; thus we might expect to find almost 12,000 occurrences of 'YHWH' in the Hebrew Bible. The actual total, however, is only about 7,000; the 3:16s turn out to be unusually rich in the number of references they make to God.

Mathematical calculations sometimes turn up in theological studies, especially with respect to questions of authorship of the Biblical books. I found many of the statistical arguments unconvincing in the works I read, because the methods used to "prove" that Paul didn't write all of the letters signed by him would also "prove" that I didn't write all of the comments on Paul's letters in this book! My vocabulary and style are different on different pages of this book because I'm writing about quite different things; and I've adopted a completely different vocabulary and style in my other books about computer science and mathematics. Yet I know that I'm the author of all those works, contrary to the statistical evidence.

Similarly, many scholars have commented that James and Peter did not have sufficient education to write the fine Greek texts that are attributed to them. But I know from my own experience that it's quite easy to do such a thing, because I once wrote a book in French—a language that I don't speak at all—with the help of three talented students whose mother tongue was French. The four of us discussed every sentence of that book (*Mariages Stables*, Montréal, 1976), and I knew that I was controlling the content and even the style although they were doing the actual writing.

After spending several months preparing the present book, I began to wonder if I might have had a subconscious reason for choosing the 3:16 rule, because I may have previously learned several of these Bible verses and noticed a 3:16 pattern. This might be a serious flaw in my methodology, so it deserved serious consideration. Indeed, I learned in 1987 of a pastor in New Hampshire who had been preaching a series of sermons on the New Testament 3:16s; he had surely not heard about my Bible class, so he must have gotten the idea independently. Moreover, when I was writing the closing chapters of this book in 1989, I stumbled across the fact that Adam Clarke had already made the following observation in his commentary of 1811:

> This 16th verse of this 3d chapter of John's First Epistle is, in the main, an exact counterpart of the 16th verse of the 3d chapter of St. John's Gospel.

Let's suppose that the 3:16s happen to be better than average verses of the Bible, purely by coincidence. Then it's not very surprising that the idea of stratified sampling by the 3:16 rule would have occurred to me. In order to assess the potential effects of such a subconscious bias, I looked at a published list of 1,861 "key verses ... selected for their doctrinal importance and for their familiarity to readers of the Bible," which appears in the *New Strong's Exhaustive Concordance* (Thomas Nelson, 1984). A truly random selection of 58 Bible verses in addition to John 3:16 would be expected to come up with only 3, 4, 5, or 6 of those key verses; but in fact the 3:16 rule hits 10 of them: Daniel, Micah, Zechariah, Malachi, Luke, John, Colossians, 1 Timothy, 2 Timothy, and 1 John. The probability that 10 or more key verses would be obtained in a truly random sample is only about 1 chance in 140, so it is indeed likely that my choice of 3:16 was not as unbiased as I thought it was. On the other hand, let's assume that I really had somehow noticed that five of the 3:16s were special, before I decided to try this experiment in a Bible class. Then the probability of hitting 10 key verses would not be unreasonable; it would come to about 22%, better than 1 chance in 5. Something like that probably happened. But even under such an assumption, 54 of the 59 verses— the vast majority—would be completely random. Therefore this hidden source of bias didn't have a significant effect.

Where do we go from here? I know what I plan to do: more of the same! One of these days I'm sure I will want to learn more about the books of the Apocrypha (Judith, Tobit, Sirach, Maccabees, etc.); clearly I'll want to do this by taking a close look at their 3:16s.

And I want to continue exploring the Old and New Testaments by using the technique of stratified sampling, since I know that this approach will never get stale. I think I'll try Chapter 16, verse 3, next; and then 7:7, etc.

Index of Bible References

INDEX OF CALLIGRAPHERS

THIS BOOK was composed with the author's TeX system, using Computer Modern typefaces developed by the author with METAFONT. The illustrations were prepared for publication with Adobe PhotoShop and Adobe Illustrator 88, using computer facilities generously provided by Adobe Systems, Inc. Artwork for the cover was contributed by Hermann Zapf.